Hi

16
16   ×16
×12   160
32   186
260
29

16   160
×12   186
32
260
29

16   16
16   ×16
9   160
×9   186
144

3¢8   3416
×10   ×7
90   186

314
×28
112
28
392

25
×25

345   346   325
×10   ×8   ×6
600   ×10

Mathematics In Our World

Robert E. Eicholz

Phares G. O'Daffer

Charles R. Fleenor

Addison-Wesley Publishing Company

Menlo Park, California · Reading, Massachusetts · London · Amsterdam · Don Mills, Ontario · Sydney

Illustration Acknowledgments

Robert Bausch: 1 top center, 6–7, 106–107, 211, 270, 319, 364–365

David Broad: 120–121, 166–167, 228–229, 368–369

Dick Cole: 2–3, 30–31, 70, 136–137, 156–157, 278–279, 328–329, 362–363

David Cunningham: 73, 80–81, 127, 146–147, 164–165, 234, 254–255, 288–289, 307 center left, 310, 336–337, 356, 358

Susan Jaekel: 115 top center, 162–163, 185 top left, 192–193, 204–205, 256–257, 330–331, 349, 353

Heather King: 45

Ken Michaelsen: 53 center left, 92–93, 150–151

Masami Miyamoto: 243 top right and bottom right, 260–261, 280–281, 282–283, 292, 300, 307 center right, 334–335, 342–343, 355, 359, 366–367, 372–373

George Roth: 60–61, 88–89, 132–133

Teresa and Wayne Snyder: 22–23, 32–33

Holly and Iver Zapp: 87, 101, 104–105, 115 center left, 175–176, 180–181

Photograph Acknowledgments

Copyright by the California Institute of Technology and Carnegie Institution of Washington. Reproduced by permission from the Hale Observatories: 346-347

Richard Crone*: 250

George B. Fry III: 324 left

George B. Fry III*: 1 top left, top right, and bottom left, 10–11, 18, 26–27, 40 bottom left and bottom right, 41 all, 42, 46 left, 47 top left, 53 top right, bottom left, and bottom right, 56, 58–59, 64 top, 74 left, 76–77, 78–79, 90, 91, 96, 102, 115 top right, left center, and bottom center, 116 top, 124–125, 128 top, 134–135 top, 138–139, 141, 142 top, 148–149, 152–153, 155 top, 158–159 top, 159 bottom left and bottom right, 160–161, 169, 170, 185 top right, center left, and bottom right, 186 top, 190, 202, 206–207, 212, 214, 218, 222 top, 238, 243 top left, bottom left, and center, 244–245 center, 254, 258, 266–267 bottom, 268–269, 284, 288, 289, 290–291, 300, 305, 307 top left, top right, and bottom left, 308–309 top center, 318 both, 324 right, 325 both, 330–331, 344, 350 top, 354 bottom

Paul Fusco/Magnum Photos: 341

Shelly Grossman/Woodfin Camp & Associates: 84–85

George Hall*: 272, 273 both

Robb Johns: 14–15

J. Messerschmidt/Bruce Coleman Inc.: 66–67

NASA: 1 center, 4–5, 34–35, 332–333

Carl Roessler: 94–95

Earle Edwin Sisley/Van Cleve Photography: 256–257

United States Navy: 246–247

Nikolay Zurek*: cover

*Photographs provided expressly for the publisher. All other illustrations and photographs by Addison-Wesley staff.

Contents

Numeration
Adding and Subtracting
Using Your Skills
Measurement

Numeration

Hot air balloon
1783

Steamboat
1807

First public railroad
1825

Getting started

Carol's chart shows an important year in the history of modern transportation.

What is the year?

Make a chart like Carol's to show another important year in the history of transportation.

THOUSANDS	HUNDREDS	TENS	ONES

| Gas-driven automobile 1887 | Airplane 1903 | Rocket engine 1929 | Jet airliner 1949 | Manned rocket flight 1961 |

Match each of the sums below with a date
on the transportation time line.

Example:

1000 + 800 + 80 + 7

Answer: 1887

1. 1000 + 700 + 80 + 3
2. 1000 + 900 + 40 + 9
3. 1000 + 800 + 7
4. 1000 + 900 + 60 + 1
5. 1000 + 800 + 20 + 5
6. 1000 + 900 + 20 + 9

Give the year of these inventions.

7. adding machine:
   1000 + 600 + 40 + 2

8. radar:
   1000 + 900 + 20 + 2

9. lightning rod:
   1000 + 700 + 50 + 2

10. air-conditioning:
    1000 + 900 + 10 + 1

11. mercury thermometer:
    1000 + 700 + 10 + 4

12. ballpoint pen:
    1000 + 800 + 80 + 8

Place value

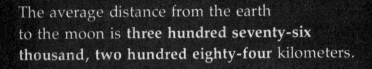

The average distance from the earth
to the moon is **three hundred seventy-six
thousand, two hundred eighty-four** kilometers.

Place Value Chart					
Thousands' period			Units' period		
hundred thousands	ten thousands	thousands	hundreds	tens	ones
3	7	6	2	8	4

The 3 in the hundred thousands' place means 300 000.
The 7 in the ten thousands' place means 70 000.
The 6 in the thousands' place means 6000.

Expanded numeral:
300 000 + 70 000 + 6000 + 200 + 80 + 4

Standard numeral:
376 284

Each group of three digits in a numeral is a **period.** In numerals
with more than 4 digits, the periods are separated by extra space.

Read each numeral. Tell what each red digit means.

Example: 2876   two thousand, eight hundred seventy-six
                The eight means eight hundred.

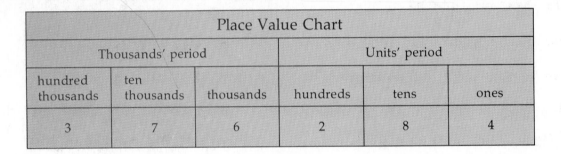

1. 7953

2. 8106

3. 24 739

4. 16 752

5. 84 731

6. 529 316

7. 741 235

8. 396

9. 838 627

10. 74 629

11. 1927

12. 207 655

Write the standard numeral.

1. 7000 + 900 + 40 + 3

2. 3000 + 600 + 10 + 7

3. 20 000 + 6000 + 500 + 20 + 7

4. 900 + 90 + 4

5. 8000 + 20 + 5

6. 40 000 + 7000 + 200 + 6

7. 500 000 + 60 000 + 5000 + 700 + 40 + 9

8. 40 000 + 400 + 4

9. 800 000 + 70 000 + 9000 + 600 + 50 + 6

10. 300 000 + 9000 + 80 + 1

Write as an expanded numeral.

11. 7856	12. 973	13. 2168	14. 3709
15. 12 426	16. 75 849	17. 60 753	18. 93 208
19. 342 748	20. 918 726	21. 201 716	22. 458 007

Write the standard numeral.

23. Deepest moon crater:
eight thousand, eight hundred
fifty-six meters

24. Moon's diameter:
three thousand, four hundred
seventy-six kilometers

Suppose you started writing
numerals in this pattern:
one 1, two 2's, three 3's, four 4's,
five 5's, and so on.

1 22 333 4444 55555 . . .

What would be the 100th numeral
in this pattern?

Rounding numbers

A record height reached
by a manned hot-air balloon
was 13 970 meters.

What is this number rounded
to the nearest thousand meters?

Finding the answer

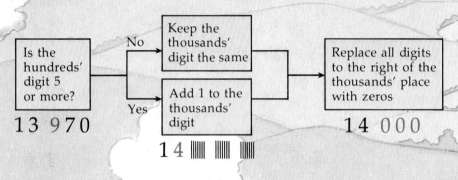

13 970 **rounded to the nearest thousand** is 14 000.

Other examples

38 276 rounded to the nearest thousand is 38 000.
623 500 rounded to the nearest thousand is 624 000.
9825 rounded to the nearest thousand is 10 000.

Round to the nearest thousand.

1. 82 728	2. 12 350	3. 459 793	4. 103 226
5. 7731	6. 2049	7. 912 819	8. 73 500

Round to the nearest hundred.

Example: 2873—The tens' digit is more than 5.
2873 rounded to the nearest hundred is 2900.

9. 6219	10. 8293	11. 5018	12. 36 788
13. 35 518	14. 4750	15. 19 984	16. 784

Round to the nearest thousand.

1. 2816
2. 5448
3. 6992
4. 27 129
5. 19 688
6. 146 725
7. 20 958
8. 753 500
9. 66 666
10. 201 278

Round to the nearest hundred.

11. 741
12. 834
13. 469
14. 2885
15. 189
16. 5650
17. 23 744
18. 8709
19. 16 193
20. 268 791

Round to the nearest ten.

21. 79
22. 262
23. 48
24. 575
25. 128
26. 2776
27. 1809
28. 355
29. 618

30. Distance record for a hot-air balloon flight: 553 km
    What is this number to the nearest hundred?

31. Largest hot-air balloon: 14 158 cubic meters (m^3)
    What is this number to the nearest thousand?

A small car costs $3492.
The mass of the car is 1200 kg.
What is the cost for each kilogram of the car?

Decimals: tenths and hundredths

one unit

1

one tenth

0.1

one hundredth

0.01

Three tenths and two hundredths
of this unit is shaded. This is
the same as thirty-two hundredths.

We write: 0.32

We say: thirty-two hundredths

units	tenths	hundredths
1	4	6

We write: 1.46
We say: one and forty-six hundredths

 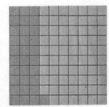

units	tenths	hundredths
2	3	1

We write: 2.31
We say: two and thirty-one hundredths

How much is shaded? Write the decimal.

1.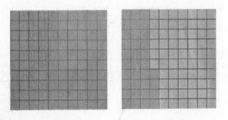

2.

3.

Write a decimal for each figure.

1.

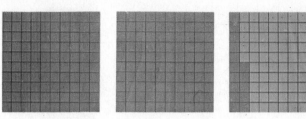

2.

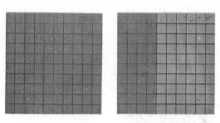

3.

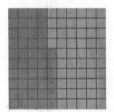

4.

Write a decimal.

5. two and seven tenths

6. eight and seventeen hundredths

7. twelve and five tenths

8. twenty-three and thirty-seven hundredths

9. seven tenths

10. nine hundredths

11. one hundred forty-seven and six tenths

12. fifty-nine and forty-four hundredths

Write a decimal for each number.

13. Gasoline purchase:
    fifteen and nine tenths liters

14. Paper thickness:
    eight hundredths of a millimeter

15. Mass of 1 ℓ of seawater:
    one and three hundredths kilograms

16. Person's height:
    one and sixty-three hundredths meters

Max has 21 coins. All of them are pennies and nickels. The coins have a value of 73 cents. How many of each kind of coin does he have?

Decimals: thousandths

Record distance traveled on a bicycle in one hour: 122.862 km

A place value chart can help you understand the meaning of this number.

hundreds	tens	ones	tenths	hundredths	thousandths
1	2	2	8	6	2

We write: 122.862

We say: one hundred twenty-two and
        eight hundred sixty-two thousandths

Read each numeral. Tell what each red digit means.

Example: 1.375
        one and three hundred seventy-five thousandths
        The five means five thousandths.

1. 0.263

2. 1.347

3. 38.49

4. 62.4

5. 763.39

6. 19.702

7. 75.91

8. 9786.4

9. 0.012

10. 0.095

11. 356.7

12. 0.569

Tell what each red digit means.

1. 4.58
2. 9.06
3. 12.34
4. 0.109
5. 25.635
6. 283.7
7. 11.739
8. 4.086
9. 497.2
10. 7.05
11. 5.345
12. 0.001

Write a decimal for each number.

13. two hundred sixty-four thousandths
14. twelve and fifty-seven thousandths
15. one thousand forty-five and eight tenths
16. eight and seventy-six hundredths
17. six thousandths
18. four and twenty-five thousandths
19. one hundred one and six hundred seven thousandths
20. three thousand two hundred fifty and four tenths
21. seven hundred eight thousandths
22. ninety-four and two hundred fifty-seven thousandths

Write a decimal for each number.

23. Record walking speed: eight and one hundred one thousandths kilometers per hour

24. Gold Cup speedboat racing record: one hundred ninety-three and six hundred ninety-four thousandths kilometers per hour

Multiply the numbers in the X pattern on the calculator.

$X = 1 \times 5 \times 9 \times 7 \times 3 = 945$

What are the products of the numbers in these patterns?

Y, H, N, T, M, Z, E

Comparing decimals

Louisville had 5.46 cm of rain in 24 hours.
Pittsburgh had 5.43 cm of rain in 24 hours.
Which city had the greater amount of rain?

Finding the answer

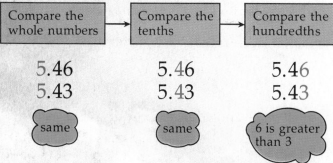

We say: 5.46 **is greater than** 5.43. We write: 5.46 > 5.43
We say: 5.43 **is less than** 5.46. We write: 5.43 < 5.46

Louisville had the greater amount of rain.

Other examples

$$2.3 > 2.1 \qquad 0.5 > 0.49 \qquad 8.326 < 8.426$$
$$0.514 < 0.517 \qquad 0.02 < 0.2 \qquad 12.45 > 12.37$$

Which number is the greater?

1. 6.5 or 6.2
2. 8.13 or 8.09
3. 729 or 792
4. 0.37 or 0.36
5. 0.5 or 0.62
6. 27.4 or 25.9

Which number is the smaller?

7. 0.043 or 0.046
8. 1.557 or 1.657
9. 83.6 or 38.6
10. 0.009 or 0.02
11. 0.742 or 0.747
12. 3.854 or 3.845

Give the correct sign (< or >) for each ●.

1. 7.8 ● 7.7
2. 0.67 ● 0.68
3. 0.832 ● 8.30

4. 60.4 ● 6.40
5. 8.32 ● 8.30
6. 832 ● 840

7. 0.32 ● 3.2
8. 83.2 ● 8.40
9. 0.005 ● 0.05

10. 12.68 ● 12.70
11. 0.1 ● 0.01
12. 0.977 ● 0.978

13. 2.079 ● 2.097
14. 147.5 ● 14.78
15. 0.803 ● 0.809

16. 3.516 ● 3.526
17. 18.4 ● 1.84
18. 63.95 ● 63.81

19. Yearly rainfall:
Wilmington, Delaware—100.61 cm
Oklahoma City, Oklahoma—100.20 cm
Which city has more rain?

20. Yearly rainfall:
Nome, Alaska—27.07 cm
Helena, Montana—27.54 cm
Which city has more rain?

21. Amounts of rain in 24 hours:
Spokane, Washington—10.39 cm
Springfield, Missouri—10.34 cm
Which city had less rain?

☆ 22. Find the yearly rainfall for
several different cities.
List the cities and their
rainfall in order from greatest
to least amount of rainfall.

Start	16	2	14	4	
	5	11	6	9	
	10	8	7	12	
	13	3	15	1→	End

What is the sum of the 7 numbers
in the path from start to end?

Find the path through 7 numbers
that has the smallest possible sum.

Rounding decimals

The record speed on skis is
194.384 km/h. What is
this speed **rounded to the
nearest tenth?**

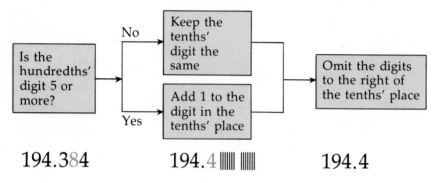

Finding the answer

194.384   194.4 ▊▊▊ ▊▊▊   194.4

The speed rounded to the nearest tenth is 194.4 km/h.

Other examples

7.241 rounded to the nearest tenth is 7.2.
0.98 rounded to the nearest tenth is 1.0.
19.55 rounded to the nearest tenth is 19.6.

Round to the nearest tenth.

1. 8.493	2. 12.92	3. 0.706	4. 43.556	5. 0.382
6. 0.78	7. 246.98	8. 35.57	9. 6.995	10. 50.737

Round to the nearest whole number.

Examples: 8.74 rounded to the nearest whole number is 9.
24.395 rounded to the nearest whole number is 24.

11. 17.2	12. 26.55	13. 89.93	14. 2.876	15. 1.018
16. 6.752	17. 5.23	18. 14.375	19. 80.138	20. 59.688

Round to the nearest whole number.

1. 4.27
2. 31.83
3. 51.866
4. 2.937
5. 47.228
6. 10.904
7. 76.31
8. 1.875
9. 6.5

Round to the nearest tenth.

10. 2.67
11. 8.318
12. 0.663
13. 95.41
14. 225.55
15. 0.193
16. 12.65
17. 91.88
18. 39.97

Round to the nearest hundredth.

Examples: 2.564 rounded to the nearest hundredth is 2.56.
1.736 rounded to the nearest hundredth is 1.74.
3.995 rounded to the nearest hundredth is 4.00.

19. 3.478
20. 6.929
21. 0.378
22. 0.049
23. 17.162
24. 247.742
25. 8.385
26. 1.997
27. 4.502

28. Record ski jump: 169.01 m
What is this number rounded
to the nearest whole number?

29. Longest downhill ski run: 12.23 km
What is this number rounded to the
nearest tenth?

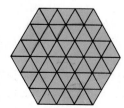

The large figure is a regular
hexagon. How many different
regular hexagons are inside it?

Self-check

Write the standard numeral.

1. seven hundred fifty-four thousand
2. twenty-six and seven tenths
3. two hundred seventy-nine thousandths
4. five and eight hundredths
5. 20 000 + 8000 + 300 + 60 + 4
6. 2000 + 700 + 50 + 3
7. 600 000 + 90 000 + 2000 + 400 + 70 + 5

Give the correct sign (> or <) for each ●.

8. 3.7 ● 3.2
9. 0.53 ● 0.55
10. 0.837 ● 0.838
11. 0.1 ● 0.01

Round to the nearest thousand.

12. 32 753
13. 181 398
14. 4547
15. 75 505

Round to the nearest tenth.

16. 0.74
17. 3.864
18. 0.61
19. 5.836
20. 1.555

Answers for Self-check—page 15

Test

Write the standard numeral.

1. four hundred thousand
2. fifty-two and three tenths
3. seventy-five hundredths
4. six and forty-two thousandths
5. 80 000 + 3000 + 900 + 6
6. 4000 + 500 + 20 + 1
7. 300 000 + 70 000 + 9000 + 400 + 80 + 8

Give the correct sign (< or >) for each ●.

8. 0.7 ● 1.01
9. 1.66 ● 1.68
10. 0.897 ● 0.899
11. 5.18 ● 5.23

Round to the nearest hundred.

12. 739
13. 32 660
14. 4456
15. 201 848

Round to the nearest hundredth.

16. 0.767
17. 1.083
18. 0.164
19. 2.185
20. 0.029

The Four-Color Game

This is a game for two or more players.

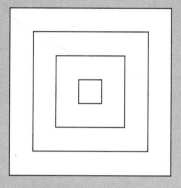

1. Start with this pattern of squares.

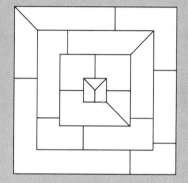

2. Divide each of the regions formed by the squares into several different smaller regions.

3. Each player takes turns coloring any small region with one of 4 different colors. No two touching regions may have the same color.

4. The first player who cannot play loses the game.

Sample Games

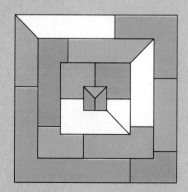

The next player to play loses this game.

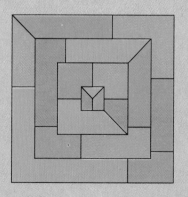

This is a tie game.

Adding and Subtracting

$$\begin{array}{r} 32 \\ 26 \\ 28 \\ 32 \\ \hline 118 \end{array}$$

23	34	27	32
15	26	19	24
17	28	21	26
21	32	25	30

Getting started

Choose one number from each row of the square.
Add the four numbers. Try to choose numbers that
will give a sum of 100.

Can you find more than one way to do this?

> **The Commutative (Order) Principle for Addition**
>
> When you add, you can change the order of the addends and the sum is the same.
>
> $$9 + 7 = 7 + 9 \qquad 34 + 27 = 27 + 34$$

Give the number for n.

1. $8 + 5 = 5 + n$

2. $27 + 19 = n + 27$

3. $438 + 156 = 156 + n$

4. Is $9 - 5$ the same as $5 - 9$?

5. Can you change the order of the numbers in subtraction and get the same difference?

> **The Associative (Grouping) Principle for Addition**
>
> When you add, you can change the grouping of the addends and the sum is the same.
>
> $$4 + (3 + 5) = (4 + 3) + 5 \qquad 34 + (15 + 21) = (34 + 15) + 21$$

Give the number for n.

6. $(7 + 4) + 6 = 7 + (n + 6)$

7. $(23 + 19) + 37 = n + (19 + 37)$

8. Is $(9 - 4) - 2$ the same as $9 - (4 - 2)$? Subtract the numbers inside the parentheses first.

9. Can you change the grouping in subtraction and get the same difference?

10. The commutative and associative principles can be used together to rearrange addends any way we choose.

    $$2 + (3 + 4) = (3 + 2) + 4 = (4 + 2) + 3$$

    Find some other ways to arrange the addends 2, 3, and 4.

More practice, page 374, page 376

Adding whole numbers

A plane flew from London to Paris to Berlin. How far did it fly in all?

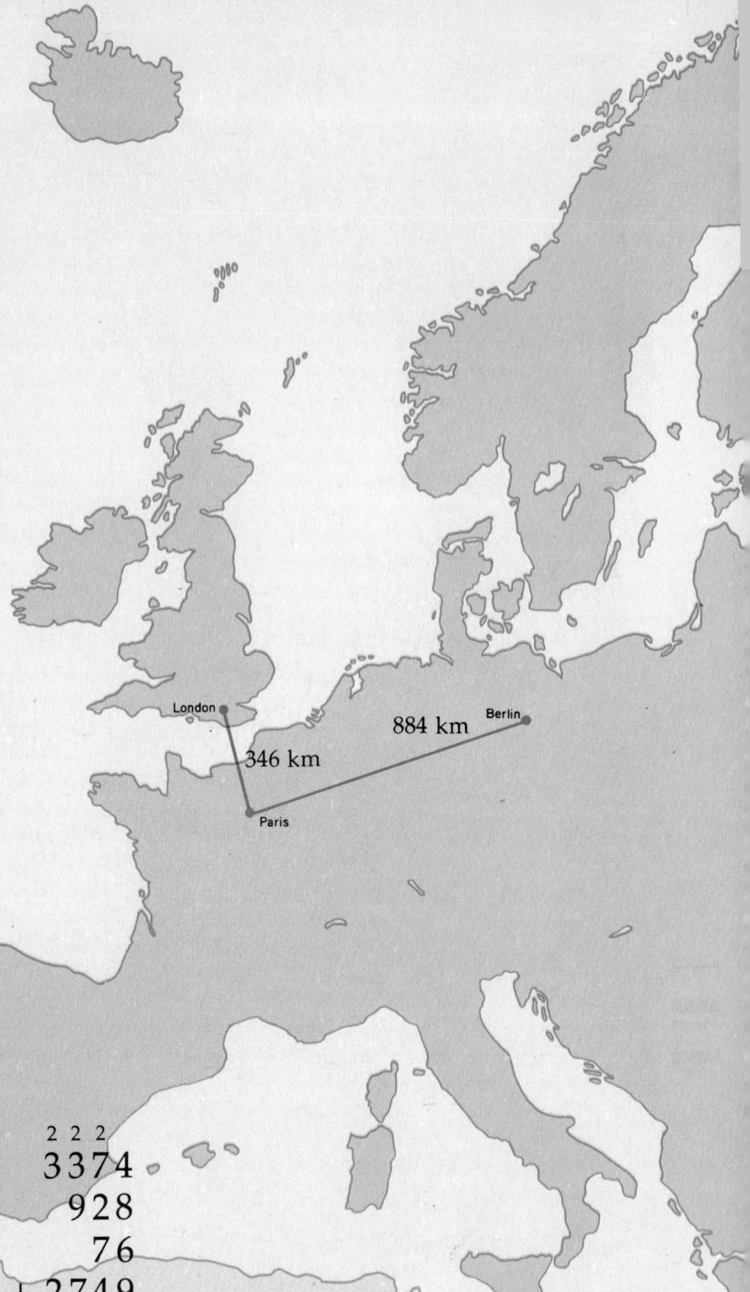

Finding the answer

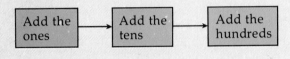

```
Add the        Add the       Add the
ones      →    tens     →    hundreds
```

```
    1              1 1            1 1
  3 4 6          3 4 6          3 4 6
+ 8 8 4        + 8 8 4        + 8 8 4
─────          ─────          ─────
      0             3 0        1 2 3 0
```

The plane flew 1230 km.

(map labels: London, Berlin, Paris, 884 km, 346 km)

Other examples

```
  1 1 1                          2 2 2
  2 7 9 5        2 5 9         3 3 7 4
+ 6 2 8 8        8 4 2           9 2 8
─────────      + 7 7 5            7 6
  9 0 8 3      ───────       + 2 7 4 9
                1 8 7 6      ─────────
                              7 1 2 7
```

Find the sums.

1. 37 + 49	2. 88 + 76	3. 237 + 593	4. 814 + 797	5. 645 + 178
6. 2782 + 1355	7. 1827 + 6655	8. 3754 + 698	9. 8709 + 4667	10. 1544 + 1776

Add.

1.	2.	3.	4.	5.
628 + 577	8281 + 4377	939 + 478	3909 + 1551	4366 + 9585

6.	7.	8.	9.	10.
27 46 + 83	58 25 + 49	123 176 + 189	319 158 + 67	433 765 + 218

11.	12.	13.	14.	15.
2741 3818 4032 + 1275	8177 943 129 + 6240	1174 2281 1984 + 1673	4295 6995 7143 + 5526	2750 4116 3457 + 2802

16.	17.	18.	1.	2.
17 429 + 38 477	27 938 + 46 375	84 929 + 19 076	51 742 + 25 558	66 741 + 28 699

21. Boston to New York: 347 km
New York to Ottawa: 785 km
Ottawa to Boston: 813 km
How far in all?

22. Los Angeles to San Francisco: 648 km
San Francisco to Vancouver: 1635 km
Vancouver to Calgary: 1193 km
How far in all?

23. Philadelphia to Detroit: 942 km
Detroit to Edmonton: 3229 km
How many kilometers in all?

☆ 24. Plan a vacation trip from your home
to several places you would like to
visit. Find the total distance of
the trip.

A number like 12321 is a **palindrome**.
It reads the same backward or
forward.

You can find palindromes by reversing
digits and adding.

start	567
reverse	+ 765
sum	1332
reverse	+ 2331
sum	3663 a palindrome!

Find palindromes using these numbers:
A 647   B 718   C 1795   D 78

More practice, page 375, Set A

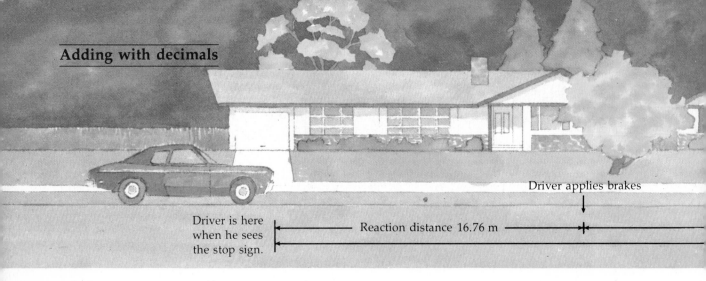

Adding with decimals

Driver applies brakes

Driver is here when he sees the stop sign.

Reaction distance 16.76 m

What is the total stopping distance?

Finding the answer

Copy. Line up the decimal points	Add the hundredths	Add the tenths	Add the whole numbers

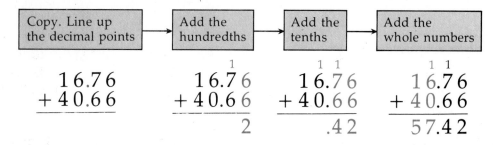

$$16.76$$
$$+40.66$$

$$16.7\overset{1}{6}$$
$$+40.66$$
$$\overline{2}$$

$$\overset{1}{1}6.\overset{1}{7}6$$
$$+40.66$$
$$\overline{.42}$$

$$\overset{1}{1}6.\overset{1}{7}6$$
$$+40.66$$
$$\overline{57.42}$$

The total stopping distance is 57.42 m.

Other examples

$$0.\overset{1}{1}26$$
$$+0.748$$
$$\overline{0.874}$$

$$3.141$$
$$+5.057$$
$$\overline{8.198}$$

$$\overset{1}{}_2\overset{1}{7}.418$$
$$18.623$$
$$+9.735$$
$$\overline{35.776}$$

Add.

1. 3.8 $+9.6$	**2.** 12.5 $+28.7$	**3.** 0.77 $+0.95$	**4.** 3.48 $+2.79$	**5.** 215.9 $+348.7$
6. 0.746 $+0.839$	**7.** 38.6 $+57.7$	**8.** 9.096 $+12.588$	**9.** 27.49 $+66.58$	**10.** 12.746 $+36.405$

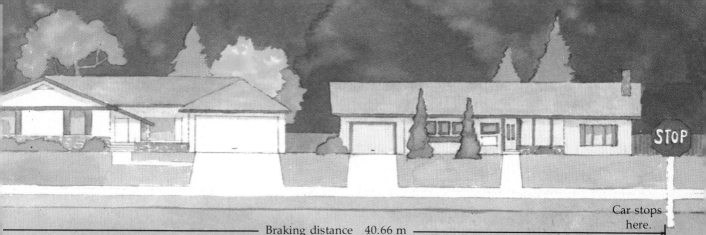

Braking distance   40.66 m
Stopping distance at 80 km/h

Car stops here.

Find the sums.

1.	3.7 + 9.6	**2.**	0.77 + 0.89	**3.**	34.4 + 72.8	**4.**	0.819 + 0.594	**5.**	66.0 + 78.5
6.	9.6 8.4 + 12.8	**7.**	0.13 0.77 + 0.45	**8.**	16.4 38.6 + 27.1	**9.**	1.875 2.500 + 4.125	**10.**	26.69 37.48 + 55.75
11.	1.81 3.76 + 5.09	**12.**	12.85 0.17 + 7.47	**13.**	9.776 12.987 + 6.452	**14.**	0.428 0.925 + 0.804	**15.**	38.493 7.838 + 19.776

Copy and add.

16. 3.84 + 9.16 + 8.49

17. 0.96 + 0.88 + 0.75

18. 4.942 + 0.975 + 0.862

19. 38.7 + 553.9 + 6.4

20. 0.65 + 1.85 + 2.76

21. 4.96 + 6.47 + 3.77 + 13.64

22. Driving 40 km/h:
Reaction distance—8.38 m
Braking distance—9.97 m
What is the total stopping distance?

23. Speeding 100 km/h:
Reaction distance—20.85 m
Braking distance—68.36 m
What is the total stopping distance?

More practice, page 375, Set B

Subtracting whole numbers

Empty container: 208 g
With 3 cups of liquid: 893 g
What is the mass of the
liquid?

Finding the answer

| You need more ones Trade a ten | → | Subtract the ones | → | Subtract the tens | → | Subtract the hundreds |

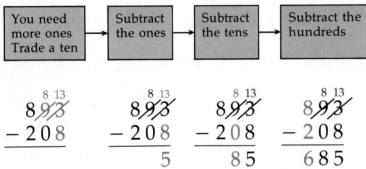

The mass of the liquid is 685 g.

Other examples

$$\begin{array}{r} \overset{3\ 12\ 12}{\cancel{432}} \\ -\ 164 \\ \hline 268 \end{array} \qquad \begin{array}{r} \overset{6\ 13\ 14}{\cancel{7448}} \\ -\ 3681 \\ \hline 3767 \end{array} \qquad \begin{array}{r} \overset{2\ 9\ 10\ 14}{\cancel{3014}} \\ -\ 1776 \\ \hline 1238 \end{array} \qquad \begin{array}{r} \overset{5\ 9\ 9\ 12}{\cancel{6002}} \\ -\ 3146 \\ \hline 2856 \end{array}$$

Find the differences.

1. 365
    − 128

2. 628
    − 241

3. 819
    − 577

4. 380
    − 229

5. 508
    − 347

6. 1295
    − 744

7. 2743
    − 1378

8. 9221
    − 3835

9. 3306
    − 2815

10. 2002
     − 1744

A Multimagic Square

This is a magic square. What is the magic sum in each row, column, and diagonal?

87.12	10.89	65.34
32.67	54.45	76.23
43.56	98.01	21.78

↓

This square was made from the magic square above. Is it a magic square?

7.1	0.8	5.3
2.6	4.4	6.2
3.5	8.0	1.7

Other squares can be made from the top magic square. Find some of them. Check to see if the squares you make are magic squares.

Using Your Skills

Downtown Exit 2.0
Westside Exit 3.5
Medford Exit 10.5

| 2 | 7 | 4 | 1 | 8 |

Odometer

Getting started

1. What will the odometer read at the Downtown exit?
2. How far is it from the Downtown exit to the Westside exit?
3. What other problems can you solve?

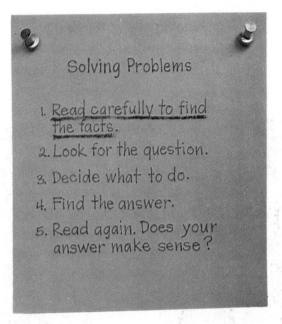

Solving Problems

1. Read carefully to find the facts.

2. Look for the question.

3. Decide what to do.

4. Find the answer.

5. Read again. Does your answer make sense?

You need to be able to find
the important facts in a problem.
Some problems may include facts
you do not need. Sometimes
the facts you need may be missing.

Which problems below have more facts than are needed?
Which do not have all the facts needed?

1. Mrs. James's odometer showed
943 km at 8:00 am. She drove
her car to work in 20 minutes.
Her odometer then read 967 km.
How far did she drive?

2. Mr. Perez saw a sign that read:
Centerville—80 km. He drove
for 30 minutes. How far was
he from Centerville then?

3. Janet had an odometer on her
bicycle. At the beginning of
a bicycle trip it read 12.7.
After the trip it read 50.1.
How far did Janet ride her bike?

4. Susan rode her bicycle 12.3 km
on Monday. She lives 1.5 km
from school. She rode to school
and back on Tuesday. What was
her bicycle odometer reading then?

Estimating sums and differences

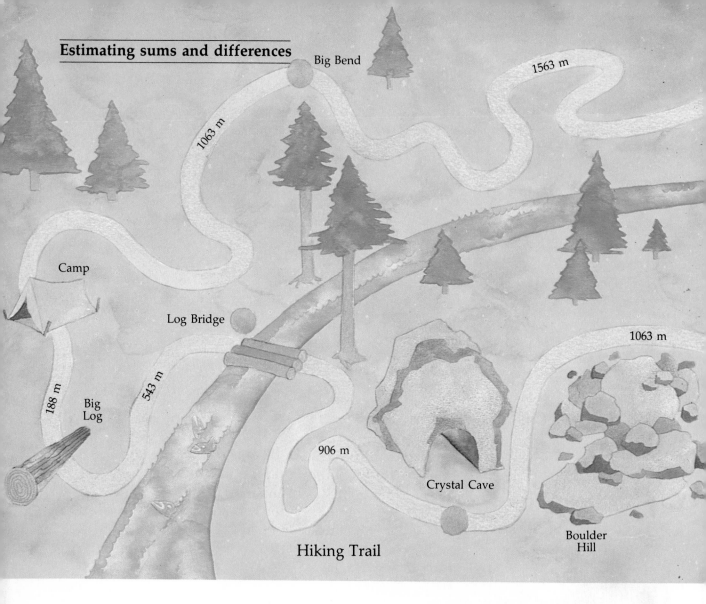

Big Bend

1563 m

1063 m

Camp

Log Bridge

188 m

Big Log

543 m

906 m

Crystal Cave

1063 m

Boulder Hill

Hiking Trail

Estimate the distance from Camp to the Log Bridge.

Estimate how much further it is from Red Rocks to Blue Falls Bridge than from Trail Junction to Red Rocks.

Problem   Estimate

Problem   Estimate

$$
\begin{array}{r}
188 \\
+\,543 \\
\end{array}
\quad
\text{Round to the nearest hundred}
\quad
\begin{array}{r}
200 \\
+\,500 \\
\hline
700 \\
\end{array}
$$

$$
\begin{array}{r}
1938 \\
-\,1375 \\
\end{array}
\quad
\text{Round to the nearest hundred}
\quad
\begin{array}{r}
1900 \\
-\,1400 \\
\hline
500 \\
\end{array}
$$

It is about 700 m from Camp to the Log Bridge.

It is about 500 m farther.

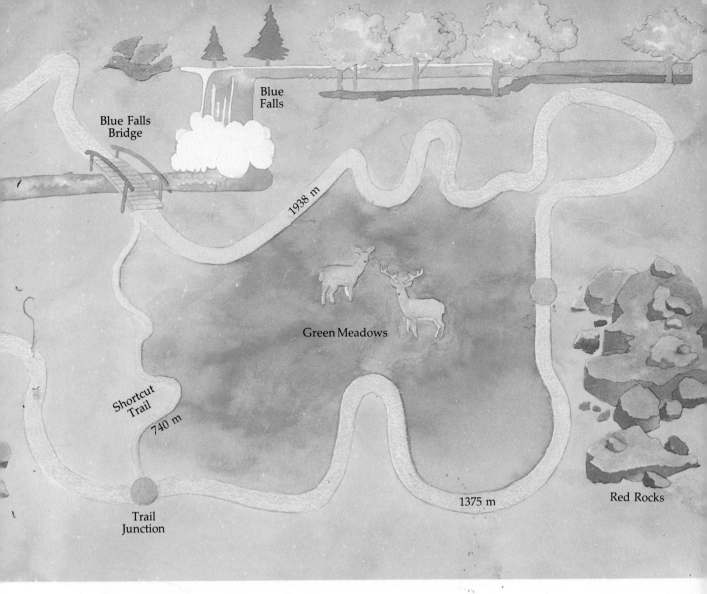

Blue Falls

Blue Falls Bridge

1938 m

Green Meadows

Shortcut Trail

740 m

1375 m

Red Rocks

Trail Junction

Estimate the total distances. Round to the nearest hundred.

1. Log Bridge to Trail Junction
2. Big Log to Crystal Cave
3. Crystal Cave to Blue Falls Bridge using Shortcut Trail

4. Trail Junction to Big Bend
5. Blue Falls Bridge to Camp
6. The shortest way from Red Rocks to Camp across Blue Falls Bridge

Estimate the difference in distances.

7. Blue Falls Bridge to Big Bend and Crystal Cave to Trail Junction
8. Trail Junction to Red Rocks and Trail Junction to Blue Falls Bridge

9. Big Bend to Camp and Log Bridge to Crystal Cave
10. Red Rocks to Blue Falls Bridge and Blue Falls Bridge to Big Bend

Solve the problems.

1. Distances from the moon
    to the earth:
    Greatest distance—406 699 km
    Least distance—356 399 km
    What is the difference
    in the distances?

2. Distances around the equators:
    Moon—10 927 km
    Earth—40 075 km
    How much farther around
    the earth's equator?

3. First man to see the moon through
    a telescope: Galileo, in 1609
    First man to walk on the moon:
    Neil Armstrong, 360 years later
    What year did the first man walk
    on the moon?

4. Crater diameters:
    Meteor Crater in Arizona—1.22 km
    Plato Crater on the moon—116.20 km
    How much farther across Plato
    Crater?

8. Moon's speed in orbit:
3700 km/h
Earth's speed in orbit:
107 200 km/h
How much faster is
the earth's speed?

5. Distance across the Grand
Canyon: 11.26 km
Distance across the moon crater
Copernicus: 78.84 km more than
across the Grand Canyon
How far is it across Copernicus?

9. Shortest stay on the moon:
Apollo 11 astronauts—21.6 h
Longest stay on the moon:
Apollo 17 astronauts—54.4 h
longer than Apollo 11
How long did the Apollo 17
astronauts stay?

6. Number of days the earth takes
to orbit the sun: 365.25
Number of days the moon takes
to orbit the earth: 29.5
What is the difference?

☆ 10. Nighttime moon temperature:
173° C below zero
Daytime moon temperature:
300° C higher than nighttime
What is the daytime moon
temperature?

7. Moon rock samples collected
by Apollo astronauts:
Apollo 11—22.0 kg
Apollo 12—33.9 kg
Apollo 14—43.6 kg
Apollo 15—77.3 kg
Apollo 16—96.8 kg
Apollo 17—110.4 kg
Find the total mass of rocks.

Banking

Would you like to be a bank teller?

Bank tellers receive cash or checks from customers. They pay out the money that customers withdraw from the bank. They also cash checks for customers.

Tellers must carefully record the amounts of money they take in and pay out. They must check **deposit slips** like this to make sure there are no mistakes in the amounts. Is the total deposit shown on this slip correct?

List checks by Bank number	Dollars	Cents
Currency	23	00
Coin	18	57
Checks		
3-169	37	56
Total Deposit	79	13

Find the total deposit for each slip.

1.

List checks by Bank number	Dollars	Cents
Currency	47	00
Coin		82
Checks		
2-034	66	25
1-963	93	48
Total Deposit		

3.

List checks by Bank number	Dollars	Cents
Currency	138	00
Coin		42
Checks		
60-9014	27	95
9-369	249	50
Total Deposit		

2.

List checks by Bank number	Dollars	Cents
Currency	295	00
Coin		62
Checks		
1-0324	148	14
5-065	342	86
39-209	166	95
Total Deposit		

4.

List checks by Bank number	Dollars	Cents
Currency		
Coin		
Checks		
3-963	42	55
20-149	154	67
16-039	20	00
72-6324	73	48
Total Deposit		

When money is **deposited** in a bank, the amount is **added** to the customer's account.

When money is **withdrawn,** the amount is **subtracted** from the customer's account.

The new amount after a deposit or withdrawal is called the **balance.**

Find each balance.

1.

Amount in savings	$ 129	42
Deposit	38	26
Balance		

5.

Amount in savings	$ 217	42
Withdrawal	32	95
Balance		

2.

Amount in savings	$ 529	11
Withdrawal	64	75
Balance		

6.

Amount in savings	$1215	44
Deposit	72	68
Balance		

3.

Amount in savings	$ 57	33
Deposit	19	88
Balance		

7.

Amount in savings	$ 318	47
Withdrawal	250	00
Balance		

4.

Amount in savings	$1708	00
Withdrawal	314	66
Balance		

8.

Amount in savings	$2933	48
Deposit	174	56
Balance		

Self-check

1. Odometer readings:
   Monday—7734.7 km
   Tuesday—8015.4 km
   How many kilometers were
   traveled?

2. Estimate the difference by
   rounding to the nearest hundred.

   $$\begin{array}{r} 2592 \\ -\,1224 \\ \hline \end{array}$$

3. Find the total deposit.

Checks	1.	$347	84
	2.	158	19
	3.	77	50
Total Deposit			

4. Estimate the sum by rounding
   to the nearest hundred.

   $$\begin{array}{r} 487 \\ +\,209 \\ \hline \end{array}$$

5. The Apollo 16 astronauts stayed
   71.03 hours on the moon. The
   Apollo 15 astronauts stayed 4.11
   hours less than that. How long were
   the Apollo 15 astronauts on the moon?

6. Find the balance.

Amount in savings	$251	22
Withdrawal	67	56
Balance		

Answers for Self-check—page 37

Test

1. Odometer reading was 896.9 km.
   Drove 74.8 km.
   What is the reading now?

2. Estimate the difference by
   rounding to the nearest hundred.

   $$\begin{array}{r} 806 \\ -\,388 \\ \hline \end{array}$$

3. Find the total deposit.

Checks	1.	$ 76	42
	2.	84	79
	3.	129	66
Total Deposit			

4. Estimate the sum by rounding
   to the nearest hundred.

   $$\begin{array}{r} 719 \\ +\,878 \\ \hline \end{array}$$

5. Crater diameters:
   Meteor Crater, Arizona—1.22 km
   Crater Lake, Oregon—9.65 km
   How much greater is the diameter
   of Crater Lake?

6. Find the balance.

Amount in savings	$88	14
Deposit	15	68
Balance		

A Cross-Number Puzzle

Trace the puzzle. Then use
the clues to fill in the blanks.

Across

1. $400\,000 + 20\,000 + 5000 + 800 + 30 + 9$
5. 706 rounded to the nearest ten
6. $1046 - 387$
8. $0.2 + 1.2 + 0.6$
9. one thousand ninety more than 3096
12. the digit in the ten thousands' place in 564 327
13. 4.505 rounded to the nearest whole number
14. $34 + 17 + 42$
15. $1.275 + 1.725$
16. five hundred seventeen thousand, twenty
19. the digit in the hundreds' place in 903 276
20. $MMM - C$
21. half of half a dozen
22. four less than five more than five
23. the difference of 16.7 and 9.8 rounded to the nearest whole number
24. your age $+ 11.9 + 11.6 - 2.4 -$ your age $- 21.1$
25. 1.500 rounded to the nearest whole number
26. $4000 + 700 + 90$

Down

1. 40.6 rounded to the nearest whole number
2. $106.4 + 97.6$
3. number of days in a leap year
4. halfway between 90 and 100
5. six dozen
7. number of hours in 4 days
10. MCMLXXIX
11. 8347 rounded to the nearest hundred
13. $10 + 9 + 8 + 7 + 6 + 5 + 4 + 3 + 2 + 1$
15. number of days in June
17. $161 + 637 + 318 + 158$
18. the first year of the 21st century
19. the number of letters in the English alphabet
21. 10 more than $10 + 10 + 1 + 1$
27. the missing number in the series 1, 3, 5, _, 9, . . .
28. the difference of 100 000 and 99 991

Measurement

Getting started

The meter (m) is the basic unit of length. It is divided into these shorter units:

decimeter (0.1 m)
centimeter (0.01 m)
millimeter (0.001 m)

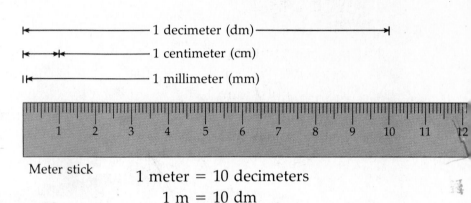

|←————————————— 1 decimeter (dm) —————————————→|

|←——→|←————— 1 centimeter (cm) —————|

|←———————— 1 millimeter (mm) ————————|

Meter stick

1 meter = 10 decimeters
1 m = 10 dm

Estimate whether these measurements for you are **equal to, more than,** or **less than** the unit shown. Measure to check your estimate.

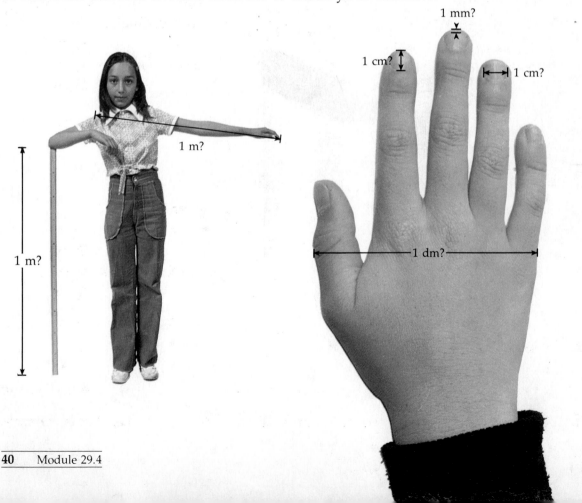

1 m?

1 m?

1 mm?

1 cm?

1 cm?

1 dm?

First estimate. Then measure.

1. width of your thumb
   your estimate: |||| cm
                  |||| mm
   actual measure: |||| cm
                   |||| mm

2. length of your ring finger
   your estimate: |||| cm
                  |||| mm
   actual measure: |||| cm
                   |||| mm

3. your armspan
   your estimate: |||| m
                  |||| cm
   actual measure: |||| m
                   |||| cm

4. your elbow to your fingertips
   your estimate: |||| m
                  |||| cm
   actual measure: |||| m
                   |||| cm

5. length of your shoe
   your estimate: |||| cm
                  |||| mm
   actual measure: |||| cm
                   |||| mm

6. your height
   your estimate: |||| m
                  |||| cm
   actual measure: |||| m
                   |||| cm

Give the correct number for each ||||.

7. 1 cm = |||| mm

8. 1 dm = |||| cm

9. 1 dm = |||| mm

10. 1 m = |||| dm

11. 1 m = |||| cm

12. 1 m = |||| mm

Length and distance

Units of Length

millimeter	(mm)	0.001 m
centimeter	(cm)	0.01 m
decimeter	(dm)	0.1 m
meter	(m)	1 m
dekameter	(dam)	10 m
hectometer	(hm)	100 m
kilometer	(km)	1000 m

The chart shows some units of length.

The most commonly used units are the centimeter, meter, and kilometer.

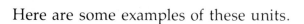

Here are some examples of these units.

The radius of a penny is about 1 cm.

A long step is about 1 m long.

If you walked for 10 city blocks, you would walk about 1 km.

1. About how many long steps would it take you to walk a kilometer?

2. About how many pennies laid side by side would make a row 1 m long?

3. About how many city blocks would you have to walk to go 10 km?

Give the missing unit, **cm, m,** or **km.**

1. A new pencil is 19 __?__ long.

2. The flagpole is 10 __?__ high.

3. Detroit is 436 __?__ from Chicago.

4. The book is 20 __?__ wide.

5. The airplane flew 740 __?__ in an hour.

6. The park bench is 2 __?__ long.

7. The paper clip is 3 __?__ long.

8. The lake is 8 __?__ wide.

9. The school bus is 12 __?__ long.

10. The cup's diameter is 8 __?__ .

Choose the correct number for each ▥.

11. 1 m = ▥ cm
    A 10
    B 100
    C 1000

12. 1 km = ▥ m
    A 10
    B 100
    C 1000

13. 1 cm = ▥ m
    A 1.0
    B 0.1
    C 0.01

14. A person who is 2 m tall is how many centimeters tall?

☆ 16. Give the measure of 10 objects or distances at your home and school. Try to find objects or distances to illustrate some of the units listed on page 42.

15. If you jog 2 km in the morning and 1 km in the evening, how many meters is that altogether?

Which would be worth more, a pile of pennies as high as you are tall or a row of dimes (laid side by side) equal to your height? Guess. Then find the actual values and their difference.

7 pennies

1 cm

dime

←1.7 cm→

Capacity: liters and milliliters

The basic unit of capacity is the liter(ℓ).

A cube 1 dm on each edge holds 1 liter (ℓ).

A cube 1 cm on each edge holds 1 milliliter (ml).

1 cm 1 cm 1 cm

$1\ \ell = 1000$ ml
1 ml $= 0.001\ \ell$

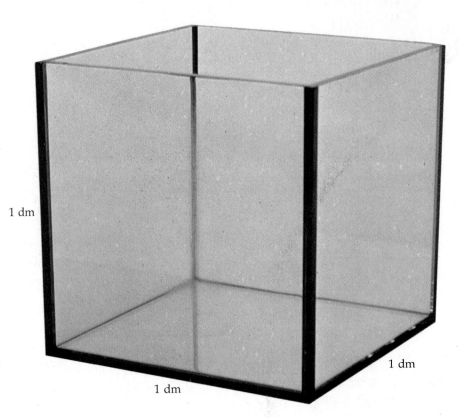

1 dm

1 dm

1 dm

How many of each would it take to fill a 1 ℓ container?

1.

250 ml

2.

500 ml

3.

100 ml

4.

10 ml

Choose the better measure of capacity for each container.

1.

2 ℓ or 2 ml?

2.

750 ℓ or 750 ml?

3.

15 ℓ or 15 ml?

4.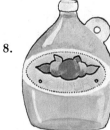

325 ℓ or 325 ml?

5.

450 ℓ or 450 ml?

6.

1 ℓ or 1 ml?

7.

250 ℓ or 250 ml?

8.

3.5 ℓ or 3.5 ml?

9. Carl bought 1.89 ℓ of milk, 0.95 ℓ of buttermilk, and 0.24 ℓ of whipping cream. How many liters did he buy in all?

10. Mila bought two cans of soft drink. Each can held 450 ml. Did she buy more or less than one liter of soft drink?

☆ 11. Jo used these amounts to make some punch. How many liters of punch did she make?

Island Punch
1.5 ℓ ginger ale
1.0 ℓ pineapple juice
450 ml orange juice
50 ml lemon juice

Practicing your skills
Add or subtract.

1.	2.	3.	4.	5.
967 + 846	532 − 197	6004 − 1976	9076 − 1887	3000 − 496

6.	7.	8.	9.	10.
94.36 + 72.98	5.98 + 0.09	80.63 − 9.79	79.07 − 49.98	4.076 − 0.948

Mass: grams and kilograms

The basic unit of mass is the kilogram (kg).
Two other commonly used units are the gram (g)
and the metric ton (t).

$$1 \text{ kg} = 1000 \text{ g} \qquad 1 \text{ g} = 0.001 \text{ kg} \qquad 1 \text{ t} = 1000 \text{ kg}$$

an 11 year old:
about 45 kg

a bunch of bananas:
about 2 kg

a letter:
about 14 g

a large man:
about 90 kg

an encyclopedia:
about 1 kg

a dime:
about 2 g

a car:
about 2 t

Give the unit, **g, kg,** or **t,** for each mass.

1. a liter carton of milk
   mass: 1 __?__

2. a ballpoint pen
   mass: 15 __?__

3. a nickel
   mass: 5 __?__

4. a camper wagon
   mass: 3 __?__

5. a baseball bat
   mass: 1 __?__

6. a canned ham
   mass: 2 __?__

7. a tube of toothpaste
   mass: 140 __?__

8. a baby
   mass: 4 __?__

9. a TV set
   mass: 50 __?__

Choose the best estimate for each object.

1.  a large dog

   A 3.5 kg

   B 35 kg

   C 350 kg

2.  a day's supply of puppy food

   A 42 g

   B 420 g

   C 4200 g

3.  6 potatoes

   A 15 g

   B 150 g

   C 1500 g

4.  a cup filled with nuts

   A 22 g

   B 220 g

   C 2200 g

5.  a portable typewriter

   A 5.4 kg

   B 54 kg

   C 540 kg

6.  a packed suitcase

   A 1.5 kg

   B 15 kg

   C 150 kg

7. Copy and complete this table.

kilograms	0.001	0.002	0.005	0.025	0.125	0.775	1.000
grams	1	2	5	▦	▦	▦	▦

8. How many grams of hamburger are in the package?

9. How many grams of flour are in the bag?

Using degrees Celsius: recording temperatures

The unit for measuring temperature
is the **degree Celsius** (° C).

This thermometer shows that water freezes
at 0° C and that comfortable room temperature
is about 20° C. Water boils at 100° C.

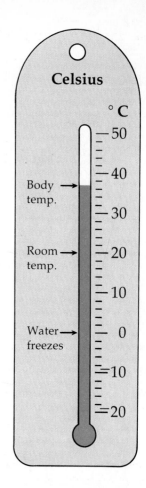

A student used a Celsius thermometer
and collected this information.

Temperature	Reading
Cold water from a faucet	12° C
Hot water from a faucet	70° C
Inside the refrigerator	5° C
Today's indoor temperature	19° C
Today's outdoor temperature	14° C

Draw some graph paper thermometers like
the one shown here and color them to show
each of the temperatures in the chart.

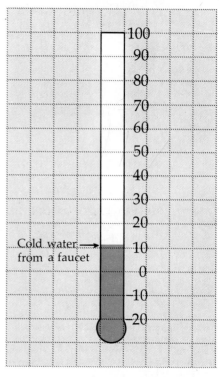

Choose the best estimate for each Celsius temperature.

1.	high fever	**A** 22° C	**B** 39° C	**C** 54° C
2.	medium-hot oven	**A** 50° C	**B** 90° C	**C** 180° C
3.	a very hot summer day	**A** 40° C	**B** 80° C	**C** 120° C
4.	inside a refrigerator	**A** ⁻10° C	**B** 2° C	**C** 15° C
5.	a cool fall day	**A** 6° C	**B** 36° C	**C** 56° C

6. This graph shows the normal monthly high temperature for Dallas, Texas, during the first 6 months of the year.

Give each temperature as accurately as you can from the graph.

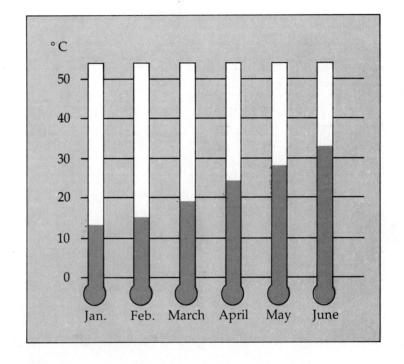

7. Record the temperature in °C at noon each day for 5 days. Make a temperature graph to show your findings.

Find the next number in this sequence.

2 856 719
2 956 819
3 056 919
3 157 019

▮▮▮ ▮▮▮ ▮▮▮ ▮▮▮ ▮▮▮ ▮▮▮ ▮▮▮

Answers for Self-check   1. 100   2. 1000   3. 1000   4. 37   5. 40   6. 2 km   7. 250 ml   8. 5500 kg
9. 5 m   10. 2.1 cm

Self-check

Choose the number for each ▓.

1. 1 m = ▓ cm
    A 10   B 100   C 1000

2. 1 ℓ = ▓ ml
    A 100   B 500   C 1000

3. ▓ g = 1 kg
    A 10   B 100   C 1000

4. human body temperature: ▓° C
    A 20   B 37   C 50

5. hot summer day: ▓° C
    A 20   B 40   C 60

Choose the best measure.

6. length of an airport runway
    A 2 cm   B 2 m   C 2 km

7. capacity of a water glass
    A 250 ml   B 250 ℓ

8. mass of an elephant
    A 5500 g   B 5500 kg

9. length of a car
    A 5 cm   B 5 m   C 5 km

10. width of a nickel
    A 2.1 cm   B 2.1 m   C 2.1 km

Answers for Self-check—page 49

Test

Choose the number for each ▓.

1. 1 km = ▓ m
    A 10   B 100   C 1000

2. 1 kg = ▓ g
    A 100   B 1000   C 10 000

3. ▓ ml = 1 ℓ
    A 100   B 1000   C 10 000

4. food freezer temperature: ▓° C
    A −10   B 10   C 20

5. comfortable room temperature: ▓° C
    A 5   B 20   C 35

Choose the best measure.

6. length of a ballpoint pen
    A 18 cm   B 18 m   C 18 km

7. capacity of a car's gas tank
    A 60 ml   B 60 ℓ

8. mass of a baseball
    A 140 g   B 140 kg

9. length of a river
    A 205 cm   B 205 m   C 205 km

10. height of a giraffe
    A 4.8 cm   B 4.8 m   C 4.8 km

Logical Reasoning

Suppose you had a set of figures like these.

3 large squares

3 large triangles

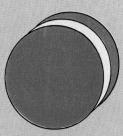

3 large circles

3 small squares

3 small triangles

3 small circles

Pretend that one of the pieces above is hidden under each of these clue cards. Which pieces are they?

Clue Card

1.
It is **not** small.
It is **not** red **or** yellow.
It is **not** a square **or** a circle.
Which is it?

Clue Card

2.
It is large **and** red.
It does **not** have corners.
Which is it?

Clue Card

3.
If it is yellow, **then** it is small.
If it is small, **then** it is a square.
It is **not** blue or red.
Which is it?

4. Choose a piece to hide. Make a clue card and see whether a friend can find which piece it is. Use some of these words on your card: **and, or, not, if-then.**

Level 29 review

Write the standard numeral.

1. six million, two hundred ninety thousand

2. thirty-five and four tenths

3. nine and forty-six hundredths

4. $50\ 000 + 8000 + 300 + 60 + 7$

Give the correct sign ($<$ or $>$) for each ◉.

5. 4.6 ◉ 4.4   6. 0.75 ◉ 0.78   7. 0.02 ◉ 0.2   8. 0.342 ◉ 0.341

Round to the nearest hundred.

9. 856   10. 85 476

Round to the nearest thousand.

11. 4463   12. 53 519

Round to the nearest tenth.

13. 0.86   14. 5.48

Round to the nearest hundredth.

15. 0.783   16. 2.045

Add.

17.
$$\begin{array}{r} 97 \\ + 54 \\ \hline \end{array}$$

18.
$$\begin{array}{r} 368 \\ + 872 \\ \hline \end{array}$$

19.
$$\begin{array}{r} 5813 \\ + 4398 \\ \hline \end{array}$$

20.
$$\begin{array}{r} 579 \\ 384 \\ + 627 \\ \hline \end{array}$$

21.
$$\begin{array}{r} 2836 \\ 3942 \\ + 7519 \\ \hline \end{array}$$

22.
$$\begin{array}{r} 3.8 \\ + 8.7 \\ \hline \end{array}$$

23.
$$\begin{array}{r} 0.56 \\ + 2.89 \\ \hline \end{array}$$

24.
$$\begin{array}{r} 2.546 \\ + 6.385 \\ \hline \end{array}$$

25.
$$\begin{array}{r} 4.7 \\ 5.2 \\ + 8.6 \\ \hline \end{array}$$

26.
$$\begin{array}{r} 16.53 \\ 21.79 \\ + 8.45 \\ \hline \end{array}$$

Subtract.

27.
$$\begin{array}{r} 76 \\ - 49 \\ \hline \end{array}$$

28.
$$\begin{array}{r} 517 \\ - 328 \\ \hline \end{array}$$

29.
$$\begin{array}{r} 3775 \\ - 2847 \\ \hline \end{array}$$

30.
$$\begin{array}{r} 4100 \\ - 2613 \\ \hline \end{array}$$

31.
$$\begin{array}{r} 83\ 127 \\ - 64\ 259 \\ \hline \end{array}$$

32.
$$\begin{array}{r} 3.6 \\ - 1.8 \\ \hline \end{array}$$

33.
$$\begin{array}{r} 0.84 \\ - 0.57 \\ \hline \end{array}$$

34.
$$\begin{array}{r} 7.43 \\ - 3.86 \\ \hline \end{array}$$

35.
$$\begin{array}{r} 0.971 \\ - 0.593 \\ \hline \end{array}$$

36.
$$\begin{array}{r} 27.305 \\ - 16.738 \\ \hline \end{array}$$

Level **30**

Multiplication Facts and Special Products
Multiplying Whole Numbers
Multiplying with Decimals
Using Your Skills
Area

Multiplication Facts and Special Products

Getting started

Think centimeters: 3 × 4 = 12

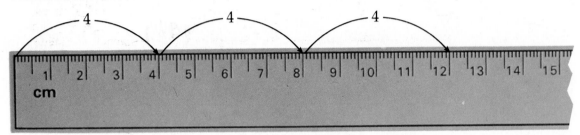

Think millimeters: 3 × 40 = 120

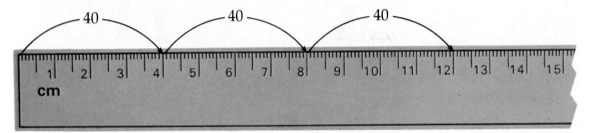

Think centimeters: Solve 5 × 3 = n.

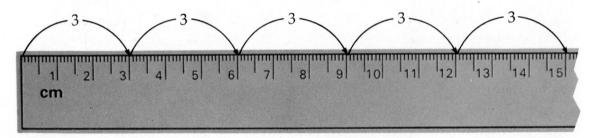

Think millimeters: Solve 5 × 30 = n.

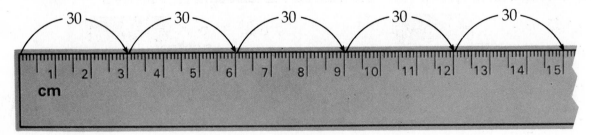

Write a "think millimeters" equation for each "think centimeters" equation.

1. Think centimeters: 6 × 7 = 42

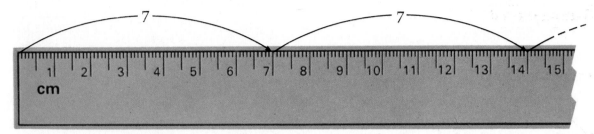

2. Think centimeters: 8 × 6 = 48

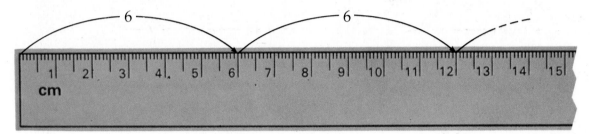

3. Think centimeters: 7 × 9 = 63

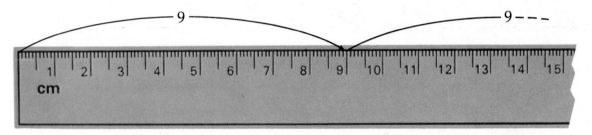

The **associative principle** helps you find special products.

Associative Principle
You can change the grouping in multiplication and the product is the same.

$3 \times 40 = 3 \times \boxed{4 \times 10}$ $6 \times 800 = 6 \times \boxed{8 \times 100}$

$3 \times 40 = \boxed{3 \times 4} \times 10$ $6 \times 800 = \boxed{6 \times 8} \times 100$

$3 \times 40 = 12 \times 10$ $6 \times 800 = 48 \times 100$

Solve: $3 \times 40 = $ |||| Solve: $6 \times 800 = $ ||||

Reviewing multiplication facts

What is the product?

$$\begin{array}{r} 5 \\ \times 9 \\ \hline \end{array}$$

If you forget 9×5,
maybe you remember 5×9.

The Commutative (Order) Principle of Multiplication
You can change the order of the factors and the product is the same.

$$9 \times 5 = 5 \times 9$$

Give these facts as quickly as you can.
You may want to time yourself.

1. 4×6 2. 5×8 3. 6×5 4. 7×7 5. 9×8

6. 8×5 7. 8×9 8. 7×8 9. 9×4 10. 5×9

11. 3×7 12. 4×0 13. 7×6 14. 8×3 15. 4×9

16. 7×9 17. 2×9 18. 5×7 19. 1×8 20. 9×7

21. 8×6 22. 5×4 23. 9×5 24. 2×6 25. 3×9

26. $\begin{array}{r} 8 \\ \times 4 \\ \hline \end{array}$
27. $\begin{array}{r} 7 \\ \times 8 \\ \hline \end{array}$
28. $\begin{array}{r} 6 \\ \times 9 \\ \hline \end{array}$
29. $\begin{array}{r} 9 \\ \times 6 \\ \hline \end{array}$
30. $\begin{array}{r} 3 \\ \times 9 \\ \hline \end{array}$

31. $\begin{array}{r} 4 \\ \times 8 \\ \hline \end{array}$
32. $\begin{array}{r} 2 \\ \times 9 \\ \hline \end{array}$
33. $\begin{array}{r} 4 \\ \times 6 \\ \hline \end{array}$
34. $\begin{array}{r} 6 \\ \times 6 \\ \hline \end{array}$
35. $\begin{array}{r} 5 \\ \times 7 \\ \hline \end{array}$

36. $\begin{array}{r} 7 \\ \times 6 \\ \hline \end{array}$
37. $\begin{array}{r} 8 \\ \times 8 \\ \hline \end{array}$
38. $\begin{array}{r} 9 \\ \times 9 \\ \hline \end{array}$
39. $\begin{array}{r} 8 \\ \times 6 \\ \hline \end{array}$
40. $\begin{array}{r} 4 \\ \times 7 \\ \hline \end{array}$

Give the products.

1. 6 × 6
2. 7 × 6
3. 8 × 6
4. 9 × 6
5. 5 × 6

6. 6 × 7
7. 7 × 7
8. 8 × 7
9. 9 × 7
10. 5 × 7

11. 6 × 8
12. 7 × 8
13. 8 × 8
14. 9 × 8
15. 5 × 8

16. 6 × 9
17. 7 × 9
18. 8 × 9
19. 9 × 9
20. 5 × 9

21. 1
    × 9

22. 2
    × 8

23. 3
    × 7

24. 4
    × 6

25. 5
    × 5

26. 6
    × 4

27. 7
    × 3

28. 8
    × 2

29. 9
    × 1

30. 8
    × 0

31. 7
    × 1

32. 6
    × 2

33. 5
    × 3

34. 4
    × 4

35. 3
    × 5

36. 2
    × 6

37. 4
    × 7

38. 5
    × 8

39. 3
    × 9

40. 9
    × 4

☆ 41. Make flash cards for any facts
you have trouble remembering.
Practice the facts with a friend.

front   back

input → Rule: ? → output
10   99

input	output
1	0
2	3
3	8
4	15
5	24

What's the
rule?

More practice, page 378, Set A

Special products

Marian practices playing the piano 40 minutes every day. How many minutes does she practice in a week (7 days)? How many minutes does she practice in a month? (Use 30 days in a month.)

Finding the answers

$$7 \times 40$$
$$7 \times 4 \times 10$$
$$28 \times 10$$
$$280$$

$$30 \times 40$$
$$30 \times 4 \times 10$$
$$120 \times 10$$
$$1200$$

$$7 \times 40 = 280 \qquad 30 \times 40 = 1200$$

Marion practices 280 minutes a week and 1200 minutes a month.

Other examples

24×10	$=$	240	5×70	$=$	350
24×100	$=$	2400	5×700	$=$	3500
24×1000	$=$	$24\ 000$	5×7000	$=$	$35\ 000$

$$60 \times 70 = 4200$$
$$20 \times 80 = 1600$$
$$20 \times 800 = 16\ 000$$

Give the products.

1. 8×10
2. 29×10
3. 4×100
4. 36×100
5. 72×100

6. 7×1000
7. 32×1000
8. 3×70
9. 9×40
10. 5×60

11. 8×70
12. 6×200
13. 7×400
14. 8×500
15. 9×700

16. 5×3000
17. 4×9000
18. 7×2000
19. 5×600
20. 3×5000

Give the products.

1. 20 × 60
2. 40 × 80
3. 30 × 60
4. 70 × 50
5. 90 × 40
6. 60 × 40
7. 70 × 90
8. 80 × 30
9. 50 × 30
10. 40 × 30
11. 70 × 20
12. 80 × 70
13. 60 × 60
14. 70 × 40
15. 50 × 90
16. 60 × 300
17. 40 × 400
18. 30 × 900
19. 80 × 600
20. 90 × 900
21. 70 × 60

22. 10 × 12
23. 68 × 10
24. 70 × 70
25. 37 × 100
26. 60 × 9
27. 600 × 7
28. 5 × 4000
29. 300 × 9
30. 80 × 80
31. 500 × 70
32. 90 × 60
33. 8000 × 7
34. 6 × 400
35. 30 × 200
36. 9 × 7000

37. Tony plays the violin. He practices 50 minutes a day. How many minutes does he practice in a week? In a month?

38. Linda is a drummer. She practices 30 minutes a day. How many minutes does she practice in a week? In a month?

Are these statements true?

15 × 15 = (10 × 20) + 25
25 × 25 = (20 × 30) + 25
35 × 35 = (30 × 40) + 25

Complete these equations to make them like the ones above. Check them.

45 × 45 = ?
55 × 55 = ?
65 × 65 = ?

More practice, page 378, Set B

Estimating products

The Italian trader Marco Polo spent
24 years on his travels through Asia.
About how many weeks was this?
(Use 52 weeks in a year.)

Finding the answer

Problem	→	Round each number to the nearest 10	→	Multiply the rounded numbers

$$24 \times 52 \qquad 20 \times 50 \qquad 1000$$

Marco Polo spent about 1000 weeks
on his travels through Asia.

Other examples

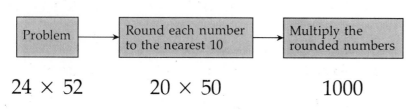

23×8 9×78 41×58 25×34
$20 \times 8 = 160$ $9 \times 80 = 720$ $40 \times 60 = 2400$ $30 \times 30 = 900$

Estimate the products.

1. 8×32 2. 57×21 3. 9×69 4. 89×22

5. 27×78 6. 7×48 7. 63×5 8. 76×43

9. 65×4 10. 39×61 11. 76×28 12. 7×44

13. 47×59 14. 35×72 15. 6×19 16. 56×24

17. 7×88 18. 63×4 19. 93×47 20. 22×87

Estimate the products.

Example: 9 × 597

Round 597 to
the nearest hundred

9 × 600 = 5400

1. 7 × 698	**2.** 6 × 489	**3.** 8 × 311
4. 5 × 403	**5.** 4 × 775	**6.** 3 × 198
7. 2 × 889	**8.** 421 × 7	**9.** 582 × 4
10. 794 × 6	**11.** 517 × 8	**12.** 331 × 9
13. 865 × 7	**14.** 921 × 5	**15.** 21 × 68
16. 43 × 18	**17.** 64 × 47	**18.** 85 × 42
19. 5 × 66	**20.** 942 × 8	**21.** 29 × 3
22. 571 × 7	**23.** 59 × 498	**24.** 31 × 695
25. 304 × 78	**26.** 813 × 52	**27.** 49 × 702

28. The voyage of the first ship to sail
around the world took 3 years.
About how many weeks was this?

☆ **29.** Find out how many days it
took the *Mayflower* to reach
the coast of New England.
About how many hours was this?

Think!

A pen cost a dollar more than
an eraser. Together they cost
one dollar and ten cents. How
much was the eraser?

Answers for Self-check 1. 54 2. 56 3. 42 4. 63 5. 64 6. 54 7. 25 8. 36 9. 270 10. 3600
11. 54 000 12. 240 13. 3600 14. 30 000 15. 2800 16. 54 000 17. 2100 18. 32 000 19. 1800
20. 10 000 21. 7200 22. 35 000 23. 26 000 24. 4200 25. 400 26. 3500 27. 4200 28. 27 000

Self-check

Find the products.

1. 9×6
2. 8×7
3. 6×7
4. 9×7
5. 8×8
6. 9×6
7. 5×5
8. 4×9
9. 27×10
10. 100×36
11. 54×1000
12. 8×30
13. 400×9
14. 6×5000
15. 40×70
16. 90×600
17. 7×300
18. 4000×8
19. 60×30
20. 500×20
21. 80×90
22. 700×50
23. 1000×26
24. 60×70

Estimate the products.

25. 8×47
26. 48×65
27. 6×689
28. 32×897

Answers for Self-check—page 61

Test

Find the products.

1. 6×8
2. 9×9
3. 7×5
4. 9×8
5. 6×6
6. 5×9
7. 8×4
8. 5×8
9. 10×56
10. 81×100
11. 48×1000
12. 9×50
13. 7×400
14. 8000×4
15. 30×90
16. 700×90
17. 500×6
18. 6×7000
19. 70×70
20. 40×500
21. 90×40
22. 300×80
23. 1000×82
24. 50×50

Estimate the products.

25. 7×64
26. 74×39
27. 967×4
28. 58×304

Prime Number Draw

Try this game for 2 or more players.

1. Make a set of 25 cards, using the prime numbers less than 100.

Prime Numbers				
2	3	5	7	11
13	17	19	23	29
31	37	41	43	47
53	59	61	67	71
73	79	83	89	97

2. Take turns drawing one card at a time from the deck.

3. Find your score for each draw by choosing the row in the table below that describes your number and gives you the most points.

Number	Description	Score
Prime	A prime number has exactly 2 different factors— the number itself and 1.	5
Even prime	The number 2 is the only even prime number.	25
One of a pair of twin primes	A twin prime is one of a pair of prime numbers that differ by 2 (like 17 or 19).	10
Reversal prime	If you reverse the digits of a reversal prime, you get another prime. The number 13 is a reversal prime because 31 is also prime.	15

4. The first player to score a total of 100 points wins the game.

olying Whole Numbers

Getting started

Make 3 sets of cards like these.

| 0 | 100 | 200 | 300 | 400 |
| 500 | 600 | 700 | 800 | 900 |

| 0 | 10 | 20 | 30 | 40 |
| 50 | 60 | 70 | 80 | 90 |

| 0 | 1 | 2 | 3 | 4 |
| 5 | 6 | 7 | 8 | 9 |

Shuffle the cards in each set and put them facedown on the table. Then draw a card from each set and roll a number cube with the faces labeled 4 through 9.

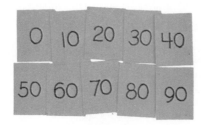

$$7 \times 3 = 21$$
$$7 \times 60 = 420$$
$$7 \times 200 = 1400$$
$$\overline{}$$
$$TOTAL \quad 1841$$

Multiply each card number by the cube number. Add the three products.

Play the game with a friend. The highest total wins.

The Distributive Principle

When you multiply, you can "break apart" one of the factors as in the examples below.

3×26 is the same as $(3 \times 20) + (3 \times 6)$.

4×352 is the same as $(4 \times 300) + (4 \times 50) + (4 \times 2)$.

This principle is used in multiplying larger numbers.

Find each score.

1. 400 20 6 7

2. 500 40 3 6

3.  700 60 4 8

4. 9 3 8  4

5. Linda found her score this way:

```
    5 3 6
  ×     8
      4 8  ← 8 × 6
    2 4 0  ← 8 × 30
  4 0 0 0  ← 8 × 500
  4 2 8 8
```

Use Linda's method to find these scores:

```
    7 4 2          8 5 7
  ×     6        ×     4
```

Multiplying by a 1-digit factor

United States senators are elected
to serve for 6 years. How many days
is this? (Use 365 days in a year.)

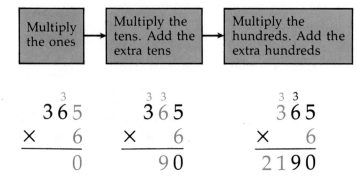

Finding the answer

Multiply the ones	Multiply the tens. Add the extra tens	Multiply the hundreds. Add the extra hundreds

$$\begin{array}{r} \overset{3}{3}65 \\ \times\ \ \ 6 \\ \hline 0 \end{array} \qquad \begin{array}{r} \overset{3\ 3}{3}65 \\ \times\ \ \ 6 \\ \hline 90 \end{array} \qquad \begin{array}{r} \overset{3\ 3}{3}65 \\ \times\ \ \ 6 \\ \hline 2190 \end{array}$$

United States senators are elected
to serve for 2190 days.

Other examples

$$\begin{array}{r} \overset{4}{3}6 \\ \times\ 8 \\ \hline 288 \end{array} \qquad \begin{array}{r} \overset{2}{1}28 \\ \times\ \ 3 \\ \hline 384 \end{array} \qquad \begin{array}{r} \overset{4}{5}07 \\ \times\ \ 6 \\ \hline 3042 \end{array} \qquad \begin{array}{r} \overset{2\ 3\ 2}{3}596 \\ \times\ \ \ \ 4 \\ \hline 14\ 384 \end{array}$$

Find the products.

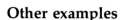

1. $\begin{array}{r} 64 \\ \times\ 3 \\ \hline \end{array}$
2. $\begin{array}{r} 73 \\ \times\ 6 \\ \hline \end{array}$
3. $\begin{array}{r} 167 \\ \times\ \ 5 \\ \hline \end{array}$
4. $\begin{array}{r} 234 \\ \times\ \ 7 \\ \hline \end{array}$
5. $\begin{array}{r} 679 \\ \times\ \ 2 \\ \hline \end{array}$

6. $\begin{array}{r} 703 \\ \times\ \ 8 \\ \hline \end{array}$
7. $\begin{array}{r} 155 \\ \times\ \ 9 \\ \hline \end{array}$
8. $\begin{array}{r} 309 \\ \times\ \ 4 \\ \hline \end{array}$
9. $\begin{array}{r} 717 \\ \times\ \ 6 \\ \hline \end{array}$
10. $\begin{array}{r} 598 \\ \times\ \ 8 \\ \hline \end{array}$

Find the products.

1.	274 × 6	**2.**	302 × 9	**3.**	67 × 8
4.	34 × 7	**5.**	136 × 5	**6.**	1234 × 6
7.	5231 × 9	**8.**	6418 × 8	**9.**	1792 × 4
10.	1368 × 3	**11.**	9216 × 2	**12.**	7435 × 7
13.	2163 × 5	**14.**	4816 × 6	**15.**	3250 × 7
16.	1408 × 8	**17.**	3506 × 9	**18.**	1079 × 2
19.	2038 × 4	**20.**	5030 × 3	**21.**	2719 × 5

22. The president of the United States is elected to serve for 4 years. How many weeks is this? (Use 52 weeks in a year.)

☆ **23.** Find out how many years the governor of your state or province is elected to serve. How many days is this? (Use 365 days in a year.)

Multiply. Write your answers in list form.

142 857 × 1	142 857 × 2	142 857 × 3
142 857 × 4	142 857 × 5	142 857 × 6

What did you discover?

More practice, page 379, Set A

Multiplying by a 2-digit factor

During a movie, 1440 separate still pictures are flashed onto the screen every minute. How many separate pictures are flashed onto the screen during a 75-minute movie?

Finding the answer

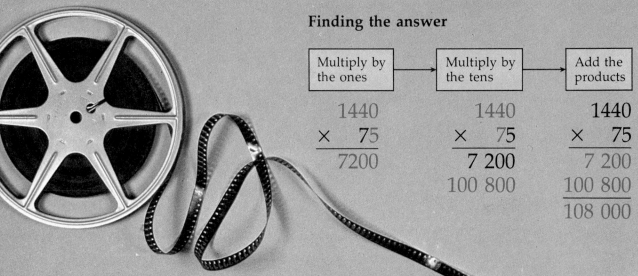

Multiply by the ones	Multiply by the tens	Add the products

```
   1440          1440          1440
 ×   75        ×   75        ×   75
   7200          7 200         7 200
               100 800       100 800
                             108 000
```

During a 75-minute movie, 108 000 separate pictures are flashed onto the screen.

Other examples

```
      43           409          3287
    × 26         ×  38        ×   64
     258         3 272        13 148
     860        12 270       197 220
    1118        15 542       210 368
```

Find the products.

1. 58
   × 24

2. 87
   × 43

3. 164
   × 26

4. 243
   × 57

5. 72
   × 49

6. 186
   × 34

7. 89
   × 76

8. 45
   × 38

9. 457
   × 38

10. 82
    × 95

Find the products.

1. 147 × 36	**2.** 237 × 31	**3.** 396 × 92	**4.** 405 × 43	**5.** 573 × 54
6. 654 × 25	**7.** 748 × 46	**8.** 830 × 57	**9.** 906 × 38	**10.** 819 × 69
11. 7014 × 78	**12.** 6738 × 27	**13.** 5803 × 86	**14.** 4029 × 35	**15.** 3867 × 94
16. 2983 × 83	**17.** 1569 × 42	**18.** 2083 × 71	**19.** 4704 × 87	

20. One of Thomas Edison's inventions (the Kinetoscope) showed pictures at a speed of 2760 pictures per minute. How many pictures would be shown in 15 minutes?

☆**21.** Watch a TV cartoon. Keep track of how long the cartoon lasts. If 24 separate pictures were needed for each second of the cartoon, how many pictures were needed in all?

If 1 goller is worth 17 tollers, and 1 toller is worth 36 zollers, would you trade 27 gollers for 16 400 zollers?

More practice, page 379, Set B

Multiplying—larger products

There are 378 students
in an elementary school.
Each student drinks an
average of 246 ml of milk
at lunch each day. How
much milk would 378
students drink in a day?

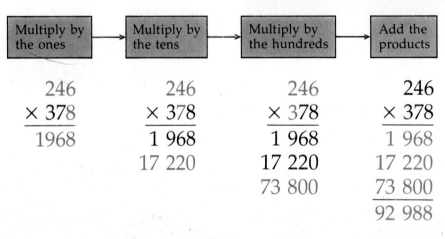

Finding the answer

Multiply by the ones	→	Multiply by the tens	→	Multiply by the hundreds	→	Add the products

$$
\begin{array}{r} 246 \\ \times\, 378 \\ \hline 1968 \end{array}
\qquad
\begin{array}{r} 246 \\ \times\, 378 \\ \hline 1\ 968 \\ 17\ 220 \end{array}
\qquad
\begin{array}{r} 246 \\ \times\, 378 \\ \hline 1\ 968 \\ 17\ 220 \\ 73\ 800 \end{array}
\qquad
\begin{array}{r} 246 \\ \times\, 378 \\ \hline 1\ 968 \\ 17\ 220 \\ 73\ 800 \\ \hline 92\ 988 \end{array}
$$

378 students would drink 92 988 ml of milk in a day.

Other examples

$$
\begin{array}{r} 453 \\ \times\, 260 \\ \hline 27\ 180 \\ 90\ 600 \\ \hline 117\ 780 \end{array}
\qquad
\begin{array}{r} 507 \\ \times\, 349 \\ \hline 4\ 563 \\ 20\ 280 \\ 152\ 100 \\ \hline 176\ 943 \end{array}
\qquad
\begin{array}{r} 786 \\ \times\, 408 \\ \hline 6\ 288 \\ 314\ 400 \\ \hline 320\ 688 \end{array}
$$

Find the products.

1.	2.	3.	4.	5.
348	694	619	752	868
× 267	× 463	× 237	× 463	× 957

Find the products.

1. 414 × 251	2. 256 × 169	3. 385 × 328	4. 520 × 589	5. 967 × 808
6. 628 × 760	7. 809 × 672	8. 790 × 957	9. 531 × 410	10. 672 × 277
11. 733 × 106	12. 864 × 355	13. 905 × 583	14. 946 × 940	15. 787 × 696
16. 948 × 814	17. 879 × 723	18. 418 × 302	19. 557 × 494	20. 696 × 535

First find the products of the numbers in parentheses.
Then multiply those products.

21. $(9 \times 8 \times 6) \times (7 \times 6 \times 4)$

22. $(7 \times 7 \times 7) \times (9 \times 9 \times 9)$

23. There are 784 students in a school. Each student drinks an average of 225 ml of milk each day. How much milk is needed each day?

☆ 24. If each student in your school drinks 245 ml of milk per day, how much milk is drunk each day? Find the cost of a liter of milk and estimate the cost of milk for your school for 1 day.

Choose any number from 1 through 9.
Multiply your number by 429.
Then multiply the product by 259.

Can you guess what the answer would be for any other number from 1 through 9?

Check your guess.

Answers for Self-check 1. 342 2. 2352 3. 3627 4. 6268 5. 5718 6. 1728 7. 3404 8. 16 392
9. 33 485 10. 126 458 11. 44 322 12. 145 382 13. 241 868 14. 267 920 15. 301 444 16. 448
17. 1075 18. 429 213

Self-check

Multiply.

1. $\begin{array}{r} 57 \\ \times\ 6 \\ \hline \end{array}$	2. $\begin{array}{r} 294 \\ \times\ 8 \\ \hline \end{array}$	3. $\begin{array}{r} 403 \\ \times\ 9 \\ \hline \end{array}$	4. $\begin{array}{r} 1567 \\ \times\ 4 \\ \hline \end{array}$	5. $\begin{array}{r} 1906 \\ \times\ 3 \\ \hline \end{array}$
6. $\begin{array}{r} 64 \\ \times\ 27 \\ \hline \end{array}$	7. $\begin{array}{r} 74 \\ \times\ 46 \\ \hline \end{array}$	8. $\begin{array}{r} 683 \\ \times\ 24 \\ \hline \end{array}$	9. $\begin{array}{r} 905 \\ \times\ 37 \\ \hline \end{array}$	10. $\begin{array}{r} 2386 \\ \times\ 53 \\ \hline \end{array}$
11. $\begin{array}{r} 178 \\ \times\ 249 \\ \hline \end{array}$	12. $\begin{array}{r} 314 \\ \times\ 463 \\ \hline \end{array}$	13. $\begin{array}{r} 506 \\ \times\ 478 \\ \hline \end{array}$	14. $\begin{array}{r} 680 \\ \times\ 394 \\ \hline \end{array}$	15. $\begin{array}{r} 748 \\ \times\ 403 \\ \hline \end{array}$

16. 7×64 17. 25×43 18. 519×827

Answers for Self-check—page 71

Test

Multiply.

1. $\begin{array}{r} 76 \\ \times\ 4 \\ \hline \end{array}$	2. $\begin{array}{r} 619 \\ \times\ 7 \\ \hline \end{array}$	3. $\begin{array}{r} 806 \\ \times\ 3 \\ \hline \end{array}$	4. $\begin{array}{r} 2756 \\ \times\ 8 \\ \hline \end{array}$	5. $\begin{array}{r} 1807 \\ \times\ 5 \\ \hline \end{array}$
6. $\begin{array}{r} 38 \\ \times\ 26 \\ \hline \end{array}$	7. $\begin{array}{r} 87 \\ \times\ 34 \\ \hline \end{array}$	8. $\begin{array}{r} 764 \\ \times\ 33 \\ \hline \end{array}$	9. $\begin{array}{r} 803 \\ \times\ 29 \\ \hline \end{array}$	10. $\begin{array}{r} 4176 \\ \times\ 49 \\ \hline \end{array}$
11. $\begin{array}{r} 263 \\ \times\ 381 \\ \hline \end{array}$	12. $\begin{array}{r} 517 \\ \times\ 435 \\ \hline \end{array}$	13. $\begin{array}{r} 605 \\ \times\ 328 \\ \hline \end{array}$	14. $\begin{array}{r} 881 \\ \times\ 263 \\ \hline \end{array}$	15. $\begin{array}{r} 428 \\ \times\ 736 \\ \hline \end{array}$

16. 8×59 17. 38×75 18. 419×767

A Rope Puzzle

Try to solve this puzzle with a friend.

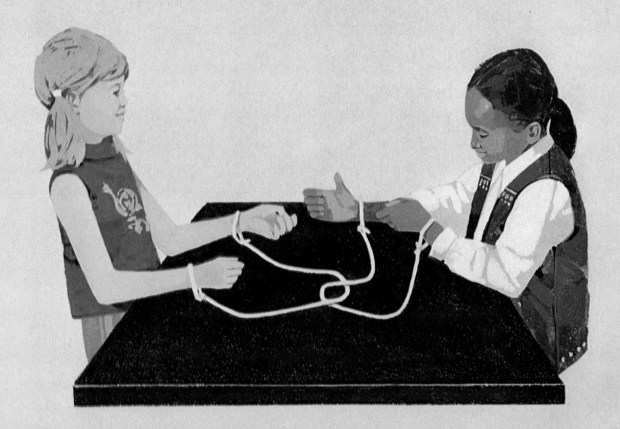

Tie pieces of rope or string around your own
wrists and a friend's wrists.

Be sure your hands cannot slip through the loops.
The ropes should cross as in the picture.

Can you separate yourself from your friend without
cutting or breaking the string, untying the knots,
or slipping your hands out of the wrist loops?

Multiplying with Decimals

You can use graph paper to help you understand multiplying with decimals.

Shade **3 tenths** of the square lightly.

3 tenths

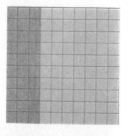

Shade **4 tenths of 3 tenths** of the square heavily.

3 tenths

4 tenths of 3 tenths

12 hundredths of the square is shaded heavily.
3 tenths × 4 tenths = 12 hundredths

Use 10 by 10 squares on your graph paper to do the following.

1. Shade 3 tenths of the square lightly.
   Shade 7 tenths of 3 tenths of the square heavily.
   How many hundredths of the square is shaded heavily?

2. Shade 6 tenths of the square lightly.
   Shade 4 tenths of 6 tenths of the square heavily.
   How many hundredths of the square is shaded heavily?

We see:	We think:	We write:

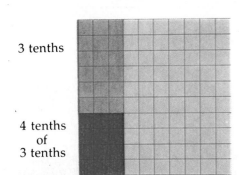

3 tenths

4 tenths
of
3 tenths

4 tenths of 3 tenths is
12 hundredths.

$\frac{3}{10} \times \frac{4}{10} = \frac{12}{100}$

or

$0.3 \times 0.4 = 0.12$

Give the missing words and numbers.

1. $\frac{4}{10} \times \frac{6}{10} = \frac{24}{100}$

    $0.4 \times 0.6 = n$

    tenths × tenths = ___?___

    1-place decimal   1-place decimal   ▥-place decimal

2. $\frac{5}{10} \times \frac{25}{100} = \frac{125}{1000}$

    $0.5 \times 0.25 = n$

    tenths × hundredths = ___?___

    1-place decimal   2-place decimal   ▥-place decimal

3. $\frac{32}{100} \times \frac{41}{100} = \frac{1312}{10\,000}$

    $0.32 \times 0.41 = n$

    hundredths × hundredths = ___?___

    2-place decimal   2-place decimal   ▥-place decimal

Give some other examples like these.
Think of a rule for multiplying with decimals.

Multiplying with decimals

A car can go 9.3 km on a
liter of gas. The tank
holds 83.6 ℓ. How far can
the car go on a full tank?

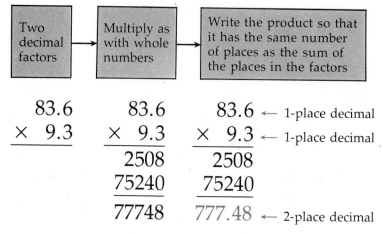

Finding the answer

| Two decimal factors | → | Multiply as with whole numbers | → | Write the product so that it has the same number of places as the sum of the places in the factors |

```
  83.6          83.6            83.6  ← 1-place decimal
× 9.3         × 9.3          × 9.3  ← 1-place decimal
              2508            2508
             75240           75240
             77748          777.48  ← 2-place decimal
```

The car can go 777.48 km on a full tank.

Other examples

```
  5.34          0.65            5.23
× 0.9         ×   9          × 1.14
 4.806         5.85           2092
                              5230
                             52300
                            5.9622
```

Find the products.

1. 7.6
   × 2.8

2. 29.3
   ×   7

3. 8.6
   × 0.7

4. 46.25
   ×   7

5. 46.3
   × 2.7

6. 5.9
   × 0.3

7. 2.05
   × 0.12

8. 17.9
   × 0.08

9. 12.57
   ×   4

10. 24.6
    × 0.38

Find the products.

1. 15.6
    × 0.35

2. 1537
    × 0.6

3. 873.4
    ×   0.8

4. 1.804
    ×   0.3

5. 19.32
    ×   5.4

6. 6.42
    × 0.57

7. 8.76
    ×   94

8. 9.83
    × 0.62

9. 5.03
    × 2.75

10. 76.3
    × 1.07

11. 8.68
    × 3.23

12. 3.27
    × 5.65

13. (0.9 × 0.3) × 0.56

14. (0.24 × 0.7) × 0.2

15. (1.67 × 0.6) × 0.3

16. (5.4 × 0.8) × 0.6

17. 6.3 × (1.5 × 2.4)

18. (9.6 × 4.1) × 5.2

19. A small car can go 14.7 km on 1 ℓ of gasoline. Its tank holds 76.5 ℓ. How far can it go on a full tank?

20. A motorcycle can go 18.9 km on 1 ℓ of gasoline. How far can it go on a tank that holds 19.2 ℓ?

21. A motor bus can go 4.3 km on 1 ℓ of gasoline. It has one tank that holds 152.5 ℓ and a spare tank that holds 75.8 ℓ. How far can it go if both tanks are full?

Think!

The sum of two decimals is 0.9. The product of the same two decimals is 0.18. Solve the equations.
a + b = 0.9
a × b = 0.18
a = ▓; b = ▓

More practice, page 380

More multiplying with decimals

A horse eats 0.012 times its mass in food each day. If a horse has a mass of 0.476 metric tons, how much would it eat each day?

Finding the answer

```
    0.476  ← 3-place decimal
  × 0.012  ← 3-place decimal
    952
   4760
 0.005712  ← 6-place decimal
```

Notice that you must use zeros to the right of the decimal point to form the correct decimal.

The horse would eat 0.005712 metric tons (about 5.7 kg) each day.

Other examples

```
   0.13          0.041          0.0012
 ×  0.6        ×  0.02        ×      13
  0.078        0.00082            36
                                 120
                              0.0156
```

Find the products.

1. 0.14
    × 0.6

2. 0.039
    × 0.2

3. 0.75
    × 0.05

4. 0.09
    × 0.06

5. 0.024
    × 3

6. 0.103
    × 0.8

7. 0.27
    × 0.4

8. 3.4
    × 0.02

Find the products.

1.	0.215 × 0.05	**2.**	0.039 × 0.002	**3.**	0.36 × 0.03
4.	0.038 × 0.02	**5.**	0.018 × 0.07	**6.**	0.007 × 0.012
7.	0.0005 × 15	**8.**	0.041 × 0.28	**9.**	0.563 × 0.011
10.	1.63 × 0.0004	**11.**	0.0063 × 1.3	**12.**	0.0075 × 0.03
13.	0.024 × 0.056	**14.**	8.65 × 0.01	**15.**	0.057 × 49
16.	0.0013 × 0.02	**17.**	59.6 × 0.003	**18.**	0.018 × 0.003

19. The mass of the food a mouse eats each day is about 0.5 times its mass. If a mouse has a mass of 0.016 kg, what is the mass of the food it eats daily?

☆ 20. If the mass of the food you eat each day were 0.025 times your mass, how much would this be? How do you think this compares with the amount you actually eat?

An old-time movie theater charged 25¢ for adults and 10¢ for children. At the end of a day, 240 tickets had been sold and $48 had been collected. How many children had bought tickets?

(**Hint:** Keep trying different numbers until you get the right answer.)

More practice, page 381, Set A

Special decimal products

A model of a container ship
is 1.35 m long. The full-sized
ship is 100 times that long.
How long is the full-sized
ship?

Finding the answer

$$1.35 \times 100 = 1.\underset{\smile}{35}. \text{ or } 135$$

To multiply by 100, move the decimal point
two places to the right.

The full-sized ship is 135 m long.

Other examples

Multiplying by 10:
$$10 \times 5.3 = 53 \qquad 10 \times 3.07 = 30.7$$

Multiplying by 100:
$$100 \times 4.236 = 423.6 \qquad 100 \times 2.4 = 240$$

Multiplying by 1000:
$$1000 \times 25.43 = 25\,430 \qquad 1000 \times 0.136 = 136$$

Give the products. Write the complete equations.

1. 100×4.67 2. 10×3.5 3. 1000×3.456 4. 100×0.09

5. 10×0.4 6. 1000×0.362 7. 10×2.76 8. 100×8.695

9. 1000×4.8367 10. 10×94.6 11. 100×0.08 12. 1000×0.123

13. 10×97.2 14. 100×1.97 15. 1000×5.407 16. 10×0.1

17. 100×0.01 18. 1000×0.001 19. 10×0.69 20. 100×0.834

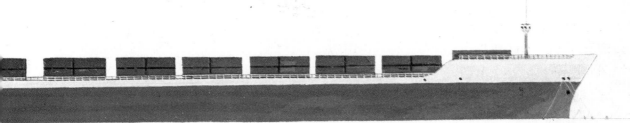

Find the products.

1. 10×0.8
2. 10×5.06
3. 9.47×10
4. 0.03×10

5. 10×0.7
6. 100×7.3
7. 0.09×100
8. 13.472×100

9. 1000×0.6
10. 1000×9.6
11. 0.07×1000
12. 54.23×1000

Give the missing numbers. To write a centimeter measurement in millimeters, multiply by 10.

13. 4.6 cm = ▓ mm
14. 54.7 cm = ▓ mm
15. 3.8 cm = ▓ mm

To write a meter measurement in centimeters, multiply by 100.

16. 57.34 m = ▓ cm
17. 83 m = ▓ cm
18. 96.5 m = ▓ cm

To write a kilometer measurement in meters, multiply by 1000.

19. 0.534 km = ▓ m
20. 8 km = ▓ m
21. 9.64 km = ▓ m

22. A model airplane is 1.07 m long. A full-sized airplane is 10 times as long as the model airplane. How long is the full-sized airplane?

23. A model railroad car is 0.24 m long. A full-sized railroad car is 100 times as long as the model car. How long is the full-sized car?

A nickel has a mass of 5 g. If you are given a bag of nickels whose mass is equal to your mass, how much money will you have?

Multiplying with decimals—practice

Find the products.

1. 0.2×0.3 2. $0.3 \times 0.4 \times 0.5$ 3. 2.3×0.4

4. $1.5 \times 2 \times 0.7$ 5. $0.7 \times 0.3 \times 4$ 6. $0.6 \times 0.1 \times 2.2$

7. $\begin{array}{r} 2.9 \\ \times\ 0.4 \\ \hline \end{array}$	8. $\begin{array}{r} 6.7 \\ \times\ 0.9 \\ \hline \end{array}$	9. $\begin{array}{r} 0.91 \\ \times\ \ \ 8 \\ \hline \end{array}$	10. $\begin{array}{r} 9.9 \\ \times\ 0.7 \\ \hline \end{array}$	11. $\begin{array}{r} 6.8 \\ \times\ 0.5 \\ \hline \end{array}$
12. $\begin{array}{r} 0.94 \\ \times\ 0.6 \\ \hline \end{array}$	13. $\begin{array}{r} 5.4 \\ \times\ \ 3 \\ \hline \end{array}$	14. $\begin{array}{r} 3.7 \\ \times\ 0.09 \\ \hline \end{array}$	15. $\begin{array}{r} 2.8 \\ \times\ 0.06 \\ \hline \end{array}$	16. $\begin{array}{r} 7.1 \\ \times\ 0.1 \\ \hline \end{array}$
17. $\begin{array}{r} 8.2 \\ \times\ 2.1 \\ \hline \end{array}$	18. $\begin{array}{r} 4.3 \\ \times\ 2.7 \\ \hline \end{array}$	19. $\begin{array}{r} 7.5 \\ \times\ 5.5 \\ \hline \end{array}$	20. $\begin{array}{r} 0.46 \\ \times\ 0.45 \\ \hline \end{array}$	21. $\begin{array}{r} 0.42 \\ \times\ 1.1 \\ \hline \end{array}$
22. $\begin{array}{r} 2.76 \\ \times\ 0.4 \\ \hline \end{array}$	23. $\begin{array}{r} 3.54 \\ \times\ 0.07 \\ \hline \end{array}$	24. $\begin{array}{r} 1.08 \\ \times\ 2.5 \\ \hline \end{array}$	25. $\begin{array}{r} 34.6 \\ \times\ 0.02 \\ \hline \end{array}$	26. $\begin{array}{r} 0.471 \\ \times\ \ \ \ 5 \\ \hline \end{array}$
27. $\begin{array}{r} 4.05 \\ \times\ 3.7 \\ \hline \end{array}$	28. $\begin{array}{r} 63.8 \\ \times\ 1.4 \\ \hline \end{array}$	29. $\begin{array}{r} 89.3 \\ \times\ 0.27 \\ \hline \end{array}$	30. $\begin{array}{r} 2.49 \\ \times\ 2.8 \\ \hline \end{array}$	31. $\begin{array}{r} 0.509 \\ \times\ 0.93 \\ \hline \end{array}$
32. $\begin{array}{r} 2.34 \\ \times\ 2.7 \\ \hline \end{array}$	33. $\begin{array}{r} 62.8 \\ \times\ 0.34 \\ \hline \end{array}$	34. $\begin{array}{r} 76.3 \\ \times\ 0.56 \\ \hline \end{array}$	35. $\begin{array}{r} 1.23 \\ \times\ 0.51 \\ \hline \end{array}$	36. $\begin{array}{r} 8.63 \\ \times\ 0.71 \\ \hline \end{array}$
37. $\begin{array}{r} \$\ 3.48 \\ \times\ \ \ \ 7 \\ \hline \end{array}$	38. $\begin{array}{r} \$\ 9.27 \\ \times\ \ \ \ 5 \\ \hline \end{array}$	39. $\begin{array}{r} \$\ 12.25 \\ \times\ \ \ \ 12 \\ \hline \end{array}$	40. $\begin{array}{r} \$\ 8.04 \\ \times\ \ \ \ 15 \\ \hline \end{array}$	41. $\begin{array}{r} \$\ 24.95 \\ \times\ \ \ \ 42 \\ \hline \end{array}$
42. $\begin{array}{r} \$\ 12.75 \\ \times\ \ \ \ 8 \\ \hline \end{array}$	43. $\begin{array}{r} \$\ 10.50 \\ \times\ \ \ \ 20 \\ \hline \end{array}$	44. $\begin{array}{r} \$\ 8.64 \\ \times\ \ \ \ 38 \\ \hline \end{array}$	45. $\begin{array}{r} \$\ 9.99 \\ \times\ \ \ \ 12 \\ \hline \end{array}$	46. $\begin{array}{r} \$\ 49.50 \\ \times\ \ \ \ 24 \\ \hline \end{array}$

Find the products.

1.   0.13
  $\times$ 0.4

2.   1.34
  $\times$ 0.06

3.   2.76
  $\times$ 0.03

4.   0.478
  $\times$ 0.1

5.   0.37
  $\times$ 0.09

6.   0.035
  $\times$ 0.7

7.   3.2
  $\times$ 0.03

8.   0.105
  $\times$ 0.24

9.   0.594
  $\times$ 0.056

10.   0.007
  $\times$ 1.5

11.   0.204
  $\times$ 0.015

12.   0.007
  $\times$ 0.16

13.   0.035
  $\times$ 0.112

14.   0.0025
  $\times$ 2.5

15.   0.479
  $\times$ .019

16. 0.03×10

17. 0.4×100

18. 0.35×10

19. 1.23×100

20. 2.45×10

21. 0.345×100

22. 2.143×1000

23. 23.4×100

24. 2.8×100

25. 18×2.7

26. 4.5×3.7

27. 45×0.27

28. 28.6×0.23

29. 6.82×8.43

30. 23.8×0.6234

Practicing your skills

Add or subtract.

1.   27
  + 58

2.   83
  − 36

3.   501
  − 314

4.   486
  + 239

5.   3079
  − 1887

6.   3.2
  + 1.8

7.   5.6
  − 3.9

8.   0.84
  + 0.47

9.   8.365
  + 6.748

10.   0.703
  − 0.435

11. $ 97
  + 86

12. $ 128
  − 59

13. $ 4.75
  + 5.50

14. $ 6.15
  − 3.89

15. $ 8.79
  + 9.57

More practice, page 381, Set B

Estimation with decimals

A group of people saw a flash of lightning. They heard a thunderclap 5 seconds later. If the sound traveled at a speed of 334.8 m/s (meters per second), about how far away was the lightning?

Finding the answer

5×334.8 $5 \times 300 = 1500$

The lightning was about 1500 m away.

Other examples

49×6.97 6.3×4.5 97.4×8.7 7.4×489.6

$50 \times 7 = 350$ $6 \times 5 = 30$ $100 \times 9 = 900$ $7 \times 500 = 3500$

Estimate these products.

1. 5×32.7 2. 78×4.3 3. 39×6.8 4. 0.98×12

5. 19×3.5 6. 73×8.9 7. 58.3×7.2 8. 9.7×6.3

9. 64.5×9.1 10. 78.6×8.1 11. 41.3×7.5 12. 32.4×9.8

13. 7×8.88 14. 42.63×6 15. 19.3×4.7 16. 5.8×50.2

Estimate the products.

1. 7.32×8.9 2. 54.1×6.73 3. 4.08×7 4. 29.34×6.5

5. 37.68×4.7 6. 92.86×5.3 7. 67.21×89.56 8. 9.732×54.65

9. 8.76×29.54 10. 1.083×42.65 11. 9×4.736 12. 46.57×95.36

13. 48×3.764 14. 52.86×78.27 15. 583.6×9.2 16. 1.8×56.387

17. 564.9×7.872 18. 67.24×43.08 19. 24.3×8.652 20. 47.34×73.5

21. Sound travels through the air at a speed of about 20.1 km/min (kilometers per minute). About how many kilometers does it travel in an hour?

22. Sound travels through water about 5.75 times faster than it travels through the air. About how many kilometers per minute does it travel through water?

Try these.

$0.1089 \times 9 = n$
$0.10989 \times 9 = n$
$0.109989 \times 9 = n$

$0.2178 \times 4 = n$
$0.21978 \times 4 = n$
$0.219978 \times 4 = n$

Do you see a pattern? Give the next equation for each list.

Self-check

Find the products.

1. 46.7
    ×   24

2. 26.8
    × 34.3

3. 1.706
    ×   0.6

4. 0.73
    ×   0.8

5. 3.68
    × 4.29

6. 0.12
    ×   0.5

7. 0.032
    ×   0.03

8. 0.417
    × 0.012

9. 10 × 4.736

10. 100 × 6.8

11. 1000 × 0.82

Estimate the products.

12. 5.8 × 3.22

13. 7.08 × 29.9

14. 213 × 4.78

Answers for Self-check—page 85

Test

Find the products.

1. 56.8
    ×   34

2. 42.3
    × 67.5

3. 2.342
    ×   0.4

4. 0.69
    ×   0.7

5. 4.38
    × 6.27

6. 0.13
    ×   0.4

7. 0.041
    ×   0.02

8. 0.376
    ×   .013

9. 10 × 5.842

10. 1000 × 7.9

11. 1000 × 4.36

Estimate the products.

12. 6.77 × 4.2

13. 31.3 × 8.19

14. 5.17 × 794

Estimation Activities

Try one of these estimation activities.

1. How many boxes 1 m
   on each edge could
   be stacked in your
   classroom?

   Make an estimate. Then
   measure to check your
   estimate. How close
   was your estimate?

2. Estimate how much water
   you would lose in one year
   from a dripping faucet.

   Plan and carry out an
   experiment to check your
   estimate. How close
   was your estimate?

3. Guess the number of pages
   in an encyclopedia.
   Then guess the number
   of words on one page
   of the encyclopedia.

   Check your guesses.
   Were your guesses good ones?

4. Estimate the total mass
   of everyone in your class.
   Then add the correct masses
   to check your estimate.

   How close was your estimate?

Using Your Skills

Getting started

1. What would be the cost of a table tennis ball, a net, and 4 paddles?

2. What would be the cost of 2 baseballs and a bat?

3. What other problems can you solve?

RACKET STRINGS
$8.98

3 BALLS
$2.79

BALLS
$0.98 each

TABLE TENNIS
SUPPLIES

SUPER PADDLES
$2.19 each

NET
$4.49

SPECIAL on
Table Tennis
Balls
$0.69 each

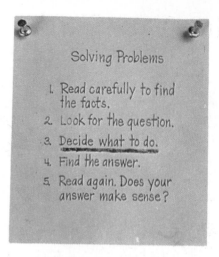

Solving Problems

1. Read carefully to find the facts.
2. Look for the question.
3. Decide what to do.
4. Find the answer.
5. Read again. Does your answer make sense?

Sometimes two or more steps
($+$, $-$, $\times$, $\div$) must be used to
solve a problem.

Try these.

1. Michelle bought 2 table tennis paddles at $2.19 each and a net for $4.49. What was the total cost?

2. Rudy bought a baseball for $4.95 and a bat for $9.95. Mario bought a glove for $13.65. Who spent the most money? What was the difference?

3. Ted bought 7 pairs of sports socks at $1.69 a pair. How much change did he get from $20.00?

4. Phyllis bought a jogging suit for $12.49. She also bought a pair of shoes that cost $2.50 more than the suit. What was the total cost of the suit and shoes?

Human body facts

1. The heart may pump 45 ℓ of blood during 1 minute of exercise. How many liters may be pumped in 27 minutes of exercise?

2. An average adult's heart beats 72 times per minute. How many beats is this per day? How many beats is this per week?

3. The length of a baby's head is about 0.25 times the total body length. If the body length is 46 cm, what is the head length?

4. The eyes of the average person blink 25 times per minute. How many blinks is this per day? Per week?

5. Human hair grows about 13 mm per month. How many millimeters does it grow in 3 years?

6. A person may take 18 breaths per minute while resting. While working, a person may take 23 breaths per minute. How many more breaths are taken per hour while working than while resting?

7. The mass of body muscle is 0.39 times the total body mass. The mass of body fat is 0.23 times the total body mass. If the total body mass is 64 kg, how many kilograms are muscle and fat?

8. If a person takes 18 breaths per minute, and takes in 0.753 ℓ of air in each breath, how many liters are taken in per hour? How many liters is this per day?

9. The radius bone (between the wrist and the elbow) on a skeleton of a prehistoric human is 26.7 cm. The early human's height can be estimated by the formula H = (3.27 × length of radius) + 85.9. About how tall was the prehistoric human?

☆ 10. Measure the length of your radius bone to the nearest centimeter, and use the formula in problem 9 to estimate your height. How close is this estimate to your measured height?

Measurement problems—unit changes

From centimeters to millimeters

Body length of a bald eagle: 89 cm
How many millimeters is this?

1 cm=10 mm

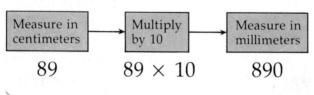

| Measure in centimeters | → | Multiply by 10 | → | Measure in millimeters |
| 89 | | 89 × 10 | | 890 |

From meters to centimeters

Wingspread of a pelican: 2.4 m
How many centimeters is this?

1 m=100 cm

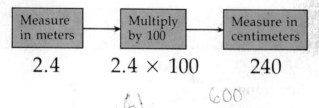

| Measure in meters | → | Multiply by 100 | → | Measure in centimeters |
| 2.4 | | 2.4 × 100 | | 240 |

61   600

From kilometers to meters

Flying speed of a spine-tailed swift: 171 km/h
How many meters per hour is this?

1 km=1000 m

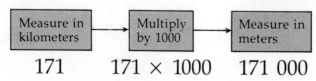

| Measure in kilometers | → | Multiply by 1000 | → | Measure in meters |
| 171 | | 171 × 1000 | | 171 000 |

1. The body length of an elf owl is about 14 cm. How many millimeters is this?

2. The body length of a swan is about 1.5 m. How many centimeters is this?

3. A penguin can swim 36 km/h. How many meters per hour is this?

4. A wren egg is about 1.5 cm long. An ostrich egg is about 10 times as long. How long is the ostrich egg?

5. If a whooping crane is 1.5 m tall, and an ostrich is 1.6 times as tall, how tall is the ostrich?

6. An ostrich can run at a speed of 80 km/h. An eagle can dive 3.625 times as fast as the ostrich can run. What is the eagle's diving speed?

7. If a mockingbird egg is 2.5 cm long, and a golden eagle egg is 3.2 times as long, how long is the eagle egg in centimeters? In millimeters?

8. The wingspread of an albatross is 3.7 m. The wingspread of a great gray owl is 152 cm. How many centimeters greater is the wingspread of the albatross?

9. The body length of a condor is about 1.5 m. The body length of a hummingbird is about 5 cm. How many centimeters longer is the condor?

The oceans of our world

The oceans cover about seven tenths of the world's surface. Many parts of them have not yet been explored. Scientists who study the oceans (oceanographers) say that in the future the oceans will provide a large part of the food, minerals, and power that we need. Many high schools and colleges offer special courses for students who wish to study the oceans.

1. Scientists say that if the ice caps in the northern and southern polar regions suddenly melted, the world's oceans would rise about 61 m. How many centimeters is this?

2. The first ship built to make scientific studies of the oceans spent 3.5 years on its first voyage. How many months was this?

3. Men in diving suits can go about 60 m below the ocean's surface. Special submarines can go 20 times that deep. How deep can the submarines go?

4. The deepest known part of the Atlantic Ocean is 7725 m below the surface. The deepest known part of the Pacific is 3308 m deeper than that. How deep is the deepest part of the Pacific?

5. A kilogram of sea water contains about 0.035 kg of salts. About how many kilograms of salts are there in 100 kg of sea water?

6. The average depth of the Indian Ocean is 3960 m. The average depth of the Pacific Ocean is 4270 m. How many meters difference?

7. One of the first diving bells could go 0.8 km below the ocean's surface. An improved diving bell could go 12.5 times as deep as the older bell. How deep could the improved bell go?

8. The surface temperature of ocean water is 30° C in the tropics. The temperature of the water 2000 m below the surface might be as low as 3.5° C. How many degrees difference?

9. The tide on Lake Superior rises and falls only 5 cm. The tide on the Bay of Fundy rises and falls 300 times that much. How many centimeters does the tide on the Bay of Fundy rise and fall?

10. The smallest ocean fish is about 1.2 cm long. The largest ocean fish is 1500 times that long. About how many centimeters long is the largest fish?

☆ 11. Tidal waves (*tsunamis*) travel at speeds up to 200 m/s (meters per second). How many **kilometers per hour** is this?

Solve these problems. (Round all sales tax figures to the nearest cent.)

1. How much more does the super 10-speed cost than the special 10-speed?

2. What would be the total cost of the special 10-speed, including a tax of 0.05 times the listed price?

3. What would be the total cost of the super 10-speed including tax?

Sales Order Form

Item Number	Item	Cost	
301	Tool kit	9	49
	Subtotal	9	49
Sales tax: 0.05 × subtotal			47
	Total	9	96

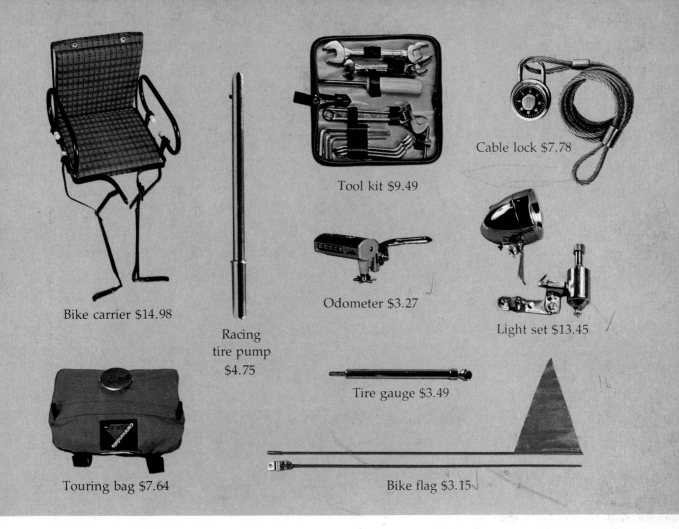

Bike carrier $14.98

Racing tire pump $4.75

Tool kit $9.49

Odometer $3.27

Cable lock $7.78

Light set $13.45

Tire gauge $3.49

Touring bag $7.64

Bike flag $3.15

4. Suppose you order a light set. What is your total cost, including tax?

5. Suppose you order a tool kit and a tire pump. What is your total cost, including tax?

6. You have $20 to spend. Can you pay for an odometer, a bike flag, and a light set, including tax?

☆ 7. Choose 2 items from the above that you would like to buy for a bike. Make an order blank like the one on page 96 and fill it out.

☆ 8. Use a mail-order catalog or the prices shown above. Fill out an order form for a 10-speed bike and the extras you would like to have. Show the price of each item, the subtotal, the amount of tax, and the total cost.

Estimating costs

Before you buy something, you often need to estimate
the total to find out about how much it is going to cost.

Try these. First choose
the best estimate. Then find
the actual total.

1. Burgers and shakes

   A   under $3
   B   about $3.50
   C   over $4

Bigger Burgers Drive In	
2 Bigger Burgers (with fries)	$1.09 each
2 shakes	$0.59 each
Total	

2. Books and supplies

   A   less than $5
   B   a little more than $5
   C   a little less than $7

The Book Bin	
2 paperbacks	$1.95 each
1 notebook	$0.98 each
1 pen	$0.49 each
Total	

3. Camera supplies

   A   about $5
   B   about $7
   C   about $9

Camera Supplies	
2 rolls of film	$2.89 each
2 batteries	$0.89 each
1 pack of flash bulbs	$1.05 each
Total	

4. Groceries

   A less than $10
   B about $12
   C more than $14

Market	
5 cartons milk	$0.97 each
4 loaves bread	$0.49 each
2 pkg wieners	$0.94 pkg
1 bottle catsup	$0.59 each
Total	

5. Clothes

   A about $30
   B about $40
   C about $50

Clothing Department	
3 T-shirts	$2.96 each
6 pr socks	$1.89 pr
2 pr jeans	$9.85 pr
Total	

6. Records and needle

   A about $10
   B about $15
   C about $20

Record Shop	
4 records (45's)	$1.08 each
2 records (LP's)	$3.98 each
1 needle	$6.97 each
Total	

Answers for Self-check 1. 44.08 kg 2. 110 000 m/h 3. 3.765 km 4. $5.04 5. B about $27

Self-check

Solve.

1. The mass of water in the human body is 0.58 times the total body mass. If the total body mass is 76 kg, what is the mass of the water?

2. The top speed of a canvasback duck is 110 km/h. How many meters per hour is this?

3. The average depth of the Indian Ocean is 3.960 km, and the depth of the deepest known part is 7.725 km. How many kilometers difference?

4. The list price of a bicycle pump is $4.80. The sales tax is 0.05 times the list price. What is the total cost?

5. Wanda bought these items:
   tennis racket—$14.85
   can of tennis balls—$3.19
   tennis shoes—$9.08
   Choose the best total cost estimate.

   A   about $24
   B   about $27
   C   about $30

Answers for Self-check—page 99

Test

Solve.

1. If a person takes 1080 breaths per hour, and takes in 0.768 ℓ of air in each breath, how many liters of air are taken in per hour?

2. The height of a flamingo is about 1.45 m. How many centimeters is this?

3. The average depth of the Pacific Ocean is 4.720 km, and the depth at the deepest known part is 11.033 km. How many kilometers difference?

4. The list price of a bicycle odometer is $3.20. The sales tax is 0.05 times the list price. What is the total cost?

5. Howard bought these items:
   calendar—$2.25
   diary—$3.15
   stationery—$2.79
   Choose the best total cost estimate.

   A   about $6
   B   about $8
   C   about $10

Find the Rule

For each **input,** this math machine uses a **rule** to give a
special **output** and prints an input-output card.

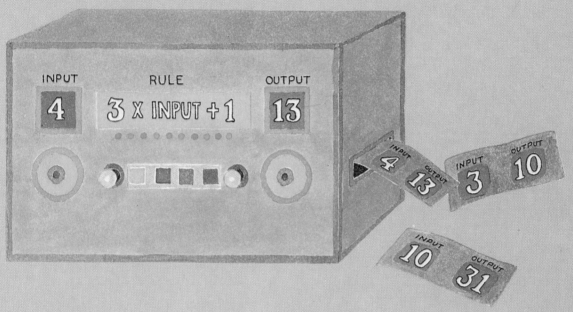

What was the rule for each of these sets of cards?

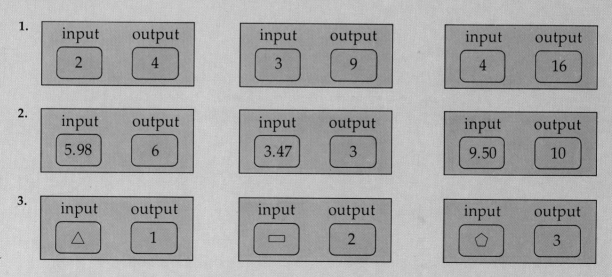

1.

input	output
2	4

input	output
3	9

input	output
4	16

2.

input	output
5.98	6

input	output
3.47	3

input	output
9.50	10

3.

input	output
△	1

input	output
▭	2

input	output
⬠	3

4. Play a math-machine game. Make up a rule and give examples of the
   input-output cards for the rule. See if a friend can guess your rule.

Area

Getting started

If this square  has an area of 1 square unit, the area of each object in this floor plan is as shown.

Shelves 2		Lamp $\frac{1}{2}$		Desk 3
Bed 8				Chair 1
Table 1	Chair 1			
		Dresser 2		

Find the area of each of these figures.

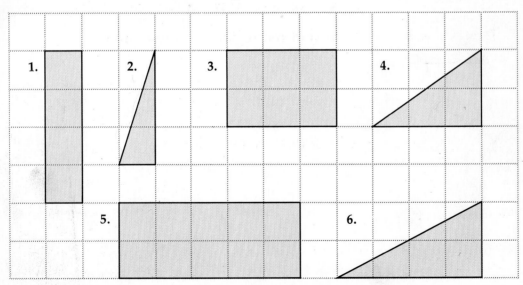

1.
2.
3.
4.
5.
6.

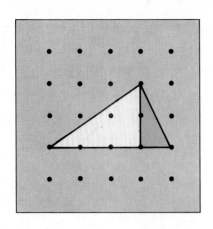

Find each area.

1. **A** area of yellow region: ▥ square units

   B area of blue region: ▥ square units

   C total area: ▥ square units

2. **A** area of yellow region: ▥ square units

   B area of brown region: ▥ square units

   C area of blue region: ▥ square units

   D total area: ▥ square units

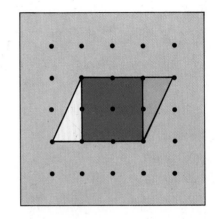

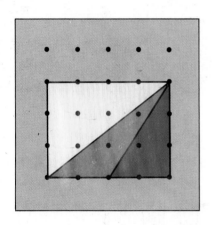

3. **A** area of the rectangular region: ▥ square units

   B area of yellow region: ▥ square units

   C area of brown region: ▥ square units

   D area of red region: ▥ square units

4. Find the area of this figure.

☆ 5. Make a figure on a geoboard or dot paper. Ask a friend to find its area.

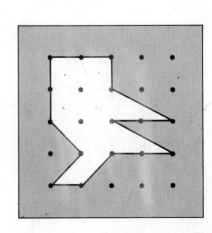

Area of a rectangle

The area of a rectangular region is
the number of unit squares and parts of
unit squares needed to cover the region.

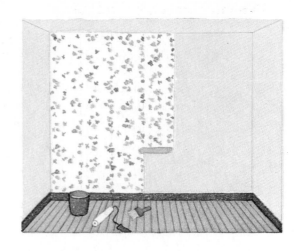

This wall is a rectangular region with a
length of 4.5 m and a width of 3.4 m.
What is its area in square meters (m²)?

Finding the answer

The area of a rectangle is the length times the width.

$$A = l \times w \qquad 4.5 \times 3.4 = 15.30$$

The area of the wall is 15.3 m².

Find the area.

1.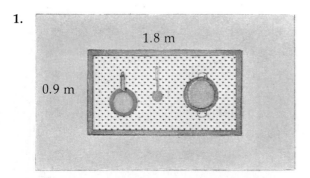

1.8 m

0.9 m

area of the pegboard: ▊ m²

2.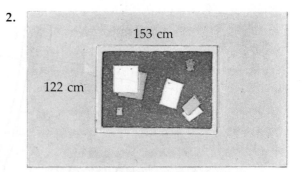

153 cm

122 cm

area of the bulletin board: ▊ cm²

3.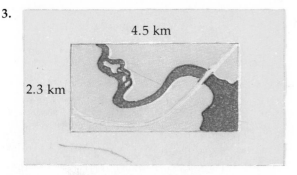

4.5 km

2.3 km

area of the map: ▊ km²

4.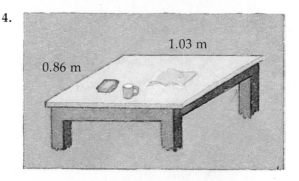

1.03 m

0.86 m

area of the table top: ▊ m²

Give the number for each ▓.

1.

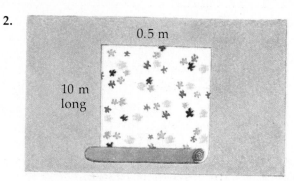

8 m

5.75 m

area of a floor: ▓ m²

2.

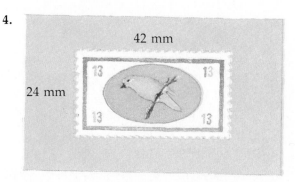

0.5 m

10 m long

area of wallpaper in a roll: ▓ m²

3.

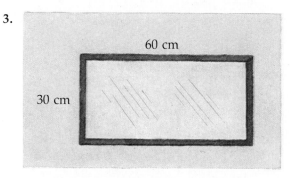

60 cm

30 cm

area of a cork panel: ▓ cm²

4.

42 mm

24 mm

area of a stamp: ▓ mm²

5.

3.5 km

2.5 km

area of an airport: ▓ km²

6.

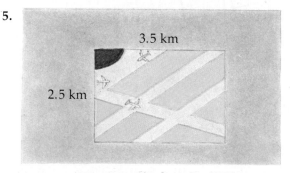

38 m

34 m

area of a lot: ▓ m²

Four sections of chain are shown.

It costs 15¢ to have a link cut open. It costs 35¢ to have a link welded together. Show how you could form one long chain for $1.50. There is a cheaper way. What would it cost?

More practice, page 382, Set A

Area of a triangle

The base of the large sail is 3 m. Its height is 8 m. What is its area?

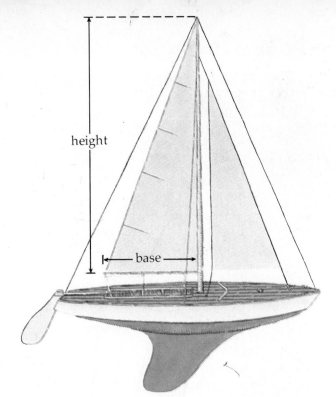

height

base

Finding the answer

The area of a triangle is the base times the height, divided by 2.

$$A = (b \times h) \div 2$$
$$(3 \times 8) \div 2 = 12$$

The area of the large sail is 12 m².

Other examples

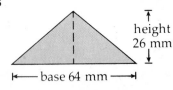

height
26 mm

base 64 mm

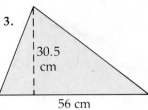

height
19 cm

base 28 cm

$$(64 \times 26) \div 2 = 832$$
$$\text{area} = 832 \text{ mm}^2$$

$$(28 \times 19) \div 2 = 266$$
$$\text{area} = 266 \text{ cm}^2$$

Find the area.

1.

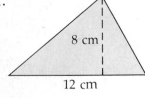

8 cm

12 cm

2.

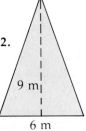

9 m

6 m

3.

30.5 cm

56 cm

4.

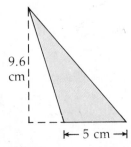

9.6 cm

5 cm

5.

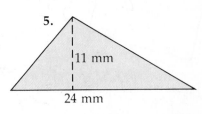

11 mm

24 mm

6.

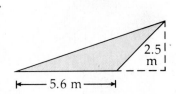

2.5 m

5.6 m

Kw K

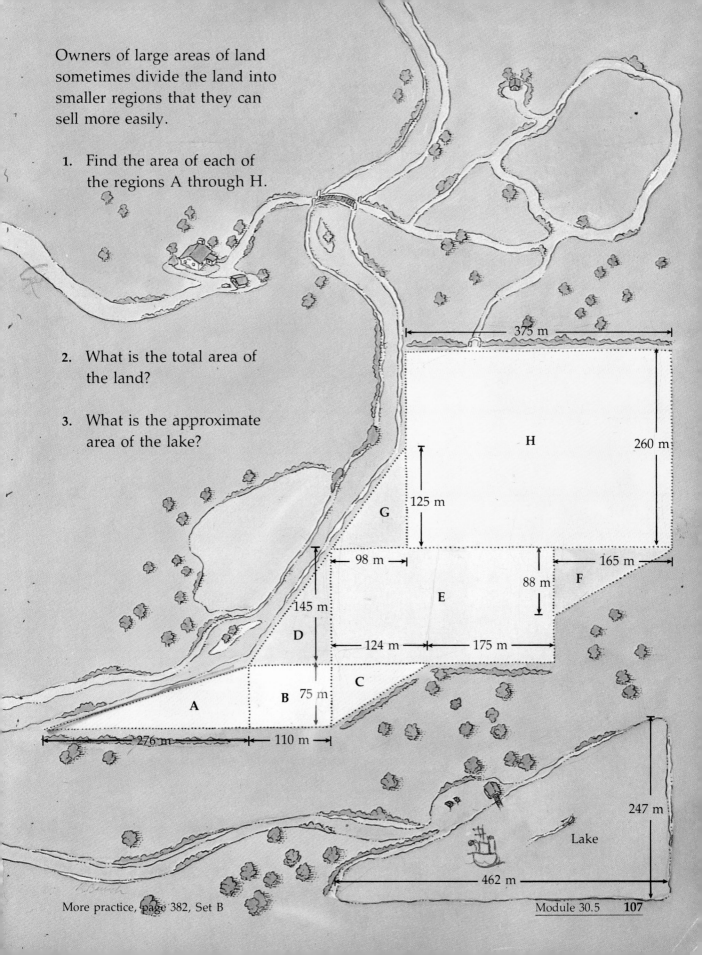

Owners of large areas of land sometimes divide the land into smaller regions that they can sell more easily.

1. Find the area of each of the regions A through H.

2. What is the total area of the land?

3. What is the approximate area of the lake?

375 m

H   260 m

125 m

G

98 m

88 m   F   165 m

E

145 m   124 m   175 m

D

C

B 75 m

A

276 m   110 m

247 m

Lake

462 m

Area of a circle

First estimate the area by
counting squares and parts
of squares. Then find the area.

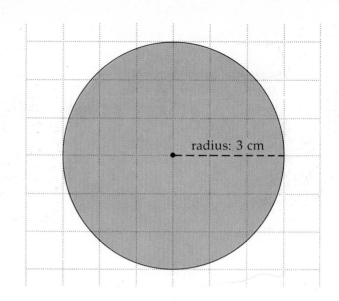

radius: 3 cm

Finding the answer

The area of a circle is the radius
multiplied by itself and then
multiplied by π (pi—about 3.14).

$$A = r \times r \times \pi$$

$$3 \times 3 \times 3.14 = 28.26$$

The area of the circle is 28.26 cm².

Find the area of each circle.

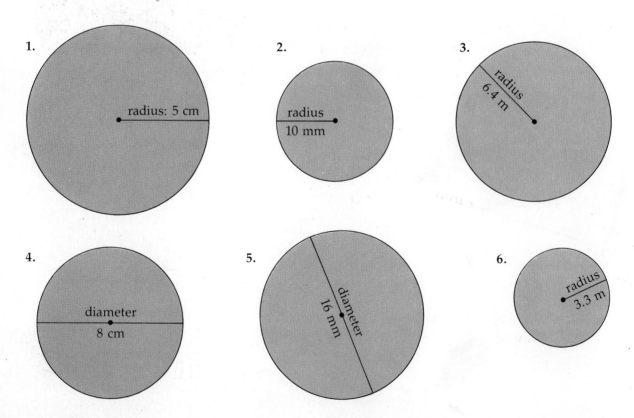

1.

radius: 5 cm

2.

radius
10 mm

3.

radius
6.4 m

4.

diameter
8 cm

5.

diameter
16 mm

diameter

6.

radius
3.3 m

Joe's Pizza Palace sells 3 sizes of pizza.

Small
24 cm diameter

Medium
30 cm diameter

Large
36 cm diameter

1. What is the area of each pizza?

2. How many more square centimeters of pizza do you get with a medium pizza and a small pizza than with one large pizza?

3. The Pizza Roma sells a family-size pizza. Its diameter is 40 cm. Which gives you more pizza, one family-size pizza or a medium pizza and a small pizza from Joe's? How much more?

Family size
40 cm diameter

4. If pizzas cost about $0.005 per square centimeter, find the cost of each pizza described above, to the nearest cent.

Find the area of each different-size circle. Then find the area of the colored regions. What is the area of the regions that are not colored?

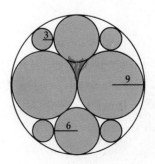

More practice, page 382, Set C

⊗ Surface area

The total area of all the surfaces of a figure is called the **surface area** of the figure.

Think of this box as being covered on all sides with graph paper. What is its surface area?

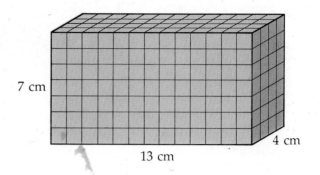

7 cm

13 cm

4 cm

Finding the answer

The surface area of a figure is the sum of the areas of all of its faces.

$$13 \times 7 = 91$$
$$13 \times 7 = 91$$
$$13 \times 4 = 52$$
$$13 \times 4 = 52$$
$$7 \times 4 = 28$$
$$7 \times 4 = \underline{28}$$
$$342$$

The surface area of the box is 342 cm².

Find the surface area of each figure.

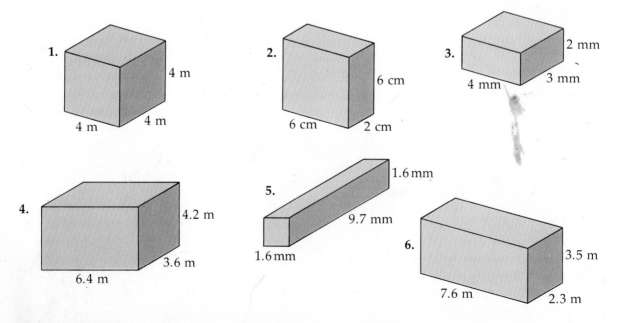

1.
4 m
4 m
4 m

2.
6 cm
6 cm
2 cm

3.
2 mm
4 mm
3 mm

4.
4.2 m
3.6 m
6.4 m

5.
1.6 mm
9.7 mm
1.6 mm

6.
3.5 m
7.6 m
2.3 m

Find the surface area of each box.

1. Tool box:
   length—95 cm
   width—42 cm
   height—56 cm

56 cm

95 cm   42 cm

2. Jewelry box:
   length—15.2 cm
   width—8.5 cm
   height—6.3 cm

6.3 cm

15.2 cm   8.5 cm

3. Music box:
   length—14 cm
   width—8 cm
   height—8 cm

4. Cake box:
   length—28 cm
   width—28 cm
   height—15 cm

5. Hobby box:
   length—28 cm
   width—16 cm
   height—7 cm

6. Cube:
   2.5 cm on
   each side

7. Find the length, width, and height of a shoe box or a cereal box. Then find the surface area of the box.

Practicing your skills

Add, subtract, or multiply.

1. 509
   − 275

2. 53.65
   − 9.78

3. 8.376
   + 7.095

4. 900
   − 275

5. 9.67
    0.89
   54.63
   + 239.45

6. 387
   ×   8

7. 423
   × 24

8. 0.95
   × 5.3

9. 2.95
   ×   28

10. 0.314
    × 2.56

Answers for Self-check   1. 25.92 cm²   2. 594 mm²   3. 11 square units   4. 96 m²   5. 58.0586 cm²
6. 128 cm²

Self-check

Find the area of each figure.

1.

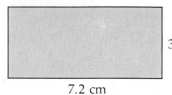

3.6 cm

7.2 cm

2.

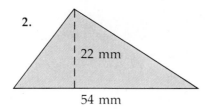

22 mm

54 mm

3.

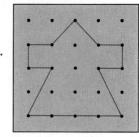

4.

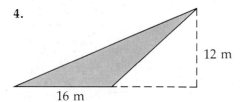

12 m

16 m

5. Use the formula
$A = r \times r \times 3.14$.

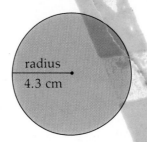

radius
4.3 cm

6. Find the surface area
of this box.

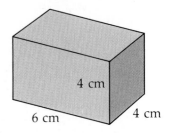

4 cm

6 cm

4 cm

Answers for Self-check—page 111

Test

Find the area of each figure.

1.

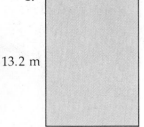

13.2 m

5.4 m

2.

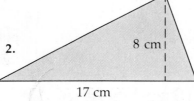

8 cm

17 cm

3.

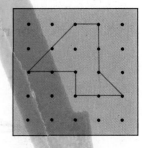

4.

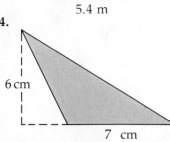

6 cm

7 cm

5.

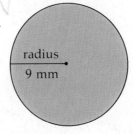

radius
9 mm

6. Find the surface area.

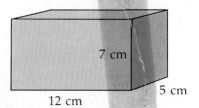

7 cm

12 cm

5 cm

Jigsaw Squares

Trace one of the following figures. Cut it apart on the dashed lines.
Try to fit the pieces together so that they cover the red square.

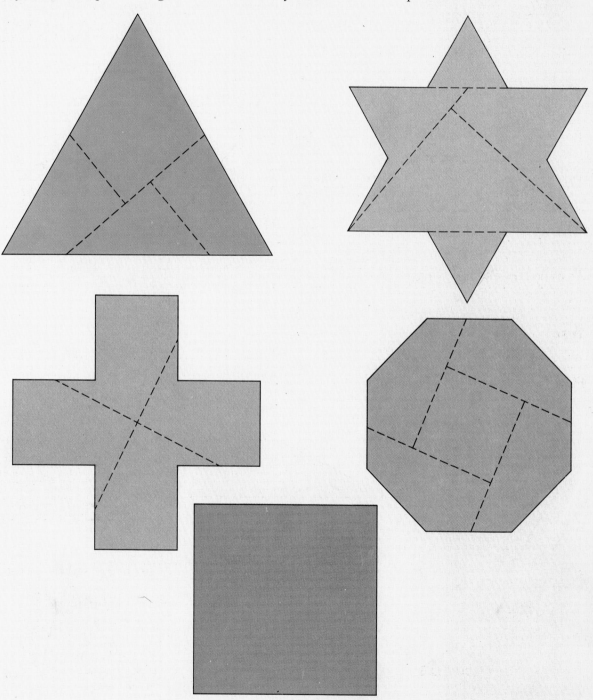

Level 30 review

Find the products.

1. 5×7 2. 8×3 3. 6×9 4. 7×8 5. 9×4

6. 6×20 7. 19×10 8. 5×40 9. 72×100 10. 5×300

11. 40×30 12. 6×7000 13. 80×50 14. 3×900 15. 80×80

16. $\begin{array}{r} 26 \\ \times\ 3 \\ \hline \end{array}$ 17. $\begin{array}{r} 44 \\ \times\ 9 \\ \hline \end{array}$ 18. $\begin{array}{r} 132 \\ \times\ 7 \\ \hline \end{array}$ 19. $\begin{array}{r} 219 \\ \times\ 5 \\ \hline \end{array}$ 20. $\begin{array}{r} 3246 \\ \times\ 4 \\ \hline \end{array}$

21. $\begin{array}{r} 62 \\ \times\ 28 \\ \hline \end{array}$ 22. $\begin{array}{r} 39 \\ \times\ 47 \\ \hline \end{array}$ 23. $\begin{array}{r} 208 \\ \times\ 17 \\ \hline \end{array}$ 24. $\begin{array}{r} 536 \\ \times\ 53 \\ \hline \end{array}$ 25. $\begin{array}{r} 7815 \\ \times\ 62 \\ \hline \end{array}$

26. $\begin{array}{r} 231 \\ \times\ 74 \\ \hline \end{array}$ 27. $\begin{array}{r} 419 \\ \times\ 265 \\ \hline \end{array}$ 28. $\begin{array}{r} 342 \\ \times\ 623 \\ \hline \end{array}$ 29. $\begin{array}{r} 507 \\ \times\ 328 \\ \hline \end{array}$ 30. $\begin{array}{r} 294 \\ \times\ 420 \\ \hline \end{array}$

31. $\begin{array}{r} 8.5 \\ \times\ 7 \\ \hline \end{array}$ 32. $\begin{array}{r} 6.3 \\ \times\ 2.9 \\ \hline \end{array}$ 33. $\begin{array}{r} 5.27 \\ \times\ 0.8 \\ \hline \end{array}$ 34. $\begin{array}{r} 4.06 \\ \times\ 3.4 \\ \hline \end{array}$ 35. $\begin{array}{r} 9.73 \\ \times\ 4.36 \\ \hline \end{array}$

36. $\begin{array}{r} 0.26 \\ \times\ 0.3 \\ \hline \end{array}$ 37. $\begin{array}{r} 0.056 \\ \times\ 0.7 \\ \hline \end{array}$ 38. $\begin{array}{r} 0.09 \\ \times\ 0.04 \\ \hline \end{array}$ 39. $\begin{array}{r} 3.5 \\ \times\ 0.08 \\ \hline \end{array}$ 40. $\begin{array}{r} 0.28 \\ \times\ 0.03 \\ \hline \end{array}$

41. 10×0.01 42. 100×3.6 43. 1000×3.657 44. 100×0.8

45. 1000×0.05 46. 10×23.47 47. 1000×0.76 48. 10×0.04

Level 31

Division and Special Quotients
Dividing Whole Numbers
Dividing Decimals
Using Your Skills
Geometry and Constructions

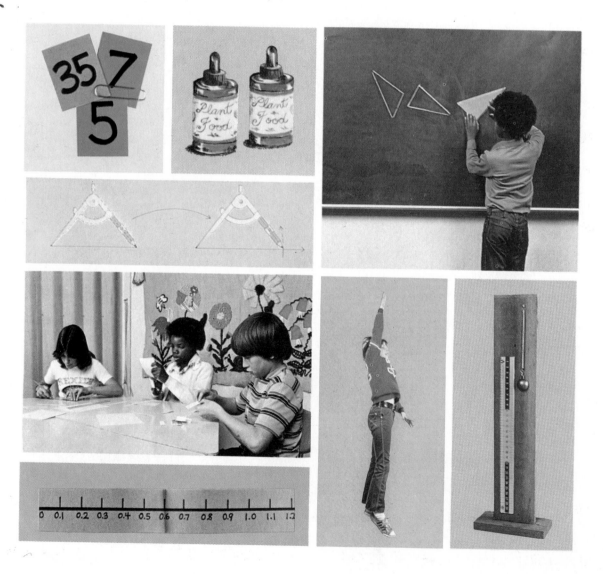

Division and Special Quotients

Getting started

Each set of cards below was used to make a multiplication equation.
The red card is the product.
What are the three numbers in each set?

1. 3 7

2. 6 30

3. 48 8

4. 36 9

5. 7 7

6. 8 56

7. Give three numbers that could be used for another set of cards.

Each set of cards below can be used to make four equations.

factor   product   factor

Fact family

$6 \times 7 = 42$ $42 \div 7 = 6$
$7 \times 6 = 42$ $42 \div 6 = 7$

factor   factor   product

Fact family

$5 \times 7 = 35$ $35 \div 7 = 5$
$7 \times 5 = 35$ $35 \div 5 = 7$

Solve the equations for this fact family.

1. $4 \times 9 = n$ 2. $9 \times 4 = n$

3. $36 \div 9 = n$ 4. $36 \div 4 = n$

Write four equations for each set of cards.

5.

6.

7.

8.

Reviewing fact families and division

Knowing fact family numbers helps you solve division equations.

If you know these,

you can solve these quickly.

┌─────── quotient ───────┐

A $48 \div 8 = n$ B $35 \div 5 = n$

C $36 \div 4 = n$ D $48 \div 6 = n$

E $30 \div 5 = n$ F $36 \div 9 = n$

G $35 \div 7 = n$ H $30 \div 6 = n$

Solve the equations.

1. $32 \div 4 = n$ 2. $36 \div 6 = n$ 3. $27 \div 3 = n$

4. $14 \div 2 = n$ 5. $49 \div 7 = n$ 6. $42 \div 6 = n$

7. $12 \div 4 = n$ 8. $40 \div 5 = n$ 9. $45 \div 9 = n$

10. $56 \div 8 = n$ 11. $12 \div 2 = n$ 12. $8 \div 4 = n$

13. $48 \div 6 = n$ 14. $18 \div 3 = n$ 15. $25 \div 5 = n$

16. $28 \div 7 = n$ 17. $24 \div 6 = n$ 18. $64 \div 8 = n$

19. $24 \div 3 = n$ 20. $40 \div 8 = n$ 21. $10 \div 2 = n$

22. $48 \div 8 = n$ 23. $16 \div 4 = n$ 24. $42 \div 7 = n$

25. $27 \div 9 = n$ 26. $21 \div 3 = n$ 27. $20 \div 4 = n$

28. $21 \div 7 = n$ 29. $56 \div 7 = n$ 30. $45 \div 5 = n$

Find the quotients.

Dividing by 1, 2, 3, 4, or 5

1. $16 \div 4$
2. $12 \div 2$
3. $6 \div 3$
4. $0 \div 3$

5. $5 \div 1$
6. $25 \div 5$
7. $20 \div 5$
8. $10 \div 5$

9. $30 \div 5$
10. $4 \div 4$
11. $35 \div 5$
12. $7 \div 1$

13. $9 \div 3$
14. $27 \div 3$
15. $14 \div 2$
16. $20 \div 4$

17. $36 \div 4$
18. $5 \div 5$
19. $8 \div 4$
20. $40 \div 5$

21. $18 \div 2$
22. $12 \div 4$
23. $0 \div 4$
24. $8 \div 2$

25. $0 \div 5$
26. $21 \div 3$
27. $24 \div 3$
28. $12 \div 3$

29. $18 \div 3$
30. $6 \div 1$
31. $10 \div 2$
32. $16 \div 2$

33. $32 \div 4$
34. $45 \div 5$
35. $28 \div 4$
36. $15 \div 5$

37. $3 \div 3$
38. $6 \div 2$
39. $15 \div 3$
40. $24 \div 4$

Dividing by 6, 7, 8, or 9

41. $28 \div 7$
42. $32 \div 8$
43. $24 \div 8$
44. $9 \div 9$

45. $72 \div 8$
46. $7 \div 7$
47. $72 \div 9$
48. $40 \div 8$

49. $45 \div 9$
50. $18 \div 9$
51. $42 \div 7$
52. $0 \div 7$

53. $12 \div 6$
54. $30 \div 6$
55. $0 \div 6$
56. $36 \div 6$

57. $48 \div 8$
58. $63 \div 9$
59. $56 \div 8$
60. $16 \div 8$

61. $27 \div 9$
62. $0 \div 8$
63. $36 \div 9$
64. $54 \div 9$

65. $14 \div 7$
66. $49 \div 7$
67. $42 \div 6$
68. $18 \div 6$

69. $48 \div 6$
70. $64 \div 8$

71. $21 \div 7$
72. $35 \div 7$

73. $0 \div 9$
74. $6 \div 6$

75. $8 \div 8$
76. $63 \div 7$

77. $24 \div 6$
78. $81 \div 9$

79. $56 \div 7$
80. $54 \div 6$

Joe Superstar makes $150 000 a year playing ball. For one game, 28 126 tickets were sold. If each ticket costs $6, would the total be enough to pay Joe's salary for the year?

Special quotients

For a school show, 160 chairs are needed. There is room for 8 rows of chairs. How many chairs should be in each row?

Finding the answer

$$160 \div 8 = n$$
Since $8 \times 20 = 160$,
then $160 \div 8 = 20$.

There should be 20 chairs in each row.

Other examples

$$180 \div 3 = 60$$
$$1800 \div 3 = 600$$
$$18\,000 \div 3 = 6000$$

Find the quotients.

1. $250 \div 5$	2. $120 \div 2$	3. $120 \div 3$	4. $300 \div 5$
5. $210 \div 3$	6. $240 \div 8$	7. $140 \div 7$	8. $360 \div 6$
9. $280 \div 7$	10. $90 \div 3$	11. $420 \div 6$	12. $320 \div 4$
13. $200 \div 4$	14. $350 \div 7$	15. $180 \div 9$	16. $160 \div 2$
17. $720 \div 9$	18. $540 \div 6$	19. $240 \div 4$	20. $400 \div 8$
21. $180 \div 2$	22. $350 \div 5$	23. $320 \div 8$	24. $540 \div 9$
25. $480 \div 8$	26. $630 \div 9$	27. $400 \div 5$	28. $210 \div 7$
29. $300 \div 6$	30. $360 \div 4$	31. $140 \div 2$	32. $240 \div 3$

Divide.

1. $180 \div 6$	**2.** $240 \div 3$	**3.** $540 \div 9$
4. $140 \div 2$	**5.** $360 \div 4$	**6.** $280 \div 7$
7. $100 \div 5$	**8.** $400 \div 8$	**9.** $560 \div 7$

10. $3200 \div 4$	**11.** $2800 \div 4$	**12.** $3600 \div 9$
13. $4500 \div 9$	**14.** $4200 \div 6$	**15.** $1800 \div 3$
16. $2500 \div 5$	**17.** $1200 \div 3$	**18.** $1800 \div 2$
19. $6300 \div 7$	**20.** $1600 \div 8$	**21.** $2000 \div 5$
22. $2400 \div 8$	**23.** $3600 \div 6$	**24.** $1400 \div 2$

25. $42\,000 \div 6$	**26.** $14\,000 \div 2$	**27.** $40\,000 \div 8$
28. $35\,000 \div 5$	**29.** $28\,000 \div 7$	**30.** $24\,000 \div 8$
31. $16\,000 \div 2$	**32.** $12\,000 \div 3$	**33.** $24\,000 \div 3$
34. $25\,000 \div 5$	**35.** $30\,000 \div 6$	**36.** $54\,000 \div 9$
37. $20\,000 \div 4$	**38.** $63\,000 \div 9$	**39.** $36\,000 \div 4$

40. Lunchroom:
300 chairs
6 chairs at
each table
How many tables?

41. Music show:
270 chairs
9 rows
How many chairs
in each row?

Give the quotients
in Roman numerals.

CC ÷ V
L ÷ V
CL ÷ V
CL ÷ III
M ÷ V

1	= I
5	= V
10	= X
50	= L
100	= C
500	= D
1000	= M

More practice, page 383, Set B

Dividing by a multiple of ten

Each unit of mass stretches the spring 30 mm. How many units of mass would it take to stretch the spring 240 mm?

Finding the answer

$$240 \div 30 = n \qquad \text{Since } 30 \times 8 = 240,$$
$$\text{then } 240 \div 30 = 8.$$

It would take 8 units of mass to stretch the spring 240 mm.

Other examples

$$280 \div 40 = 7$$
$$2800 \div 40 = 70$$
$$28\,000 \div 40 = 700$$

Find the quotients.

1. $240 \div 30$	2. $140 \div 20$	3. $360 \div 40$
4. $300 \div 60$	5. $210 \div 70$	6. $400 \div 50$
7. $630 \div 90$	8. $480 \div 80$	9. $540 \div 90$
10. $320 \div 80$	11. $350 \div 50$	12. $180 \div 20$
13. $400 \div 80$	14. $240 \div 40$	15. $540 \div 60$	16. $720 \div 90$	17. $160 \div 20$
18. $180 \div 90$	19. $350 \div 70$	20. $200 \div 40$	21. $320 \div 40$	22. $420 \div 60$
23. $270 \div 30$	24. $280 \div 70$	25. $360 \div 60$	26. $140 \div 70$	27. $240 \div 80$
28. $210 \div 30$	29. $300 \div 50$	30. $120 \div 30$	31. $120 \div 20$	32. $250 \div 50$

Divide.

1. $420 \div 60$ 2. $560 \div 80$ 3. $160 \div 20$ 4. $210 \div 70$

5. $280 \div 40$ 6. $210 \div 30$ 7. $270 \div 90$ 8. $100 \div 50$

9. $3000 \div 60$ 10. $4000 \div 80$ 11. $3600 \div 40$ 12. $4500 \div 90$

13. $1800 \div 30$ 14. $1000 \div 20$ 15. $3500 \div 70$ 16. $4500 \div 50$

17. $2000 \div 40$ 18. $5400 \div 90$ 19. $5400 \div 60$ 20. $1400 \div 20$

21. $1400 \div 70$ 22. $2000 \div 50$ 23. $1500 \div 30$ 24. $6400 \div 80$

25. $48\,000 \div 80$ 26. $40\,000 \div 50$ 27. $48\,000 \div 60$ 28. $15\,000 \div 50$

29. $12\,000 \div 30$ 30. $49\,000 \div 70$ 31. $18\,000 \div 20$ 32. $18\,000 \div 90$

33. $24\,000 \div 40$ 34. $32\,000 \div 40$ 35. $72\,000 \div 80$ 36. $12\,000 \div 20$

37. $36\,000 \div 60$ 38. $36\,000 \div 90$ 39. $24\,000 \div 30$ 40. $28\,000 \div 70$

41. Each unit of mass stretches the spring 20 mm. How many units of mass are needed to stretch the spring 140 mm?

Long elevator ride: 442 m
High-flying jet: 12 000 m

About how many elevator rides, one on top of the other, would it take to get as high as the jet?

42. If a unit of mass stretches a rubber band 40 mm, how many of the units would it take to stretch the rubber band 160 mm?

Estimation—using special quotients

The girl is riding her bicycle to Riverside. She has 57 more kilometers to go. If she averages 18 km an hour, about how long will it take her to get to Riverside?

Finding the answer

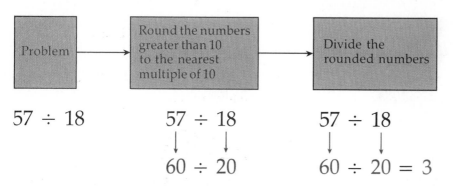

| Problem | Round the numbers greater than 10 to the nearest multiple of 10 | Divide the rounded numbers |

$$57 \div 18 \qquad\qquad 57 \div 18 \qquad\qquad 57 \div 18$$
$$\downarrow \quad \downarrow \qquad\qquad \downarrow \quad \downarrow$$
$$60 \div 20 \qquad\qquad 60 \div 20 = 3$$

It will take her about 3 hours to get to Riverside.

Other examples

$$83 \div 41 \qquad\qquad 118 \div 3 \qquad\qquad 297 \div 5$$
$$\downarrow \quad \downarrow \qquad\qquad \downarrow \quad \downarrow \qquad\qquad \downarrow \quad \downarrow$$
$$80 \div 40 = 2 \qquad 120 \div 3 = 40 \qquad 300 \div 5 = 60$$

Estimate each quotient.

1. $243 \div 8$
$$\downarrow \quad \downarrow$$
$$240 \div 8 = n$$

2. $139 \div 7$
$$\downarrow \quad \downarrow$$
$$140 \div 7 = n$$

3. $321 \div 38$
$$\downarrow \quad \downarrow$$
$$320 \div 40 = n$$

4. $198 \div 41$

5. $354 \div 49$

6. $78 \div 19$

7. $477 \div 6$

8. $631 \div 9$

9. $403 \div 8$

Estimate each quotient.

1. $239 \div 4$ 2. $141 \div 2$ 3. $148 \div 5$

4. $182 \div 3$ 5. $179 \div 2$ 6. $162 \div 4$

7. $211 \div 3$ 8. $399 \div 5$ 9. $100 \div 19$

10. $100 \div 48$ 11. $150 \div 29$ 12. $160 \div 41$

13. $148 \div 30$ 14. $202 \div 40$ 15. $319 \div 80$

16. $271 \div 90$ 17. $299 \div 51$ 18. $242 \div 28$

19. $299 \div 62$ 20. $161 \div 79$ 21. $541 \div 88$

22. Fred types about 39 words a minute. About how long will it take him to type a 1600-word paper?

23. Ms. Lee drove 241 km in 3 hours. About how far did she drive each hour?

24. Betty has $3.00. How many colored pencils can she buy if each one costs 47 cents?

25. Jerry has $4.00. How many tickets can he buy if each one costs 78 cents?

26. Rose swims the length of the pool and back in 59 seconds. About how many times can she do this in 180 seconds?

Look for the pattern. Then guess the missing numbers. Check your guess.

$74 \times 74 = 5476$ $43 \times 43 = 1849$
$73 \times 75 = 5475$ $42 \times 44 = 1848$

$87 \times 87 = 7569$ $68 \times 68 = n$
$86 \times 88 = n$ $67 \times 69 = 4623$

Answers for Self-check   1. 8   2. 5   3. 9   4. 6   5. 8   6. 7   7. 8   8. 9   9. 5   10. 6   11. 7   12. 4
13. 60   14. 50   15. 60   16. 80   17. 80   18. 50   19. 70   20. 40   21. 70   22. 700   23. 300   24. 800   25. 50
26. 70   27. 6

Self-check

Find the quotients.

1. $24 \div 3$ 2. $30 \div 6$ 3. $63 \div 7$ 4. $48 \div 8$

5. $56 \div 7$ 6. $14 \div 2$ 7. $40 \div 5$ 8. $36 \div 4$

9. $25 \div 5$ 10. $54 \div 9$ 11. $42 \div 6$ 12. $32 \div 8$

13. $240 \div 4$ 14. $150 \div 3$ 15. $300 \div 5$

16. $160 \div 2$ 17. $480 \div 6$ 18. $350 \div 7$

19. $2100 \div 30$ 20. $2000 \div 50$ 21. $2800 \div 40$

22. $42\,000 \div 60$ 23. $21\,000 \div 70$ 24. $16\,000 \div 20$

Estimate each quotient.   25. $152 \div 3$ 26. $281 \div 4$ 27. $119 \div 20$

Answers for Self-check—page 125

Test

Find the quotients.

1. $16 \div 2$ 2. $45 \div 9$ 3. $10 \div 5$ 4. $56 \div 8$

5. $72 \div 8$ 6. $20 \div 4$ 7. $42 \div 6$ 8. $21 \div 3$

9. $36 \div 6$ 10. $28 \div 7$ 11. $49 \div 7$ 12. $18 \div 9$

13. $350 \div 5$ 14. $120 \div 2$ 15. $360 \div 6$

16. $270 \div 3$ 17. $280 \div 7$ 18. $320 \div 4$

19. $1200 \div 40$ 20. $1800 \div 30$ 21. $3000 \div 50$

22. $24\,000 \div 60$ 23. $12\,000 \div 20$ 24. $28\,000 \div 70$

Estimate each quotient.   25. $199 \div 4$ 26. $152 \div 3$ 27. $149 \div 50$

Hidden Faces

Suppose you stack 27 cubes like this. Then you mark an "X" on every cube face that shows (on all four sides and on top).

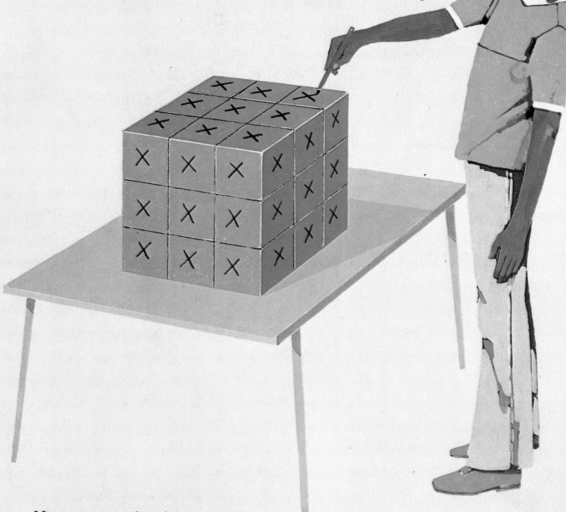

1. How many cubes have no X?
2. How many cubes have only 1 X?
3. How many cubes have only 2 X's?
4. How many cubes have only 3 X's?
5. How many cubes have 4 or more X's?

The sum of all your answers should be 27.

Getting started

The students in Room 38 are making nail boards. Each board takes 25 nails.

1. How many nail boards can they make from this box of nails?

2. How many nail boards can they make from this box of nails?

Marti made a 6-by-6 nail board. She used 36 nails. She wondered how many nail boards she could make from a box of 480 nails.

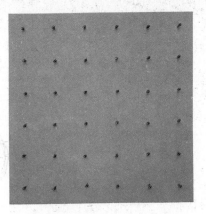

First she figured this way.

$$
\begin{array}{r}
480 \\
-360 \quad \leftarrow 10 \text{ boards} \\
\hline
120 \\
-108 \quad \leftarrow 3 \text{ boards} \\
\hline
12 \quad \leftarrow \text{ extra nails}
\end{array}
$$

Then she tried dividing.

$$
\begin{array}{r}
13 \\
36 \overline{)480} \\
36 \\
\hline
120 \\
108 \\
\hline
12
\end{array}
$$

Did she get the same answer both ways?

1. How many 3-by-3 nail boards could you make from 480 nails?

2. How many 4-by-4 nail boards could you make from 480 nails?

1-digit divisors

Joe bought a 454-g package
of gumdrops. He found that
the mass of 1 gumdrop was 6 g.
About how many gumdrops were
in the package?

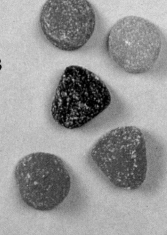

Finding the answer

Divide the tens	→	Multiply and subtract	→	Divide the ones, multiply, and subtract

$$
\begin{array}{r}
7 \\
6\overline{)454}
\end{array}
\qquad
\begin{array}{r}
7 \\
6\overline{)454} \\
42 \\
\hline
3
\end{array}
\qquad
\begin{array}{r}
75\ \text{R4} \\
6\overline{)454} \\
42 \\
\hline
34 \\
30 \\
\hline
4
\end{array}
$$

There were about 75 gumdrops in the package.

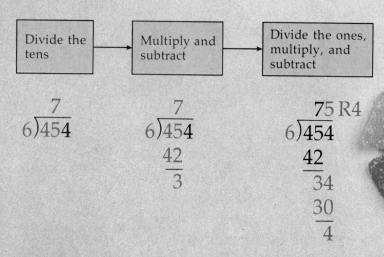

Other examples

$$
\text{divisor} \longrightarrow
\begin{array}{r}
66 \longleftarrow \text{quotient} \\
4\overline{)267} \\
24 \\
\hline
27 \\
24 \\
\hline
3 \longleftarrow \text{remainder}
\end{array}
\qquad
\begin{array}{r}
513 \\
7\overline{)3591} \\
35 \\
\hline
9 \\
7 \\
\hline
21 \\
21 \\
\hline
0
\end{array}
\qquad
\begin{array}{r}
904\ \text{R3} \\
5\overline{)4523} \\
45 \\
\hline
2 \\
0 \\
\hline
23 \\
20 \\
\hline
3
\end{array}
$$

Divide.

1. $4\overline{)273}$ 2. $7\overline{)447}$ 3. $2\overline{)158}$ 4. $6\overline{)435}$ 5. $9\overline{)234}$

6. $6\overline{)1550}$ 7. $3\overline{)2116}$ 8. $8\overline{)5176}$ 9. $7\overline{)4230}$ 10. $5\overline{)4397}$

Divide.

1. $6\overline{)280}$ 2. $4\overline{)283}$ 3. $9\overline{)795}$ 4. $3\overline{)111}$

5. $3\overline{)191}$ 6. $2\overline{)153}$ 7. $4\overline{)116}$ 8. $8\overline{)727}$

9. $6\overline{)113}$ 10. $8\overline{)476}$ 11. $7\overline{)1854}$ 12. $4\overline{)1503}$

13. $3\overline{)2586}$ 14. $4\overline{)2909}$ 15. $5\overline{)3292}$ 16. $5\overline{)3619}$

17. $9\overline{)3114}$ 18. $2\overline{)1057}$ 19. $5\overline{)4663}$ 20. $2\overline{)1306}$

21. $8\overline{)5669}$ 22. $3\overline{)2012}$ 23. $6\overline{)5418}$ 24. $9\overline{)2141}$

25. $7\overline{)3920}$ 26. $7\overline{)4954}$ 27. $5\overline{)4015}$ 28. $7\overline{)6625}$

29. $6\overline{)4561}$ 30. $2\overline{)1842}$ 31. $4\overline{)2617}$ 32. $8\overline{)5792}$

33. Jellybeans: 2 grams each
About how many are
there in a 454-g bag?

☆ 34. Find the mass of a bag
of your favorite candy
and the mass of one piece.
Then find out about how
many pieces there are
in the bag.

Joe's age is three times
Sue's. Four years from now,
Joe will be twice as old as
Sue. How old is Joe now?

More practice, page 384, Set A

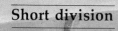

The pony express riders of the Old West carried mail between St. Joseph, Missouri, and San Francisco, California. The distance was 3164 km. The trip took 8 days. What was the average distance traveled each day?

Finding the answer

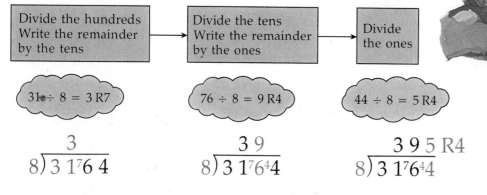

Divide the hundreds Write the remainder by the tens	Divide the tens Write the remainder by the ones	Divide the ones

$31 \div 8 = 3 \text{ R}7$ $76 \div 8 = 9 \text{ R}4$ $44 \div 8 = 5 \text{ R}4$

$$8) \overline{3\ 1^76\ 4}$$ → 3

$$8) \overline{3\ 1^76^44}$$ → 3 9

$$8) \overline{3\ 1^76^44}$$ → 3 9 5 R4

The average distance traveled each day was about 395 km.

Other examples

$$6) \overline{2\ 7^39} \quad 4\ 6 \text{ R}3$$

$$4) \overline{2\ 4\ 1^18} \quad 6\ 0\ 4 \text{ R}2$$

$$5) \overline{2\ 7^23^33^38} \quad 5\ 4\ 6\ 7 \text{ R}3$$

Find the quotients and remainders.

1. $6) \overline{380}$

2. $4) \overline{239}$

3. $2) \overline{655}$

4. $6) \overline{5052}$

5. $7) \overline{1706}$

6. $5) \overline{3522}$

7. $9) \overline{3066}$

8. $3) \overline{2411}$

9. $8) \overline{18\ 532}$

10. $7) \overline{37\ 115}$

Divide.

1. $6\overline{)219}$ 2. $4\overline{)289}$ 3. $3\overline{)152}$ 4. $7\overline{)406}$ 5. $5\overline{)199}$

6. $4\overline{)1055}$ 7. $9\overline{)3758}$ 8. $9\overline{)7578}$ 9. $7\overline{)4605}$ 10. $2\overline{)1845}$

11. $5\overline{)1735}$ 12. $3\overline{)2045}$ 13. $8\overline{)5719}$ 14. $8\overline{)5217}$ 15. $6\overline{)4583}$

16. $3\overline{)2414}$ 17. $6\overline{)1846}$ 18. $8\overline{)4962}$ 19. $6\overline{)3232}$ 20. $4\overline{)3049}$

21. $5\overline{)4515}$ 22. $9\overline{)7442}$ 23. $2\overline{)740}$ 24. $7\overline{)6456}$ 25. $9\overline{)3668}$

26. $5\overline{)18\ 144}$ 27. $7\overline{)12\ 067}$ 28. $8\overline{)66\ 434}$ 29. $6\overline{)42\ 038}$ 30. $4\overline{)37\ 483}$

31. Pioneer wagon trains:
Average speed—3 km/h
Distance—1740 km
How many hours?

☆ 32. Estimate your average speed
for a long bicycle ride. Choose
a distant city and figure out how
many hours it would take you
to get there on your bicycle.

Guess the missing products.
Then check your guess.

$(15\ 873 \times 7) \times 1 = 111\ 111$
$(15\ 873 \times 7) \times 2 = 222\ 222$
$(15\ 873 \times 7) \times 3 = 333\ 333$
$(15\ 873 \times 7) \times 4 = n$
$(15\ 873 \times 7) \times 5 = n$
$(15\ 873 \times 7) \times 6 = n$

2-digit divisors

Two students cut ribbons for the school sports day. Each piece of ribbon had to be 31 cm long. How many could they cut from 750 cm of ribbon?

Finding the answer

Estimate the tens	Multiply and subtract	Estimate the ones	Multiply and subtract

$$
\begin{array}{r} 2 \\ 31\overline{)750} \end{array}
\qquad
\begin{array}{r} 2 \\ 31\overline{)750} \\ 62 \\ \hline 13 \end{array}
\qquad
\begin{array}{r} 24 \\ 31\overline{)750} \\ 62\!\downarrow \\ \hline 130 \end{array}
\qquad
\begin{array}{r} 24\,\text{R6} \\ 31\overline{)750} \\ 62 \\ \hline 130 \\ 124 \\ \hline 6 \end{array}
$$

They could cut 24 ribbons (6 cm left over).

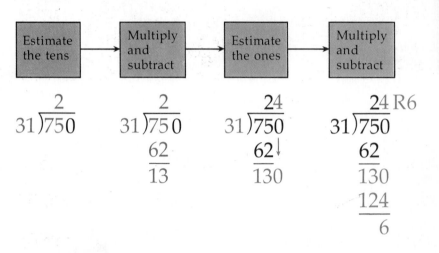

Other examples

$$
\begin{array}{r} 57\,\text{R5} \\ 63\overline{)3596} \\ 315 \\ \hline 446 \\ 441 \\ \hline 5 \end{array}
\qquad
\begin{array}{r} 83\,\text{R27} \\ 41\overline{)3430} \\ 328 \\ \hline 150 \\ 123 \\ \hline 27 \end{array}
\qquad
\begin{array}{r} 60\,\text{R25} \\ 52\overline{)3145} \\ 312 \\ \hline 25 \\ 0 \\ \hline 25 \end{array}
$$

Divide.

1. $42\overline{)1435}$ 2. $34\overline{)1740}$ 3. $23\overline{)980}$ 4. $93\overline{)2430}$ 5. $64\overline{)2380}$

6. $72\overline{)3816}$ 7. $65\overline{)1347}$ 8. $84\overline{)2880}$ 9. $53\overline{)4452}$ 10. $71\overline{)2903}$

Divide.

1. $52\overline{)3288}$ 2. $23\overline{)968}$ 3. $84\overline{)2324}$ 4. $40\overline{)3341}$ 5. $41\overline{)2624}$

6. $32\overline{)489}$ 7. $61\overline{)1856}$ 8. $75\overline{)1917}$ 9. $33\overline{)2376}$ 10. $96\overline{)7727}$

11. $41\overline{)1115}$ 12. $81\overline{)2247}$ 13. $22\overline{)1562}$ 14. $73\overline{)4398}$ 15. $53\overline{)3962}$

16. $95\overline{)7769}$ 17. $30\overline{)1163}$ 18. $54\overline{)2268}$ 19. $62\overline{)1110}$ 20. $34\overline{)1728}$

21. $60\overline{)2067}$ 22. $54\overline{)2808}$ 23. $23\overline{)553}$ 24. $70\overline{)5809}$ 25. $85\overline{)7735}$

26. $63\overline{)4431}$ 27. $72\overline{)6265}$ 28. $41\overline{)425}$ 29. $32\overline{)1984}$ 30. $94\overline{)2149}$

31. Dan and Sue had 800 cm of red ribbon. They cut 32-cm pieces. How many second-place ribbons could they make?

☆ 32. Cut a piece of string that is twice as long as you are tall. Divide to find out how many 21-cm pieces you could cut. Check your work by cutting the string.

Start with a sheet of cardboard 1 mm thick.

Double once—2 sheets, 2 mm
Double twice—4 sheets, 4 mm
Double three times—8 sheets, 8 mm

If you double the cardboard 25 times, how high is the stack?

A   as tall as you?
B   as tall as a skyscraper?
C   as high as a high-flying plane?

More about 2-digit divisors

A dairy farmer got 880 ℓ of milk from the morning milking. The milk is stored in cans that hold 38 ℓ each. How many cans will the farmer be able to fill?

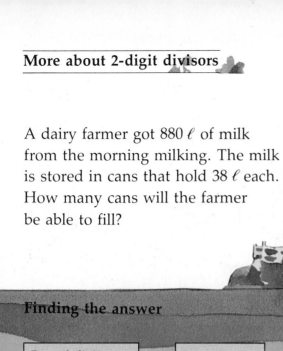

Finding the answer

Round divisor to the nearest 10 Estimate the tens	→	Multiply and subtract	→	Estimate the ones	→	Multiply and subtract

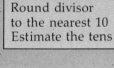

$$
\begin{array}{r}
2 \\
38\overline{)880}
\end{array}
\qquad
\begin{array}{r}
2 \\
38\overline{)880} \\
76 \\
\hline
12
\end{array}
\qquad
\begin{array}{r}
23 \\
38\overline{)880} \\
76\downarrow \\
\hline
120
\end{array}
\qquad
\begin{array}{r}
23\,\text{R}6 \\
38\overline{)880} \\
76 \\
\hline
120 \\
114 \\
\hline
6
\end{array}
$$

The farmer will be able to fill 23 cans.

Other examples

$$
\begin{array}{r}
41\,\text{R}11 \\
57\overline{)2348} \\
228 \\
\hline
68 \\
57 \\
\hline
11
\end{array}
\qquad
\begin{array}{r}
74\,\text{R}31 \\
39\overline{)2917} \\
273 \\
\hline
187 \\
156 \\
\hline
31
\end{array}
\qquad
\begin{array}{r}
30\,\text{R}28 \\
65\overline{)1978} \\
195 \\
\hline
28 \\
0 \\
\hline
28
\end{array}
$$

Divide.

1. $49\overline{)978}$
2. $27\overline{)1432}$
3. $38\overline{)1627}$
4. $62\overline{)3465}$
5. $79\overline{)825}$

6. $53\overline{)3426}$
7. $45\overline{)1378}$
8. $26\overline{)2589}$
9. $58\overline{)3460}$
10. $94\overline{)7026}$

Divide.

1. 87)6432   2. 54)708

3. 52)3206   4. 93)4007

5. 26)625   6. 45)2003

7. 30)1340   8. 19)1347

9. 71)6000   10. 68)780

11. 63)2465   12. 50)1776

13. 98)3742   14. 27)2654   15. 82)6232

16. 34)2644   17. 49)3000   18. 61)1942

19. 75)1982   20. 16)489   21. 64)1792

22. 43)1926   23. 92)4324   24. 70)6300

25. 28)1495   26. 56)2650   27. 75)1886

28. 17)500   29. 79)7426   30. 81)3767

31. A class of students visited a dairy. They learned that a herd of 25 dairy cows gives about 1925 ℓ of milk a week. What is the average amount of milk given by 1 cow in a week? In a day?

32. The class also learned that the average person eats about 13 000 ml of ice cream in a year. How much ice cream is this per week?

Think !

The missing digits are 1, 2, 3, 4, and 8. What was the problem?

▐▌▐▌ ▐▌▐▌ ▐▌▐▌ ▐▌▐▌
                    × ▐▌▐▌
3   4   5   6   8

More practice, page 384, Set B

3-digit quotients

In one day, an airline had 32 flights between San Francisco and Los Angeles. A total of 4064 people traveled on these flights. What was the average number of people on each flight?

Finding the answer

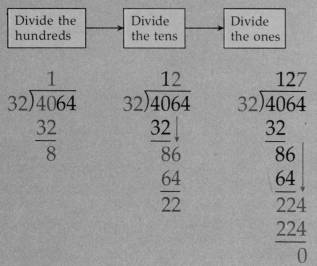

The average number of people on each flight was 127.

Other examples

```
      526 R13              407 R25             370
48)25 261            65)26 480           24)8880
   24 0                 26 0                72
    1 26                  48                168
      96                   0                168
     301                 480                  0
     288                 455
      13                  25
```

Divide.

1. 73)23 197   2. 85)36 501   3. 70)58 269   4. 28)18 228   5. 41)16 280

6. 36)28 923   7. 92)84 712   8. 17)10 285   9. 69)20 717   10. 54)41 257

Divide.

1. $56\overline{)23\ 934}$ 2. $63\overline{)24\ 459}$ 3. $15\overline{)7897}$ 4. $61\overline{)43\ 614}$ 5. $27\overline{)24\ 978}$

6. $84\overline{)30\ 617}$ 7. $79\overline{)41\ 256}$ 8. $90\overline{)88\ 520}$ 9. $38\overline{)16\ 233}$ 10. $42\overline{)32\ 004}$

11. $94\overline{)66\ 519}$ 12. $52\overline{)43\ 687}$ 13. $31\overline{)8285}$ 14. $76\overline{)68\ 715}$ 15. $39\overline{)13\ 265}$

16. $45\overline{)28\ 169}$ 17. $27\overline{)3564}$ 18. $80\overline{)24\ 320}$ 19. $18\overline{)13\ 776}$ 20. $63\overline{)15\ 562}$

21. $54\overline{)6534}$ 22. $82\overline{)27\ 880}$ 23. $49\overline{)31\ 901}$ 24. $30\overline{)23\ 429}$ 25. $16\overline{)9665}$

26. $63\overline{)44\ 537}$ 27. $71\overline{)24\ 948}$ 28. $68\overline{)13\ 660}$ 29. $95\overline{)27\ 542}$ 30. $27\overline{)20\ 576}$

31. One airline carried 2464 people on 14 flights between the East Coast and the West Coast. What was the average number on each flight?

☆ 32. Find out how many buses would be needed to take all the students in your school on a picnic.

Suppose a jet airliner cost $20 000 000. About how many $85 tickets would it take to equal that amount?

If the plane holds 184 people, about how many trips would it have to make to pay for itself?

Answers for Self-check   1. 52 R4   2. 61 R2   3. 48   4. 70 R3   5. 634 R1   6. 792   7. 308 R5
8. 950 R3   9. 28 R21   10. 69 R56   11. 43   12. 70 R7   13. 476 R42   14. 381   15. 507 R18   16. 620

More practice, page 384, Set C

Self-check

Divide.

1. $6 \overline{)316}$

2. $7 \overline{)429}$

3. $9 \overline{)432}$

4. $4 \overline{)283}$

5. $8 \overline{)5073}$

6. $3 \overline{)2376}$

7. $6 \overline{)1853}$

8. $5 \overline{)4753}$

9. $37 \overline{)1057}$

10. $92 \overline{)6404}$

11. $65 \overline{)2795}$

12. $24 \overline{)1687}$

13. $83 \overline{)39\ 550}$

14. $16 \overline{)6096}$

15. $71 \overline{)36\ 015}$

16. $48 \overline{)29\ 760}$

Answers for Self-check—page 139

Test

Divide.

1. $5 \overline{)286}$

2. $8 \overline{)344}$

3. $3 \overline{)92}$

4. $6 \overline{)507}$

5. $7 \overline{)5896}$

6. $4 \overline{)2609}$

7. $9 \overline{)6325}$

8. $6 \overline{)5520}$

9. $45 \overline{)3804}$

10. $71 \overline{)1926}$

11. $17 \overline{)1365}$

12. $53 \overline{)2438}$

13. $86 \overline{)46\ 416}$

14. $24 \overline{)6624}$

15. $62 \overline{)25\ 189}$

16. $39 \overline{)28\ 882}$

A Game of Nim

Play this game with a friend.

Place 15 markers in 3 rows as shown.

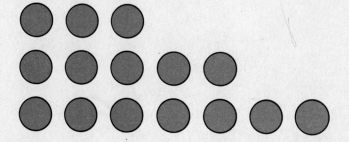

Rules:

1. Two players take turns.
2. At each turn, a player picks up one or more markers from one row only.
3. Whoever has to pick up the last marker loses the game.

Dividing Decimals

Getting started

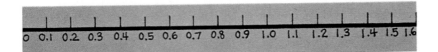

1. If you folded this 1.6 number strip in half, the fold would be on which mark?

2. If you folded it twice (fourths), where would the fold marks be?

3. Where would the marks be if you folded it 3 times (eighths)?

4. Answer the questions above for this 2.4 number strip.

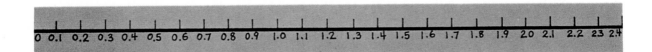

Make and fold a 1.6 or 2.4 number strip to check your answers.

When you fold a strip in half,
you can think of dividing by 2.

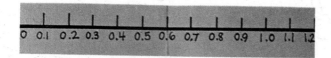

$1.2 \div 2 = 0.6$

Check: $\begin{array}{r} 0.6 \\ \times\ \ 2 \\ \hline 1.2 \end{array}$

Solve the equations. Use multiplication to check your answers.

1.

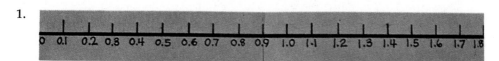

$$1.8 \div 2 = n$$

2.

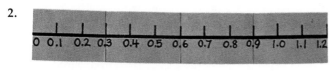

$$1.2 \div 4 = n$$

3.

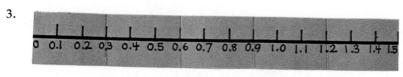

$$1.5 \div 5 = n$$

4.

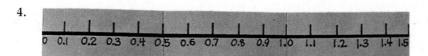

$$1.5 \div 3 = n$$

Dividing decimals by whole numbers

The pitcher holds 1.6 ℓ. If the same amount is poured into each of 8 glasses, how much will there be in each glass?

Finding the answer

| Divide as with whole numbers | → | Place the decimal point directly above the decimal point in the dividend | → | Write in the usual form |

$$\begin{array}{r} 2 \\ 8\overline{)1.6} \\ 1\ 6 \\ \hline 0 \end{array} \qquad \begin{array}{r} .2 \\ 8\overline{)1.6} \\ 1\ 6 \\ \hline 0 \end{array} \qquad \begin{array}{r} 0.2 \\ 8\overline{)1.6} \\ 1\ 6 \\ \hline 0 \end{array}$$

There will be 0.2 ℓ in each glass.

Other examples

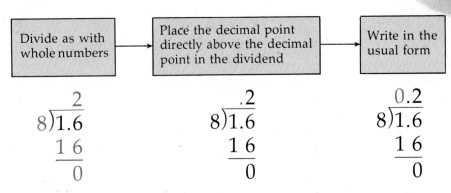

$$\begin{array}{r} 3.6 \\ 7\overline{)25.2} \\ 21 \\ \hline 4\ 2 \\ 4\ 2 \\ \hline 0 \end{array} \quad \begin{array}{r} \text{Check:}\ \ 3.6 \\ \times\ \ \ 7 \\ \hline 25.2 \\ \\ \text{same} \end{array} \quad \begin{array}{r} 0.36 \\ 7\overline{)2.52} \\ 2\ 1 \\ \hline 42 \\ 42 \\ \hline 0 \end{array} \quad \begin{array}{r} 0.076 \\ 28\overline{)2.128} \\ 1\ 96 \\ \hline 168 \\ 168 \\ \hline 0 \end{array} \quad \begin{array}{r} 4.29 \\ 52\overline{)223.08} \\ 208 \\ \hline 15\ 0 \\ 10\ 4 \\ \hline 4\ 68 \\ 4\ 68 \\ \hline 0 \end{array}$$

Divide. Check your answers.

1. $4\overline{)3.2}$ 2. $7\overline{)2.8}$ 3. $6\overline{)16.2}$ 4. $3\overline{)1.44}$ 5. $8\overline{)25.6}$

6. $23\overline{)16.1}$ 7. $58\overline{)139.2}$ 8. $41\overline{)1.517}$ 9. $72\overline{)4.464}$ 10. $69\overline{)656.88}$

Copy the problems.

Put the decimal points in the correct place.
Check by multiplying.

1. $\begin{array}{r} 2\ 56 \\ 5\overline{)12.80} \end{array}$

2. $\begin{array}{r} 34\ 7 \\ 3\overline{)104.1} \end{array}$

3. $\begin{array}{r} 0\ 408 \\ 6\overline{)2.448} \end{array}$

4. $\begin{array}{r} 65\ 1 \\ 4\overline{)260.4} \end{array}$

5. $\begin{array}{r} 2\ 07 \\ 7\overline{)14.49} \end{array}$

6. $\begin{array}{r} 21\ 8 \\ 55\overline{)1199.0} \end{array}$

7. $\begin{array}{r} 4\ 19 \\ 37\overline{)155.03} \end{array}$

8. $\begin{array}{r} 80\ 6 \\ 53\overline{)4271.8} \end{array}$

9. $\begin{array}{r} 4\ 52 \\ 28\overline{)126.56} \end{array}$

10. $\begin{array}{r} 0\ 307 \\ 86\overline{)26.402} \end{array}$

Divide.

11. $6\overline{)4.8}$

12. $3\overline{)1.5}$

13. $5\overline{)0.15}$

14. $7\overline{)4.2}$

15. $9\overline{)0.36}$

16. $4\overline{)11.2}$

17. $8\overline{)5.92}$

18. $2\overline{)7.2}$

19. $6\overline{)0.546}$

20. $5\overline{)8.5}$

21. $86\overline{)34.4}$

22. $92\overline{)6.44}$

23. $19\overline{)9.5}$

24. $34\overline{)2.04}$

25. $51\overline{)40.8}$

26. $65\overline{)175.5}$

27. $48\overline{)16.32}$

28. $30\overline{)177.0}$

29. $27\overline{)1.674}$

30. $73\overline{)255.5}$

31. Had 1.80 ℓ of cocoa.
Poured the same amount
into each of 12 cups.
How much in each cup?

☆ 32. Find the number of liters
a large pitcher holds.
Use it to fill some cups
(or glasses). Divide to
find out how much
each cup holds.

How long would it take you to
walk around the earth? If you
were to start now and walk 6 km
each day, how old would you be
when you completed the trip?
(Use 40 074 km as the distance
around the earth.)

More practice, page 385, Set A

More about dividing decimals

A mail carrier in the city spends 4 hours delivering the mail each day. In that time, the carrier may walk about 15 km. What is the average number of kilometers the carrier walks each hour?

Finding the answer

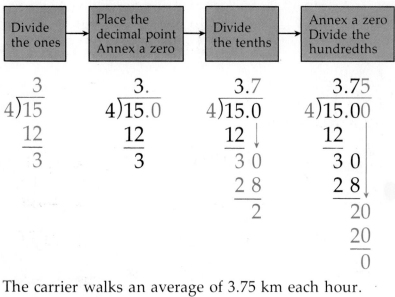

Divide the ones	Place the decimal point Annex a zero	Divide the tenths	Annex a zero Divide the hundredths

$$
\begin{array}{r} 3 \\ 4\overline{)15} \\ 12 \\ \hline 3 \end{array}
\qquad
\begin{array}{r} 3. \\ 4\overline{)15.0} \\ 12 \\ \hline 3 \end{array}
\qquad
\begin{array}{r} 3.7 \\ 4\overline{)15.0} \\ 12\downarrow \\ \hline 3\ 0 \\ 2\ 8 \\ \hline 2 \end{array}
\qquad
\begin{array}{r} 3.75 \\ 4\overline{)15.00} \\ 12 \\ \hline 3\ 0 \\ 2\ 8 \\ \hline 20 \\ 20 \\ \hline 0 \end{array}
$$

The carrier walks an average of 3.75 km each hour.

Other examples

$$
\begin{array}{r} 0.25 \\ 4\overline{)1.00} \\ 8 \\ \hline 20 \\ 20 \\ \hline 0 \end{array}
\qquad
\begin{array}{r} 0.15 \\ 12\overline{)1.80} \\ 1\ 2 \\ \hline 60 \\ 60 \\ \hline 0 \end{array}
\qquad
\begin{array}{r} 0.025 \\ 22\overline{)0.550} \\ 44 \\ \hline 110 \\ 110 \\ \hline 0 \end{array}
$$

Find the quotients.

Annex zeros as needed and divide until the remainder is zero.

1. $5\overline{)7}$

2. $2\overline{)31}$

3. $6\overline{)27}$

4. $8\overline{)34}$

5. $12\overline{)54}$

6. $15\overline{)36}$

7. $6\overline{)0.45}$

8. $15\overline{)3.45}$

Find the quotients.
Continue dividing until the remainder is zero.

1. 8)‾42‾
2. 4)‾66‾
3. 5)‾204‾
4. 4)‾2.2‾

5. 25)‾56‾
6. 50)‾7.5‾
7. 14)‾5.25‾
8. 48)‾36‾

9. 15)‾51.6‾
10. 24)‾66‾
11. 86)‾21.5‾
12. 70)‾3.5‾

13. 65)‾70.2‾
14. 60)‾8.4‾
15. 26)‾27.3‾
16. 90)‾0.81‾

17. 32)‾0.48‾
18. 40)‾2.2‾
19. 54)‾0.27‾
20. 95)‾480.7‾

21. A mail carrier in the country may drive 47 km delivering the mail. If the job takes 5 hours, what is the average distance the carrier drives each hour?

22. Find out how long your mail carrier takes to deliver the mail. Estimate the total distance. Figure out the approximate distance your carrier travels per hour.

Find pairs of numbers that can be used as both addends and factors to give the sums and products shown below.

	sums	+ ×	products
A	0.5	✳	0.06
B	0.7	✳	0.12
C	1	✳	0.24
D	1.1	✳	0.24
E	0.6	✳	0.09
F	0.02	✳	0.0001

More practice, page 385, Set B

Rounding decimals

Larry works in a candy store. He wants to divide 8 kg of peanuts, equally, into 6 bags. How many kilograms (to the nearest hundredth) should he put in each bag?

Finding the answer

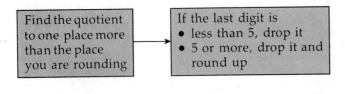

$$\frac{1.333}{6)8.^20^20^20} \longrightarrow 1.33 \text{ (rounded to the nearest hundredth)}$$

Larry should put 1.33 kg of nuts in each bag.

Other examples

$$\frac{1.42}{7)10.^30^20} \longrightarrow 1.4 \text{ (rounded to the nearest tenth)}$$

$$\frac{0.666}{9)6.0^60^60} \longrightarrow 0.67 \text{ (rounded to the nearest hundredth)}$$

$$\frac{0.75}{8)6.0^40} \longrightarrow 0.8$$

$$\frac{1.714}{7)12.^50^10^30} \longrightarrow 1.71$$

Divide and round to the nearest tenth.

1. $8)\overline{10}$ 2. $6)\overline{20}$ 3. $7)\overline{150}$ 4. $3)\overline{1.6}$

Divide and round to the nearest hundredth.

5. $6)\overline{10}$ 6. $7)\overline{18}$ 7. $6)\overline{14}$ 8. $7)\overline{2}$

Divide and round to the nearest tenth.

1. $9\overline{)12}$
2. $9\overline{)15}$
3. $9\overline{)16}$
4. $9\overline{)14}$
5. $3\overline{)10}$
6. $7\overline{)4}$
7. $6\overline{)4}$
8. $7\overline{)1.1}$
9. $8\overline{)4.6}$
10. $6\overline{)5.2}$
11. $16\overline{)8.3}$
12. $25\overline{)7.32}$
13. $12\overline{)9.5}$
14. $23\overline{)7.15}$
15. $11\overline{)50}$
16. $19\overline{)4.8}$

Divide and round to the nearest hundredth.

17. $8\overline{)13}$
18. $7\overline{)15}$
19. $8\overline{)15}$
20. $6\overline{)14}$
21. $12\overline{)10}$
22. $12\overline{)67}$
23. $13\overline{)7.6}$
24. $5\overline{)4.28}$
25. $9\overline{)2.47}$
26. $52\overline{)6.73}$
27. $13\overline{)84.9}$
28. $76\overline{)2.75}$

29. Rita wanted to put 9 kg of pecans into 7 bags. How many kilograms (to the nearest tenth) should she put into each bag?

☆ 30. Fill a large sack with something like beans or sand. Find its mass in kilograms. Plan to divide it equally into smaller containers. Figure out how much should be put into each one. Check your work.

Guess the missing numbers. Then check your guess.

$6 \times 7 = 42$
$66 \times 67 = 4422$
$666 \times 667 = 444\ 222$
$6666 \times 6667 = n$
$66\ 666 \times 66\ 667 = n$

Dividing by decimals

A fast land snail can travel
176.05 m in 3.5 hours.
What is its average speed
in meters per hour?

Finding the answer

Multiply the divisor by the multiple of 10 that will make it a whole number	Multiply the dividend by the same number	Divide as with whole numbers. Place the decimal point above its new position in the dividend

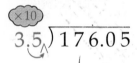

$$3.5\overline{)176.05}$$

$$3.5\overline{)176.05}$$

$$\begin{array}{r} 50.3 \\ 3.5\overline{)176.05} \\ \underline{175} \\ 10 \\ \underline{0} \\ 105 \\ \underline{105} \\ 0 \end{array}$$

The snail's average speed is 50.3 m/h.

Other examples

$$\begin{array}{r} 0.07 \\ 2.6\overline{)0.182} \\ \underline{182} \\ 0 \end{array}$$

$$\begin{array}{r} 6.8 \\ 0.43\overline{)2.924} \\ \underline{2\,58} \\ 344 \\ \underline{344} \\ 0 \end{array}$$

$$\begin{array}{r} 21.7 \\ 0.06\overline{)1.302} \\ \underline{12} \\ 10 \\ \underline{6} \\ 42 \\ \underline{42} \\ 0 \end{array}$$

Divide.

1. $0.7\overline{)4.34}$

2. $0.04\overline{)3.704}$

3. $6.8\overline{)36.72}$

4. $0.36\overline{)1.152}$

5. $4.3\overline{)27.95}$

6. $7.1\overline{)0.8023}$

7. $3.4\overline{)20.4}$

8. $0.05\overline{)0.155}$

Divide.

1. $6.4 \overline{)17.92}$ 2. $0.83 \overline{)4.067}$ 3. $3.1 \overline{)2.263}$ 4. $7.5 \overline{)3.375}$

5. $0.57 \overline{)0.684}$ 6. $0.03 \overline{)0.174}$ 7. $2.5 \overline{)0.600}$ 8. $0.52 \overline{)1.82}$

9. $0.29 \overline{)0.1392}$ 10. $3.4 \overline{)258.4}$ 11. $4.8 \overline{)14.4}$ 12. $0.07 \overline{)0.336}$

13. $7.3 \overline{)4.015}$ 14. $0.05 \overline{)0.135}$ 15. $0.61 \overline{)0.4575}$ 16. $9.2 \overline{)0.736}$

17. $0.34 \overline{)0.1836}$ 18. $7.6 \overline{)47.12}$ 19. $0.54 \overline{)0.270}$ 20. $6.3 \overline{)0.378}$

21. $0.65 \overline{)16.25}$ 22. $0.36 \overline{)1.8252}$ 23. $2.5 \overline{)0.175}$ 24. $0.17 \overline{)3.468}$

25. A giant tortoise traveled 0.675 km in 2.5 hours. What was its average speed in kilometers per hour?

26. A three-toed sloth might take 4.5 hours to go 0.711 km. What is its average speed in kilometers per hour?

Think !

Sue thought of a number,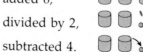

multiplied the number by 4,

added 6,

divided by 2,

subtracted 4.

If the result was 39, what number was Sue thinking of?

More practice, page 386, Set A

More dividing by decimals

A school service club collects empty soda cans to recycle aluminum. They want to collect 2.5 kg of cans each week. If an empty can has a mass of 0.005 kg, how many cans does the club need to collect each week?

Finding the answer

Multiply the divisor by the multiple of 10 that will make it a whole number	→	Multiply the dividend by the same number. Annex zeros if needed	→	Divide as with whole numbers. Place the decimal point above its new position in the dividend

$$\overset{\times 1000}{0.005\,)\,2.5}$$

$$\overset{\times 1000}{0.005\,)\,2.500}$$

$$\overset{500}{0.005\,)\,2.500}$$

They need to collect 500 cans each week.

Other examples

$$\overset{\times 10}{4.5\,)\,\overset{2}{9.0}}$$
$$\underline{9\,0}$$
$$0$$

$$\overset{\times 100}{3.25\,)\,\overset{4}{13.00}}$$
$$\underline{13\,00}$$
$$0$$

$$\overset{\times 1000}{0.015\,)\,\overset{50}{0.750}}$$
$$\underline{75}$$
$$0$$

Divide.

1. $0.25\,)\,5$

2. $1.5\,)\,6$

3. $0.04\,)\,0.72$

4. $0.008\,)\,0.4$

5. $0.75\,)\,31.5$

6. $0.6\,)\,2.1$

7. $0.15\,)\,3.6$

8. $2.2\,)\,44$

Divide. Check by multiplying.

1. $0.007 \overline{)2.1}$ 2. $3.8 \overline{)19}$

3. $0.82 \overline{)12.3}$ 4. $0.35 \overline{)7}$

5. $4.5 \overline{)99}$ 6. $0.66 \overline{)33}$

7. $7.5 \overline{)165}$ 8. $0.84 \overline{)63}$

9. $0.009 \overline{)0.72}$ 10. $0.12 \overline{)78}$

11. $0.34 \overline{)18.7}$ 12. $0.14 \overline{)13.3}$

13. $4.5 \overline{)153}$ 14. $5.5 \overline{)242}$

15. Mass of a large bag of cans: 6 kg
    Mass of each can: 0.004 kg
    How many cans?

☆ 16. Find the mass of a drink can that is not aluminum. How many of these cans would you need to collect to have a mass equal to your body's mass?

$1 ⟶ 1$ coin (silver dollar)
$1 ⟶ 2$ coins (2 half dollars)
$1 ⟶ 3$ coins (2 quarters, 1 half)
$1 ⟶ 4$ coins (4 quarters)
$1 ⟶ 5$ coins (1 half, 1 quarter, 2 dimes, 1 nickel)
Can you continue the pattern up to 20 coins?

Practicing your skills

Add, subtract, or multiply.

1. $\begin{array}{r} 3972 \\ + 8456 \end{array}$ 2. $\begin{array}{r} 2743 \\ - 1865 \end{array}$ 3. $\begin{array}{r} 28.39 \\ + 47.65 \end{array}$ 4. $\begin{array}{r} 5.364 \\ - 2.958 \end{array}$

5. $\begin{array}{r} 382 \\ \times \quad 9 \end{array}$ 6. $\begin{array}{r} 46 \\ \times 27 \end{array}$ 7. $\begin{array}{r} 6.42 \\ \times \quad 27 \end{array}$ 8. $\begin{array}{r} 0.573 \\ \times 0.43 \end{array}$

Answers for Self-check   1. 0.7   2. 0.03   3. 3.7   4. 6.2   5. 5.4   6. 3.5   7. 0.64   8. 0.005   9. 3.4
10. 0.2   11. 2.14   12. 0.21   13. 0.9   14. 42   15. 0.31   16. 6.2   17. 5   18. 90   19. 45   20. 940

More practice, page 386, Set B

Self-check

Divide.

1. $6\overline{)4.2}$
2. $8\overline{)0.24}$
3. $7\overline{)25.9}$
4. $23\overline{)142.6}$
5. $5\overline{)27}$
6. $12\overline{)42}$
7. $25\overline{)16}$
8. $22\overline{)0.11}$

Divide and round to the nearest tenth.

9. $8\overline{)27}$
10. $6\overline{)1.3}$

Divide and round to the nearest hundredth.

11. $7\overline{)15}$
12. $12\overline{)2.5}$

Divide.

13. $0.5\overline{)0.45}$
14. $0.09\overline{)3.78}$
15. $3.2\overline{)0.992}$
16. $0.17\overline{)1.054}$
17. $0.8\overline{)4}$
18. $0.06\overline{)5.4}$
19. $2.8\overline{)126}$
20. $0.35\overline{)329}$

Answers for Self-check—page 153

Test

Divide.

1. $9\overline{)6.3}$
2. $6\overline{)0.18}$
3. $4\overline{)33.2}$
4. $3\overline{)266.4}$
5. $8\overline{)52}$
6. $35\overline{)224}$
7. $90\overline{)1.8}$
8. $45\overline{)0.18}$

Divide and round to the nearest tenth.

9. $6\overline{)35}$
10. $14\overline{)40}$

Divide and round to the nearest hundredth.

11. $34\overline{)15}$
12. $21\overline{)6.4}$

Divide.

13. $0.7\overline{)5.6}$
14. $0.06\overline{)1.68}$
15. $4.9\overline{)2.058}$
16. $0.28\overline{)1.036}$
17. $0.4\overline{)1}$
18. $0.12\overline{)4.2}$
19. $7.4\overline{)185}$
20. $0.26\overline{)14.3}$

Complete the Squares

Use dot paper and try this game with a classmate.

At your turn, you must connect two adjacent dots in the same row or same column. If the connection results in a square, place your initial inside and score one point. Each time you score, take another turn. The first player to score 9 points wins.

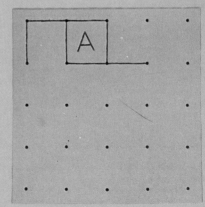

Using Your Skills

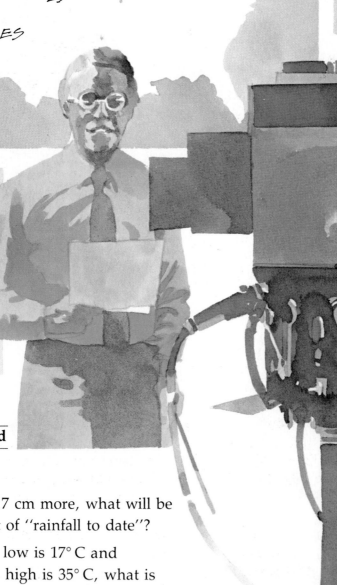

VANCOUVER
18°

TORONTO
27°

NEW
YORK
28°

CHICAGO
31°

DENVER
25°

LOS ANGELES
29°

TODAY'S HIGH 33°
LAST NIGHT'S LOW 18°
TONIGHT'S LOW 15°-19°
TOMORROW'S HIGH MID 30'S

AVERAGE YEARLY
RAINFALL
87.3 cm

RAINFALL
TO DATE
39.8 cm

Getting started

1. If it rains 3.7 cm more, what will be the amount of "rainfall to date"?

2. If tonight's low is 17° C and tomorrow's high is 35° C, what is the difference in temperatures?

3. What other problems can you solve?

Solving Problems

1. Read carefully to find the facts.
2. Look for the question.
3. Decide what to do.
4. Find the answer.
5. Read again. Does your answer make sense?

For each problem, tell which of the numbers are needed to find the answer to the question.

1. Toledo had 4.2 cm of rain in 30 minutes. During that time, the temperature fell from 34° C to 25° C. How many degrees did the temperature fall?

2. The average yearly rainfall for Dallas is 87.6 cm. In a two-year period, the city had 82.9 cm and 78.6 cm of rain. What was the average rainfall for those two years?

3. During a storm, Boston had 7.6 cm of rain in 12 hours. The barometer reading was 28.9. What was the average amount of rainfall per hour?

4. During a freak storm in Kansas, only 0.5 cm of rain fell but the barometer reading dropped from 31.2 to 28.5. How much did the barometer reading drop?

Finding averages

These are the heights of the
children on the volleyball team.

Nora—156 cm   Anna—147 cm

Jay—138 cm   Scott—149 cm

Neil—154 cm   Chris—150 cm

What is the average height of the children
on the team?

Finding the answer

Find the sum of all the numbers	→	Divide by the number of addends	→	The quotient is the average of the numbers

$$
\begin{array}{r}
156 \\
138 \\
154 \\
147 \\
149 \\
+\ 150 \\
\hline
894
\end{array}
$$

$$
\begin{array}{r}
149 \\
6\overline{)894}
\end{array}
$$

149

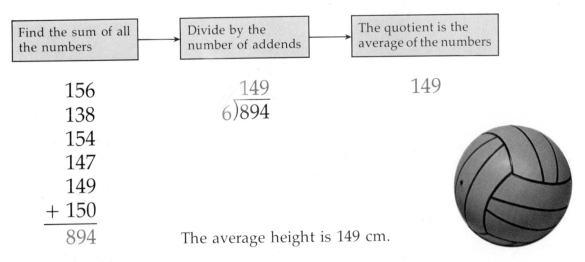

The average height is 149 cm.

Another example   Find the average (to the nearest tenth).

84, 39, 52, 46

$$
\begin{array}{r}
84 \\
39 \\
52 \\
+\ 46 \\
\hline
221
\end{array}
$$

$$
\begin{array}{r}
55.25 \\
4\overline{)221.00}
\end{array}
$$

average: 55.3

Find the average.

Find the average (to the nearest tenth).

1.
148, 175, 164, 161

2.
23, 32, 26, 30, 24

3.
275, 318, 290

4.
49, 62, 57, 46, 73, 38

Find these averages (to the nearest tenth if necessary).

1. Jumping height
   (standing start)

   Paul—214 cm
   Sandy—218 cm
   Rick—203 cm
   Ed—210 cm
   Susan—202 cm
   Linda—220 cm

2. Span
   (thumb to little finger)

   Robin—16.2 cm
   Steve—15.7 cm
   Sally—15.4 cm
   Trina—16.6 cm
   Judy—14.8 cm

3. Find one of the averages above for yourself and some classmates.

Our water supply

Wherever we live, fresh water is one of the
most important things in our lives. Only
about 0.03 of the water on the earth is
fresh. We need to do everything we can
to keep this water clean and ready for use.
This is not easy to do in places where
many people live in a small area.
The problems contain some
interesting facts about our
water supply and the
way we use it.

1. The average person in the United States
   uses about 260 ℓ of water every day.
   How much water is this in a week?
   A month (30 days)? A year (365 days)?

2. In an average lifetime, a person drinks
   about 60 600 ℓ of water. If the average
   lifetime is 75 years, about how much
   water does a person drink each year?

3. It takes about 38 ℓ of water to wash the dishes. It takes 110 ℓ to run a washing machine. How much water is used in a week if the washer is run 5 times and the dishes are washed twice a day?

4. You use about 130 ℓ of water to take a bath. You use about 19 ℓ of water per minute when you take a shower. About how long can you stay in the shower and still use the same amount of water as you do when you take a bath?

5. About 2 out of every 3 kg of your body mass is water. How much of you is water if your mass is 45 kg?

After water is used, it must be treated before it is returned to our water supply. When untreated water (sewage) is put into the water supply, pollution results. Polluted water is unfit for human use and often kills plant and animal life.

6. Of every 100 ℓ of sewage, about 89 ℓ is treated before it is put back into the rivers and lakes. How much of the 100 ℓ is untreated?

7. How much untreated sewage would there be from 1000 ℓ? From 1 000 000 ℓ?

Making the most of your money

Stores sometimes sell items at a lower price per unit if you buy more than one.

Example:

Encyclopedia of Gardening
Set of 6 $22.95 $4.00 each

If you buy the complete set, how much do you save on each book, to the nearest cent?

$$3.825 \longrightarrow \$3.83$$
$$6\overline{)\$22.950}$$

$$
\begin{array}{r}
\$\ 4.00 \\
-\ 3.83 \\
\hline
\$\ 0.17
\end{array}
$$

You save $0.17 on each book.

Find out how much you save on each one if you buy the full amount.

1.

Seeds

10¢ each   4 for 35¢

2.

Herb Garden

$0.50 each   6 for $2.79

3.

Lily Bulbs

$0.20 each   5 for $0.88

4.

Plant Food

$0.75 each   2 for $1.39

5.

Plants

$1.95 each   3 for $5

6.

Rose Bush Clippings

$0.35 each   6 for $1.95

Which is the better buy?

1.

Carnations

A 4 for 69¢   B 6 for $1.00

2.

Rosebuds

A 6 for $1.85   B 12 for $3.25

If you buy two, how much do you save on each one?

3.

Ceramic Pots

$2.98 each   2 for $5.00

4.

Bags of Soil

$0.99 each   2 for $1.76

Solve.

5. Ellie bought 3 ivy plants that cost $0.49 each. How much change should she get if she paid with a $5 bill?

6. Russ bought a bag of soil for $0.99 and 2 gardenia plants for $1.95 each. How much money did he spend?

An amazing pump

The human heart is a pump that sends blood to all parts of the body.

It works 24 hours a day. The only rest it gets is between beats. More facts about this amazing pump are given in the problems that follow.

1. The heart of a 12-year-old beats about 80 times a minute. An adult's heart beats about 0.9 times as fast. How many beats a minute is that?

2. If someone's heart beats 80 times a minute, how many times does it beat in an hour? In a day?

3. Suppose your pulse rate is 80. Find these pulse rates.

    A small bird's: 2.5 times yours

    B cat's: 1.63 times yours

    C horse's: 0.43 times yours

    D elephant's: 0.31 times yours

A person's heart is about the size of the person's fist. These are the approximate masses of the heart at different ages.

Age	Mass
Birth	19 g
2 years	44 g
9 years	93 g
15 years	200 g
Adult female	265 g
Adult male	310 g

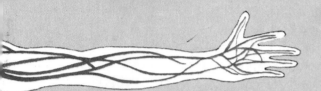

4. How many grams does the heart gain between birth and 15 years? Between 2 years and 9 years?

5. The mass of an adult female's heart is how many times as great as its mass at birth?

6. The mass of an adult male's heart is how many times as great as its mass at birth?

7. An adult's heart pumps about 4.7 ℓ of blood every minute. How many liters is this in an hour? In a day?

8. An adult's body contains about 4.73 ℓ of blood. People who give blood to a blood bank give about 0.1 of their blood. What part of a liter is this (to the nearest tenth)?

9. About 0.9 of a person's blood is water. How much water is there in 2.5 ℓ of blood?

☆ 10. Find your own pulse rate and the pulse rates of some of your classmates. Find the average of these pulse rates.

☆ 11. Estimate the mass of your heart. Completely fill a container with water. Put your fist into the water up to your wrist. Use another container to catch the water that flows over the brim. Find the mass of that water. Its mass is about the same as the mass of your heart.

Using estimation

You can solve many number problems without pencil and paper. Often, you do not need to find an exact answer. You can use **estimation** to find an answer that is close enough to meet your need. The following problems show some ways you might use estimation in your daily life.

1. You wake up a little before 7:00. You went to sleep a little after 9:00. About how many hours of sleep did you get?

2. The label on your cereal box says that the box contains 596 g. You estimate that you eat about 50 g of cereal each morning. About how many days will a full box of cereal last you?

3. You live almost 1 km from school. You walk there in about 15 minutes. About how many kilometers per hour do you walk?

4. At school you read a story that has about 4000 words. It takes you 21 minutes. About how many words do you read a minute?

5. In health class, you find the height of some of your classmates:
Judy: 132 cm
Herb: 129 cm
Fred: 133 cm
Sue: 127 cm
Estimate their average height.

6. Your teacher asks you to write a book report about 200 words long. You write about 9 words per line. About how many lines do you need to write?

7. After school you buy some pencils. The price is 3 for 59¢. About how much does each pencil cost?

8. You buy the pencils for 59¢ and 2 tablets for 49¢ each. About how much do you spend?

9. A friend from another school asks you how many students there are in your school. You remember that there are 21 classes and that each class has between 25 and 35 students. What answer should you give your friend?

☆ 10. Make up an estimation problem about something that might happen during a day in your life.

Answers for Self-check   1. 176   2. 47.3   3. 18.7   4. $0.19   5. **B**   90 minutes

Self-check

1. Find the average: 175, 168, 182, 179

2. Find the average (to the nearest tenth): 43, 56, 39, 48, 53, 45

3. Suppose you used 224 ℓ of water for a 12-minute shower. How many liters (to the nearest tenth) did you use per minute?

4.

Dish Towels

$1.69 each

2 for $3.00

How much do you save
on each one if you buy 2?

5. Reading: 29 min
   Math: 41 min
   Spelling: 18 min

Which is the best estimate for the total?

A 80 min

B 90 min

C 70 min

Answers for Self-check—page 167

Test

1. Find the average: 246, 219, 231

2. Find the average (to the nearest tenth): 60, 84, 73, 81, 79, 92

3. If you use 245 ℓ of water each day for 14 days, what is the total number of liters you use?

4.

Plants

$2.75 each

2 for $4.98

How much do you save
on each one when you
buy 2?

5. Traveled 78 km/h for 3 hours. Which is the best estimate of the distance traveled?

A 200 km

B 240 km

C 280 km

Making a Magic Square

Here is a way to make a 4-by-4 magic square.

Number a 4-by-4 square consecutively, as shown in square **A**.

Exchange positions of the pairs of numerals connected by the arrows to get square **B**.

What is the magic sum in each row, column, and diagonal of square **B**?

Start with a different number and try to make your own magic square.

A

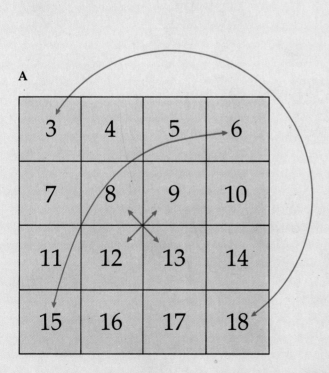

3	4	5	6
7	8	9	10
11	12	13	14
15	16	17	18

B

18	4	5	15
7	13	12	10
11	9	8	14
6	16	17	3

Geometry and Constructions

Getting started

Which of the colored figures has the same size and shape as the figure at the left? First guess, then check your guess by tracing.

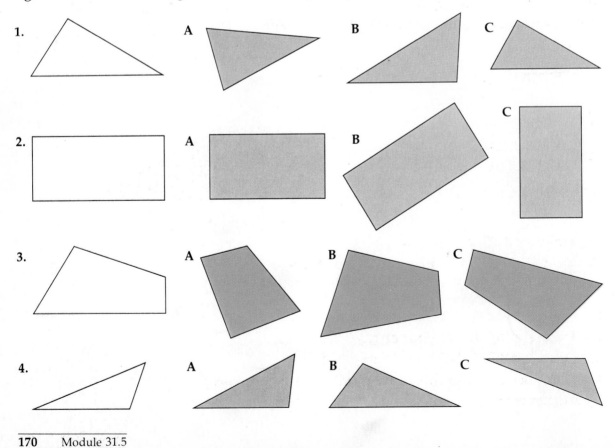

1.   A   B   C

2.   A   B   C

3.   A   B   C

4.   A   B   C

Two figures that fit exactly on each other are **congruent**.

Segments can be congruent to each other.

A •————————————————————• B
C •— — — — — — — — — — •D

We write: $\overline{AB} \cong \overline{CD}$
We read: Segment *AB* is congruent to segment *CD*.

Angles can be congruent to each other.

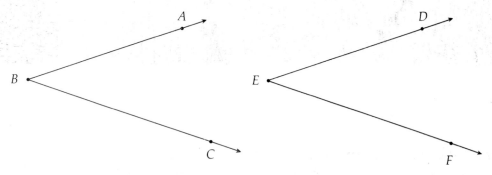

We write: $\angle ABC \cong \angle DEF$
We read: Angle *ABC* is congruent to angle *DEF*.

Triangles can be congruent to each other.

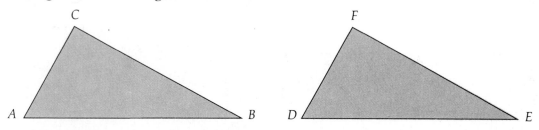

We write: $\triangle ABC \cong \triangle DEF$
We read: Triangle *ABC* is congruent to triangle *DEF*.

1. Trace $\overline{AB}$ above. Label your segment *EF*.
2. Trace $\angle ABC$. Label your angle *GHI*.
3. Trace $\triangle ABC$. Label your triangle *GHI*.
4. Write three statements that describe the congruences in exercises 1, 2, and 3.

Angle measure

Rays *BA* and *BC* intersect at point *B* to form ∠*ABC*.

The **protractor** shows that the measure of ∠*ABC* is 45°.

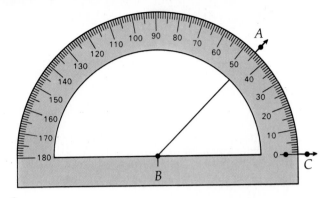

Give the measure of each of these angles.

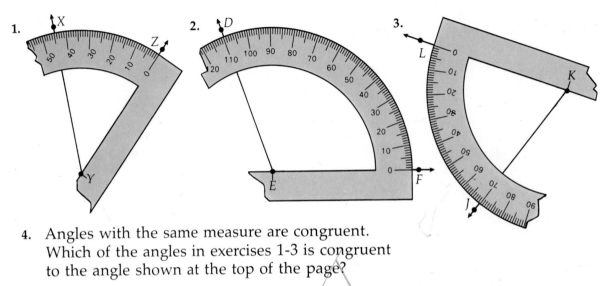

1.

2.

3.

4. Angles with the same measure are congruent. Which of the angles in exercises 1-3 is congruent to the angle shown at the top of the page?

Give the measure of each of these angles.

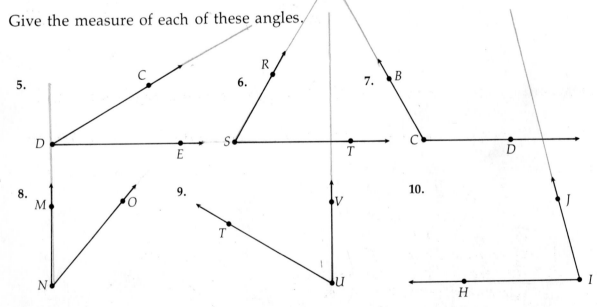

5.

6.

7.

8.

9.

10.

11. Which two angles above are congruent?

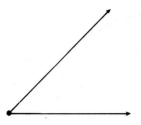

An acute angle has a measure less than 90°.

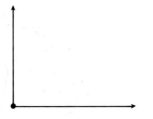

A right angle has a measure of 90°.

An obtuse angle has a measure greater than 90°.

Write **obtuse, right,** or **acute** for each angle.

1.

120°

2.

60°

3.

90°

4.

170°

5.

30°

6.

75°

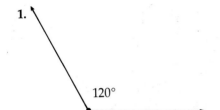

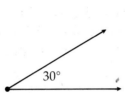
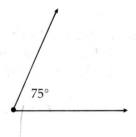

Draw angles with these measures. Label each one as **obtuse, right,** or **acute**.

7. ∠XYZ: 35°   8. ∠ABC: 90°   9. ∠HIJ: 155°   10. ∠DEF: 60°

11. ∠RST: 110°   12. ∠JKL: 10°   13. ∠MNO: 30°   14. ∠PQR: 150°

15. Measure each angle of △ABC.
Find the sum of those three measures.
If you measured carefully, your sum should be very close to 180°.

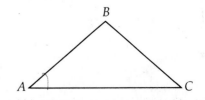

Constructing congruent segments and angles

To **construct** geometric figures, you need to use only a **compass** and the edge of a **ruler** or **straightedge.** You should not measure.

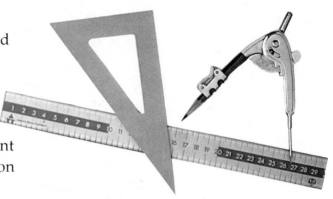

The figures below show how to construct a segment that is congruent to a given segment. This construction is called "copying a segment."

Copying a segment

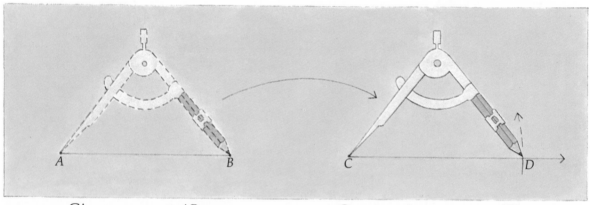

Given segment *AB*

Constructing segment *CD* congruent to segment *AB*

Congruent segments have the same length. $\overline{AB} \cong \overline{CD}$

Trace each segment. Then construct congruent segments as indicated.

1. Construct $\overline{GH}$ so that $\overline{EF} \cong \overline{GH}$.

    E •————————————• F

2. Construct $\overline{KL}$ so that $\overline{IJ} \cong \overline{KL}$.

    I •————• J

3. Construct $\overline{OP}$ so that $\overline{MN} \cong \overline{OP}$.

    M •————————————• N

4. Construct $\overline{ST}$ so that $\overline{QR} \cong \overline{ST}$.

    Q •————————————• R

The figures below show how to construct an angle congruent to a given angle.

Copying an angle

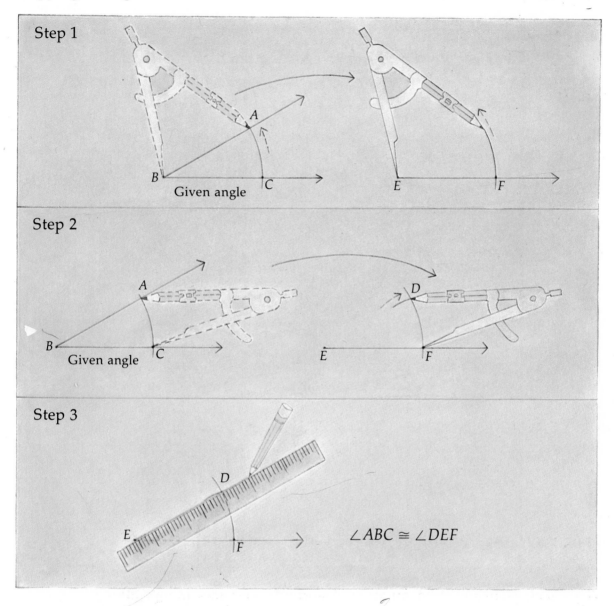

Step 1

Step 2

Step 3

$\angle ABC \cong \angle DEF$

Trace the given angles. Then construct angles congruent to the given angles. Label your angles so that each statement about congruence is true.

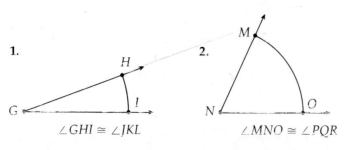

1.

$\angle GHI \cong \angle JKL$

2.

$\angle MNO \cong \angle PQR$

3. Draw an angle. Label it $\angle STU$. Draw another angle VWX such that $\angle STU \cong \angle VWX$.

Constructing congruent triangles

The figures below show
how to construct a triangle *DEF*
congruent to triangle *ABC*.

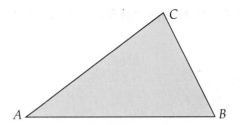

Copying a triangle

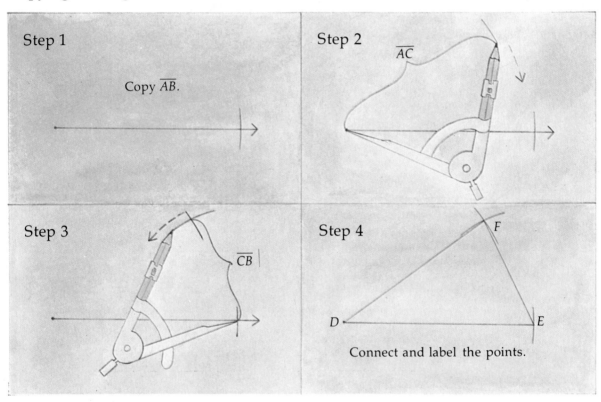

Step 1

Copy $\overline{AB}$.

Step 2

$\overline{AC}$

Step 3

$\overline{CB}$

Step 4

F

D   *E*

Connect and label the points.

Trace the given triangles. Then do each construction.

1.

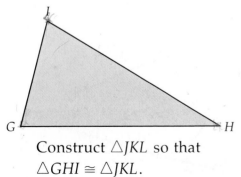

Construct △*JKL* so that
△*GHI* ≅ △*JKL*.

2.

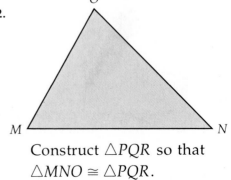

Construct △*PQR* so that
△*MNO* ≅ △*PQR*.

Trace each of these special triangles. Then construct congruent triangles.

1. Acute triangle:
   all acute angles

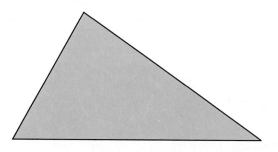

2. Right triangle:
   one right angle

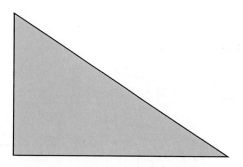

3. Obtuse triangle:
   one obtuse angle

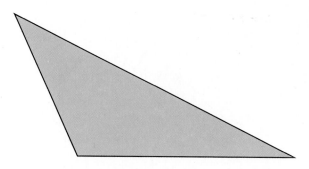

4. Scalene triangle:
   no sides congruent

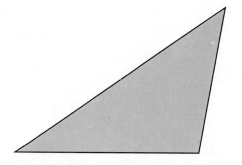

5. Isosceles triangle:
   two sides congruent

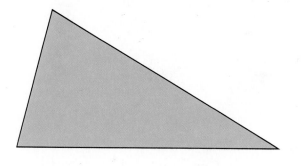

6. Equilateral triangle:
   all sides congruent

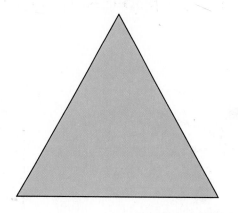

Congruent triangles

Triangle *ABC* is placed over triangle *DEF*.
It fits. The triangles are congruent.

The matching sides are congruent.

$\overline{AB} \cong \overline{DE}$

$\overline{BC} \cong \overline{EF}$

$\overline{CA} \cong \overline{FD}$

The matching angles are congruent.

$\angle CAB \cong \angle FDE$

$\angle ABC \cong \angle DEF$

$\angle BCA \cong \angle EFD$

These two triangles are congruent.
Give the missing pair of congruent
sides and angles.

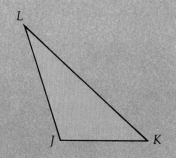

Sides	Angles
$\overline{GH} \cong \overline{JK}$	$\angle IGH \cong LJK$
$\overline{HI} \cong \overline{KL}$	$\angle GHI \cong JKL$
? $\cong$?	? $\cong$?

These pairs of triangles are congruent. Give the pairs
of congruent sides and congruent angles.

1.

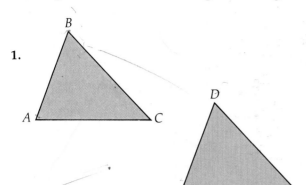

2.

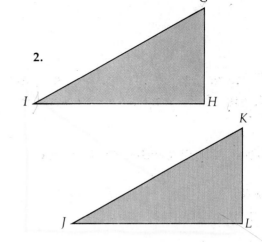

3.

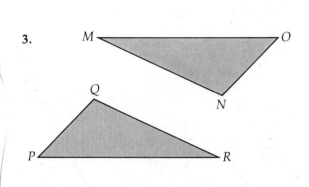

4.

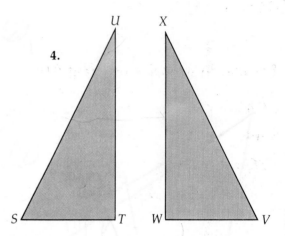

Practicing your skills

Add.

1.	856	2.	2674	3.	8234	4.	379
	97		5862		764		2486
	+ 438		+ 3049		+ 2980		+ 95

Subtract.

5.	3426	6.	403	7.	7387	8.	5038
	− 1783		− 156		− 2699		− 1762

✷ Some special constructions

The **bisector** of an angle *ABC* is a
ray *BD* such that $\angle ABD \cong \angle DBC$.

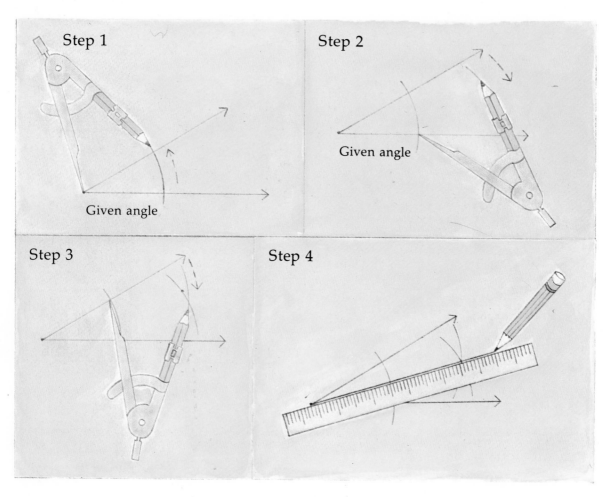

Bisecting an angle

Step 1

Given angle

Step 2

Given angle

Step 3

Step 4

Trace each of these angles.
Then construct the bisector of each one.

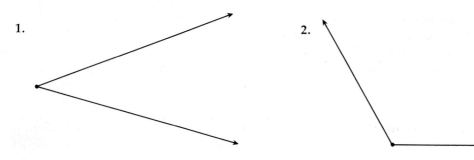

1.

2.

Constructing a perpendicular bisector

The perpendicular bisector of a segment AB is a line through the midpoint C ($\overline{AC} \cong \overline{CB}$) that forms right angles with $\overline{AB}$.

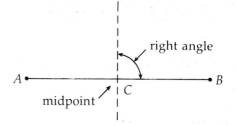

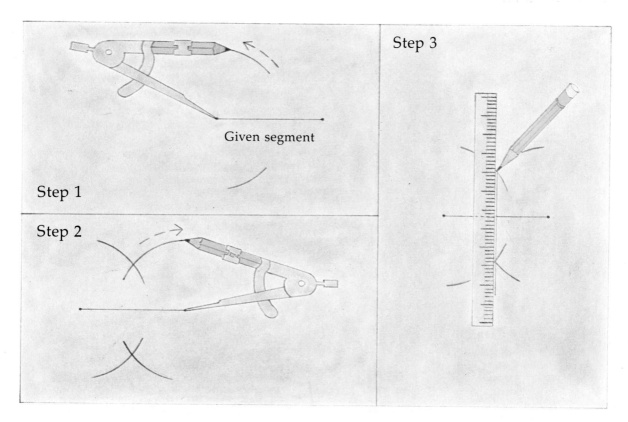

Trace each segment. Then construct its perpendicular bisector.

1. ├────────────────────┤   2. ├────────────────────────────┤

Draw any 4-sided figure. Connect in red the middle points of the 4 sides. Try it more than once. What did you find out about the red figure?

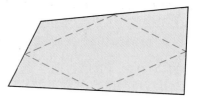

Self-check

1. Trace segment $\overline{MN}$. Then construct a segment PQ so that $\overline{PQ} \cong \overline{MN}$.

M ├─────────────────┤ N

Use a protractor and give the measure of each angle.

2.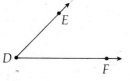

3.

4.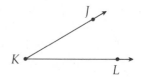

5. Which of the angles above is an obtuse angle?

$\triangle ABC \cong \triangle DEF$

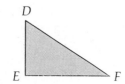

Complete each statement.

6. $\overline{AB} \cong$?

7. $\angle ABC \cong$?

8. $\overline{BC} \cong$?

9. $\angle ACB \cong$?

Answers for Self-check—page 181

Test

1. Trace angle ABC. Then construct an angle DEF so that $\angle ABC \cong \angle DEF$.

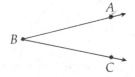

Use a protractor and give the measure of each angle.

2.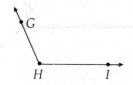

3.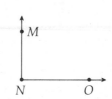

4.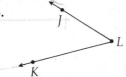

5. Which of the angles above is a right angle?

$\triangle RST \cong \triangle WXY$

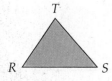

Complete the statements.

6. $\angle RTS \cong$?

7. $\overline{ST} \cong$?

8. $\overline{RT} \cong$?

9. $\angle SRT \cong$?

Tessellations

A tessellation is a repeated pattern of geometric figures.
It can be used to cover any flat surface.

These tiles can be used
to make repeating patterns.

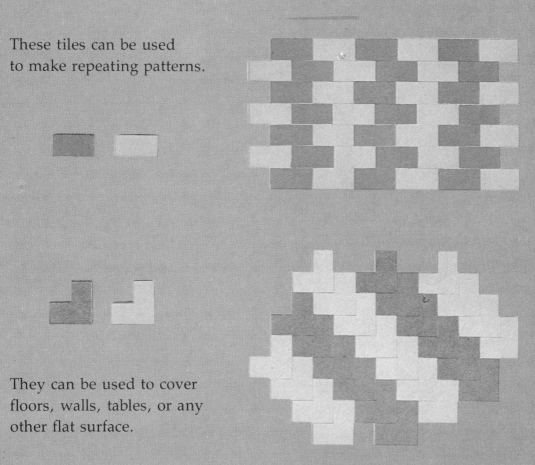

They can be used to cover
floors, walls, tables, or any
other flat surface.

These pairs of tiles can also be used to make tessellations.

Use graph paper and crayons to make a tile pattern of your own.
Use the tiles shown above or make up your own tile shape.

Level 31 review

Find the quotients.

1. $35 \div 7$ 2. $54 \div 6$ 3. $48 \div 8$ 4. $63 \div 9$

5. $60 \div 3$ 6. $150 \div 5$ 7. $360 \div 4$ 8. $1200 \div 3$

9. $320 \div 40$ 10. $720 \div 90$ 11. $210 \div 30$ 12. $2500 \div 50$

13. $3\overline{)273}$ 14. $6\overline{)435}$ 15. $4\overline{)2519}$ 16. $7\overline{)3940}$

17. $34\overline{)1742}$ 18. $22\overline{)1559}$ 19. $61\overline{)1108}$ 20. $95\overline{)7768}$

21. $83\overline{)35\ 500}$ 22. $52\overline{)40\ 254}$ 23. $79\overline{)42\ 356}$ 24. $38\overline{)16\ 240}$

Divide until the remainder is zero.

25. $8\overline{)6.4}$ 26. $6\overline{)1.92}$ 27. $24\overline{)103.2}$ 28. $17\overline{)140.25}$

29. $2\overline{)21}$ 30. $6\overline{)15}$ 31. $12\overline{)666}$ 32. $90\overline{)7.38}$

33. $0.4\overline{)1.5}$ 34. $0.03\overline{)0.72}$ 35. $0.61\overline{)21.35}$ 36. $7.6\overline{)59.28}$

37. $0.25\overline{)4}$ 38. $0.08\overline{)4.4}$ 39. $4.2\overline{)189}$ 40. $0.34\overline{)22.1}$

Divide and round to the
nearest tenth.

41. $6\overline{)19}$ 42. $7\overline{)130}$

Divide and round to the
nearest hundredth.

43. $9\overline{)12}$ 44. $8\overline{)113}$

Fractional Number Concepts
Adding and Subtracting Fractional Numbers
Multiplying Fractional Numbers
Dividing Fractional Numbers
Space Geometry

Fractional Number Concepts

Getting started

A game of concentration can be played with fractional numbers and regions.

This pair of cards is a matching pair.
3 parts out of 4 equal parts are shaded.

What fractional number cards will match these cards?

A   B   C    D   E

F   G   H   I   J

Region card   Fractional number card

3 parts out of 5 equal parts are shaded.

← numerator
← denominator

The region card and fractional number card match.

Match the region card with the correct fractional number card.

1.

2.

3.

4.

5.

6.

7.

8.

9.

10.

11.

12.

13.

14.

15.

A $\frac{3}{8}$

B $\frac{3}{4}$

C $\frac{1}{10}$

D $\frac{3}{3}$

E $\frac{1}{4}$

F $1\frac{1}{5}$

G $\frac{4}{3}$

H $\frac{1}{6}$

I $\frac{7}{10}$

J $\frac{2}{5}$

K $\frac{1}{2}$

L $\frac{5}{8}$

M $\frac{5}{6}$

N $\frac{4}{5}$

O $\frac{3}{10}$

Equivalent fractions

The same part of a region may suggest more than one fraction.

$\frac{3}{4}$ of a cake $\frac{6}{8}$ of a cake

$\frac{3}{4}$ and $\frac{6}{8}$ are **equivalent fractions.**

We write: $\frac{3}{4} = \frac{6}{8}$

What is another fraction that is equivalent to $\frac{3}{4}$?

Finding the answer

Start with any fractional number	Multiply the numerator and the denominator by any number except zero	You have found a fractional number equivalent to the first one

$$\frac{3}{4} \qquad\qquad \frac{3 \times 3}{4 \times 3} = \frac{9}{12} \qquad\qquad \frac{3}{4} = \frac{9}{12}$$

Another fraction that is equivalent to $\frac{3}{4}$ is $\frac{9}{12}$.

Other examples

$$\frac{3}{4} = \frac{3 \times 4}{4 \times 4} = \frac{12}{16} \qquad\qquad \frac{4}{5} = \frac{4 \times 6}{5 \times 6} = \frac{24}{30} \qquad\qquad \frac{7}{10} = \frac{7 \times 10}{10 \times 10} = \frac{70}{100}$$

Give the missing numerators.

1. $\dfrac{2}{3} = \dfrac{}{15}$

2. $\dfrac{3}{5} = \dfrac{}{10}$

3. $\dfrac{1}{4} = \dfrac{}{24}$

4. $\dfrac{1}{2} = \dfrac{}{10}$

5. $\dfrac{5}{6} = \dfrac{}{18}$

6. $\dfrac{3}{4} = \dfrac{}{100}$

7. $\dfrac{10}{10} = \dfrac{}{100}$

8. $\dfrac{5}{3} = \dfrac{}{12}$

9. $\dfrac{7}{8} = \dfrac{}{16}$

10. $\dfrac{1}{3} = \dfrac{}{18}$

11. $\dfrac{4}{5} = \dfrac{}{20}$

12. $\dfrac{7}{4} = \dfrac{}{12}$

Give the missing numerator or denominator.

13. $\dfrac{2}{5} = \dfrac{}{20}$

14. $\dfrac{3}{10} = \dfrac{}{100}$

15. $\dfrac{2}{2} = \dfrac{}{8}$

16. $\dfrac{3}{4} = \dfrac{}{32}$

17. $\dfrac{3}{8} = \dfrac{}{24}$

18. $\dfrac{1}{4} = \dfrac{}{16}$

19. $\dfrac{4}{5} = \dfrac{}{25}$

20. $\dfrac{9}{10} = \dfrac{}{100}$

21. $\dfrac{1}{2} = \dfrac{4}{}$

22. $\dfrac{3}{5} = \dfrac{6}{}$

23. $\dfrac{5}{6} = \dfrac{25}{}$

24. $\dfrac{7}{10} = \dfrac{70}{}$

25. $\dfrac{4}{25} = \dfrac{}{100}$

26. $\dfrac{1}{5} = \dfrac{20}{}$

27. $\dfrac{4}{5} = \dfrac{}{100}$

28. $\dfrac{3}{4} = \dfrac{15}{}$

29. $\dfrac{9}{50} = \dfrac{18}{}$

30. $\dfrac{7}{12} = \dfrac{}{24}$

31. $\dfrac{1}{3} = \dfrac{}{15}$

32. $\dfrac{7}{8} = \dfrac{28}{}$

33. $\dfrac{1}{8} = \dfrac{3}{}$

34. $\dfrac{5}{8} = \dfrac{}{16}$

35. $\dfrac{2}{3} = \dfrac{16}{}$

36. $\dfrac{1}{2} = \dfrac{50}{}$

37. What pair of equivalent fractions is suggested by the shaded squares in the figures?

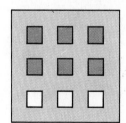 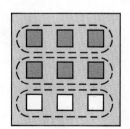

What is the missing numerator or denominator?

A $\dfrac{7}{16} = \dfrac{}{208}$

B $\dfrac{23}{24} = \dfrac{}{600}$

C $\dfrac{3}{7} = \dfrac{57}{}$

D $\dfrac{19}{40} = \dfrac{475}{}$

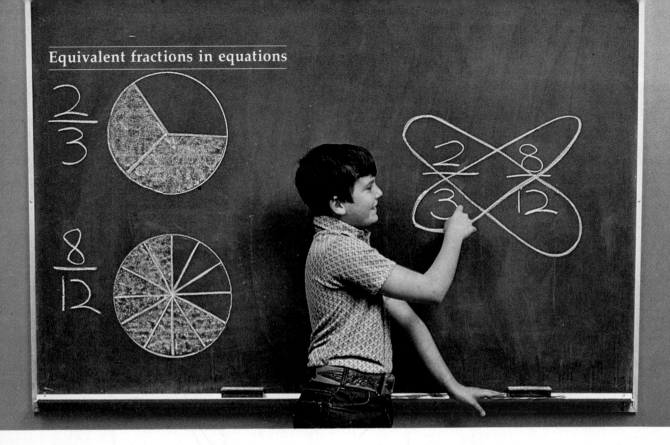

Equivalent fractions in equations

$$\frac{2}{3}$$

$$\frac{8}{12}$$

Jason is showing a quick way to see if two fractions are equivalent.
Since the cross products are equal ($3 \times 8 = 24$, $2 \times 12 = 24$), $\frac{2}{3} = \frac{8}{12}$.

Other examples

$\frac{6}{8} \bowtie \frac{9}{12}$ ⟶ $8 \times 9 = 72$
⟶ $6 \times 12 = 72$

$\frac{2}{3} \bowtie \frac{15}{18}$ ⟶ $3 \times 15 = 45$
⟶ $2 \times 18 = 36$

$\frac{6}{8}$ is equivalent to $\frac{9}{12}$.

$\frac{2}{3}$ is not equivalent to $\frac{15}{18}$.

$\frac{6}{8} = \frac{9}{12}$

$\frac{2}{3} \neq \frac{15}{18}$

Use the cross-products method to find pairs of fractions that are equivalent.
Give the correct sign, = or ≠, for each ⬤.

1. $\frac{3}{5}$ ⬤ $\frac{9}{15}$

2. $\frac{3}{12}$ ⬤ $\frac{1}{4}$

3. $\frac{3}{8}$ ⬤ $\frac{2}{6}$

4. $\frac{6}{9}$ ⬤ $\frac{9}{12}$

5. $\frac{1}{3}$ ⬤ $\frac{5}{15}$

6. $\frac{4}{6}$ ⬤ $\frac{3}{4}$

7. $\frac{3}{10}$ ⬤ $\frac{30}{100}$

8. $\frac{5}{8}$ ⬤ $\frac{15}{24}$

9. $\frac{3}{2}$ ⬤ $\frac{15}{10}$

10. $\frac{4}{5}$ ⬤ $\frac{3}{4}$

11. $\frac{9}{16}$ ⬤ $\frac{1}{4}$

12. $\frac{2}{5}$ ⬤ $\frac{8}{20}$

13. $\frac{1}{3}$ ⬤ $\frac{30}{100}$

14. $\frac{10}{16}$ ⬤ $\frac{15}{24}$

15. $\frac{15}{21}$ ⬤ $\frac{5}{7}$

Solve the equations.

Examples:

Solve: $\frac{3}{4} = \frac{n}{12}$

$$4 \times n = 36$$
$$n = 36 \div 4$$
$$n = 9$$

Solve: $\frac{2}{3} = \frac{10}{n}$

$$2 \times n = 30$$
$$n = 30 \div 2$$
$$n = 15$$

Check: $\frac{3}{4} = \frac{9}{12}$ ⟶ $4 \times 9 = 36$
⟶ $3 \times 12 = 36$

$\frac{2}{3} = \frac{10}{15}$ ⟶ $3 \times 10 = 30$
⟶ $2 \times 15 = 30$

1. $\frac{1}{3} = \frac{n}{9}$

2. $\frac{6}{8} = \frac{n}{12}$

3. $\frac{4}{5} = \frac{n}{25}$

4. $\frac{3}{2} = \frac{n}{10}$

5. $\frac{2}{6} = \frac{3}{n}$

6. $\frac{5}{10} = \frac{4}{n}$

7. $\frac{6}{15} = \frac{2}{n}$

8. $\frac{1}{7} = \frac{7}{n}$

9. $\frac{2}{5} = \frac{n}{20}$

10. $\frac{6}{6} = \frac{n}{7}$

11. $\frac{3}{10} = \frac{30}{n}$

12. $\frac{5}{1} = \frac{n}{4}$

13. $\frac{4}{16} = \frac{1}{n}$

14. $\frac{0}{5} = \frac{n}{10}$

15. $\frac{3}{8} = \frac{18}{n}$

16. $\frac{5}{6} = \frac{30}{n}$

☆ 17. Which two of these fractions are equivalent?

$\frac{18}{24}, \quad \frac{25}{30}, \quad \frac{20}{36}, \quad \frac{15}{18}$

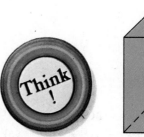

☆ 18. The missing number in each fraction is the same. What is it?

$\frac{4}{n} = \frac{n}{36}$

30

Trace or draw the cube. Then number the 8 corners of the cube from 1 to 8 so that the sum of any four numbers at the corners of each face is 18.

More practice, page 386, Set C

Lowest-terms fractions

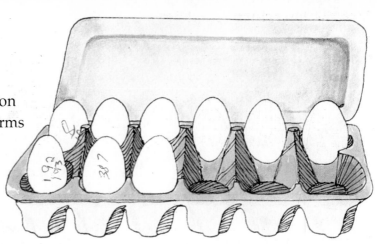

The picture shows $\frac{9}{12}$ of a carton of eggs. What is the lowest-terms fraction for $\frac{9}{12}$?

Finding the answer

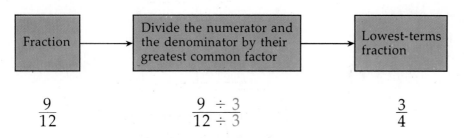

| Fraction | → | Divide the numerator and the denominator by their greatest common factor | → | Lowest-terms fraction |

$$\frac{9}{12} \qquad\qquad \frac{9 \div 3}{12 \div 3} \qquad\qquad \frac{3}{4}$$

The **lowest-terms fraction** for $\frac{9}{12}$ is $\frac{3}{4}$.

Other examples

$$\frac{15}{25} = \frac{15 \div 5}{25 \div 5} = \frac{3}{5} \qquad\qquad \frac{27}{18} = \frac{27 \div 9}{18 \div 9} = \frac{3}{2} \qquad\qquad \frac{70}{100} = \frac{70 \div 10}{100 \div 10} = \frac{7}{10}$$

Find the lowest-terms fraction for each.

1. $\frac{8}{10}$ 2. $\frac{9}{15}$ 3. $\frac{20}{40}$ 4. $\frac{12}{16}$ 5. $\frac{20}{25}$

6. $\frac{6}{9}$ 7. $\frac{12}{18}$ 8. $\frac{14}{16}$ 9. $\frac{90}{100}$ 10. $\frac{12}{10}$

11. $\frac{30}{36}$ 12. $\frac{45}{60}$ 13. $\frac{18}{24}$ 14. $\frac{27}{30}$ 15. $\frac{50}{100}$

16. $\frac{4}{6}$ 17. $\frac{32}{40}$ 18. $\frac{16}{32}$ 19. $\frac{80}{100}$ 20. $\frac{21}{12}$

Give the lowest-terms fraction.

1.

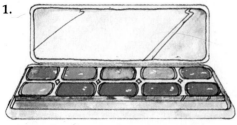

What part is brown?

2.

What part of the pan is filled?

3.

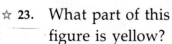

What part is red?

4.

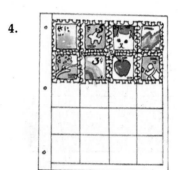

What part of the page
is filled with stamps?

Find the lowest-terms fraction for each.

5. $\frac{25}{50}$ 6. $\frac{20}{25}$ 7. $\frac{4}{8}$ 8. $\frac{25}{100}$ 9. $\frac{8}{24}$ 10. $\frac{5}{20}$

11. $\frac{8}{16}$ 12. $\frac{20}{24}$ 13. $\frac{4}{28}$ 14. $\frac{6}{18}$ 15. $\frac{18}{24}$ 16. $\frac{30}{100}$

17. $\frac{18}{27}$ 18. $\frac{6}{30}$ 19. $\frac{70}{100}$ 20. $\frac{16}{24}$ 21. $\frac{16}{40}$ 22. $\frac{24}{36}$

☆ 23. What part of this
figure is yellow?

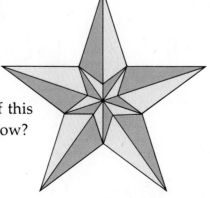

Janet had 69¢.
Sally asked her for change
for a 50-cent piece. Janet
tried to make change but
found she could not. What
coins did she have if they
were all less than 50¢ ?

More practice, page 387, Set A

Mixed numerals to improper fractions

The red string will just go around the circle.

The string is about $3\frac{1}{7}$ times as long as the diameter of the circle.

What is the improper fraction for $3\frac{1}{7}$?

Finding the answer

Mixed numeral	Multiply the whole number by the denominator, and add the numerator	Write the sum over the denominator

$$3\frac{1}{7} \qquad (7 \times 3) + 1 = 22 \qquad \frac{22}{7}$$

The improper fraction for $3\frac{1}{7}$ is $\frac{22}{7}$. $\qquad 3\frac{1}{7} = \frac{22}{7}$

Other examples

$$2\frac{3}{4} = \frac{11}{4} \qquad\qquad 3\frac{3}{10} = \frac{33}{10} \qquad\qquad 6\frac{17}{100} = \frac{617}{100}$$

Write as improper fractions.

1. $2\frac{1}{3}$
2. $3\frac{1}{4}$
3. $2\frac{2}{5}$
4. $1\frac{7}{10}$
5. $2\frac{5}{8}$

6. $6\frac{7}{10}$
7. $9\frac{2}{3}$
8. $33\frac{1}{3}$
9. $5\frac{1}{6}$
10. $8\frac{3}{4}$

11. $1\frac{7}{8}$
12. $16\frac{1}{2}$
13. $9\frac{9}{10}$
14. $2\frac{47}{100}$
15. $3\frac{747}{1000}$

Write an improper fraction for each mixed numeral.

1. $1\frac{3}{4}$

2. $2\frac{1}{10}$

3. $1\frac{1}{2}$

4. $4\frac{1}{3}$

5. $5\frac{1}{4}$

6. $2\frac{3}{5}$

7. $6\frac{3}{10}$

8. $3\frac{1}{7}$

9. $4\frac{3}{8}$

10. $5\frac{9}{10}$

11. $6\frac{2}{3}$

12. $5\frac{5}{8}$

13. $3\frac{23}{100}$

14. $7\frac{1}{6}$

15. $10\frac{1}{4}$

16. $9\frac{1}{2}$

17. $8\frac{4}{5}$

18. $3\frac{3}{5}$

19. $1\frac{31}{1000}$

20. $66\frac{2}{3}$

Write the number in each sentence as an improper fraction.

21. 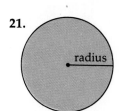 The distance around a circle is about $6\frac{2}{7}$ times the radius of the circle.

22. 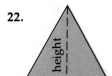 The length of one side of an equilateral triangle is about $1\frac{3}{20}$ times the height of the triangle.

23.  The diagonal of a regular pentagon is about $1\frac{3}{5}$ times the length of one side of the pentagon.

24.  The diagonal of a cube is about $1\frac{7}{10}$ times as long as an edge of the cube.

☆ 25. Cut a piece of string as long as the distance around some square object. About how many times as long as the diagonal of the square is the string? Give your answer as a mixed numeral and as an improper fraction.

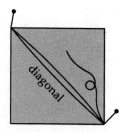

Susan has 6 coins. Only 2 of them are alike. What coins does she have if she has 96¢ in all?

More practice, page 387, Set B

Improper fractions to mixed numerals

Which is the point on the number line for $\frac{37}{4}$? To help you decide, find a mixed numeral for $\frac{37}{4}$.

Finding the answer

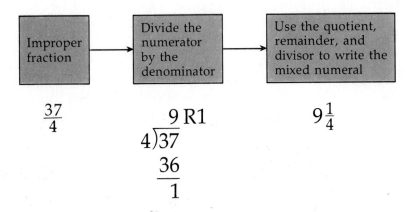

| Improper fraction | Divide the numerator by the denominator | Use the quotient, remainder, and divisor to write the mixed numeral |

$$\frac{37}{4}$$

$$\begin{array}{r} 9 \text{ R}1 \\ 4\overline{)37} \\ 36 \\ \hline 1 \end{array}$$

$$9\frac{1}{4}$$

$\frac{37}{4} = 9\frac{1}{4}$. The point for $\frac{37}{4}$ is **J**.

Other examples

$$\frac{23}{5} = 4\frac{3}{5} \qquad \frac{33}{10} = 3\frac{3}{10} \qquad \frac{37}{2} = 18\frac{1}{2} \qquad \frac{46}{9} = 5\frac{1}{9}$$

Give a mixed numeral for each improper fraction.

1. $\frac{11}{3}$ 2. $\frac{27}{5}$ 3. $\frac{9}{2}$ 4. $\frac{15}{4}$ 5. $\frac{23}{10}$

6. $\frac{43}{8}$ 7. $\frac{17}{2}$ 8. $\frac{19}{10}$ 9. $\frac{7}{4}$ 10. $\frac{19}{6}$

11. $\frac{32}{3}$ 12. $\frac{117}{100}$ 13. $\frac{73}{2}$ 14. $\frac{50}{3}$ 15. $\frac{59}{12}$

Divide. Write the quotient as a mixed numeral.

Examples:

$$\begin{array}{r} 9\text{ R2} \\ 5\overline{)47} \\ 45 \\ \hline 2 \end{array}\qquad 9\tfrac{2}{5}$$

$$\begin{array}{r} 7\text{ R6} \\ 10\overline{)76} \\ 70 \\ \hline 6 \end{array}\qquad 7\tfrac{6}{10}\text{ or }7\tfrac{3}{5}$$

1. $5\overline{)28}$ 2. $4\overline{)19}$ 3. $3\overline{)25}$ 4. $9\overline{)62}$ 5. $8\overline{)53}$

6. $10\overline{)61}$ 7. $2\overline{)51}$ 8. $4\overline{)18}$ 9. $8\overline{)42}$ 10. $5\overline{)84}$

11. $3\overline{)76}$ 12. $8\overline{)127}$ 13. $5\overline{)143}$ 14. $10\overline{)313}$ 15. $12\overline{)149}$

16. $4\overline{)233}$ 17. $2\overline{)97}$ 18. $100\overline{)719}$ 19. $20\overline{)84}$ 20. $25\overline{)640}$

21. $3\overline{)101}$ 22. $7\overline{)86}$ 23. $30\overline{)267}$ 24. $15\overline{)49}$ 25. $24\overline{)125}$

26. $6\overline{)201}$ 27. $9\overline{)118}$ 28. $40\overline{)130}$ 29. $27\overline{)159}$ 30. $16\overline{)180}$

Give a mixed numeral
for each improper fraction.

31. $\dfrac{53}{4}$ 32. $\dfrac{164}{8}$

33. $\dfrac{76}{5}$ 34. $\dfrac{66}{10}$

35. $\dfrac{423}{2}$ 36. $\dfrac{134}{8}$

37. $\dfrac{750}{100}$ 38. $\dfrac{97}{10}$

39. $\dfrac{125}{3}$ 40. $\dfrac{241}{6}$

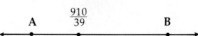

$$\text{A}\qquad \tfrac{910}{39}\qquad\qquad \text{B}$$

Between which two consecutive whole
numbers does the point for $\frac{910}{39}$ lie?

More practice, page 387, Set C

Comparing fractional numbers

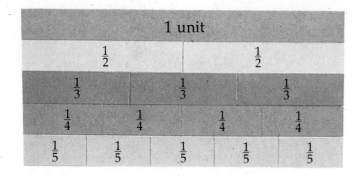

We see from the figure that $\frac{3}{5}$ **is less than** $\frac{2}{3}$.

We write: $\frac{3}{5} < \frac{2}{3}$.

How can these two fractional numbers be compared without a picture?

Finding the answer

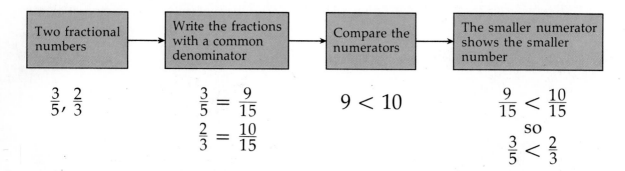

Two fractional numbers	Write the fractions with a common denominator	Compare the numerators	The smaller numerator shows the smaller number

$\frac{3}{5}, \frac{2}{3}$ $\qquad$ $\frac{3}{5} = \frac{9}{15}$ $\qquad$ $9 < 10$ $\qquad$ $\frac{9}{15} < \frac{10}{15}$

$\qquad\qquad\qquad$ $\frac{2}{3} = \frac{10}{15}$ $\qquad\qquad\qquad\qquad$ so

$\qquad\qquad\qquad\qquad\qquad\qquad\qquad\qquad\qquad$ $\frac{3}{5} < \frac{2}{3}$

Other examples

$\frac{7}{10},$ $\qquad$ $\frac{5}{8}$ $\qquad\qquad\qquad$ $\frac{2}{3},$ $\qquad$ $\frac{3}{4}$

$\downarrow \qquad\quad \downarrow$ $\qquad\qquad\qquad$ $\downarrow \qquad\quad \downarrow$

$\frac{28}{40} > \frac{25}{40},$ so $\frac{7}{10} > \frac{5}{8}$ $\qquad$ $\frac{8}{12} < \frac{9}{12},$ so $\frac{2}{3} < \frac{3}{4}$

$\frac{7}{10}$ is greater than $\frac{5}{8}$. $\qquad\qquad$ $\frac{2}{3}$ is less than $\frac{3}{4}$.

Give the correct sign, $<$ or $>$, for each ◍.

1. $\frac{2}{5}$ ◍ $\frac{1}{2}$ $\qquad$ 2. $\frac{3}{10}$ ◍ $\frac{1}{3}$ $\qquad$ 3. $\frac{1}{2}$ ◍ $\frac{3}{4}$ $\qquad$ 4. $\frac{9}{10}$ ◍ $\frac{7}{8}$ $\qquad$ 5. $\frac{2}{3}$ ◍ $\frac{5}{8}$

$\quad\downarrow \qquad \downarrow$ $\qquad\quad\;\downarrow \qquad \downarrow$ $\qquad\quad\;\downarrow \qquad \downarrow$ $\qquad\quad\;\downarrow \qquad \downarrow$ $\qquad\quad\;\downarrow \qquad \downarrow$

$\quad\frac{4}{10} \qquad \frac{5}{10}$ $\qquad$ $\frac{9}{30} \qquad \frac{10}{30}$ $\qquad$ $\frac{2}{4} \qquad \frac{3}{4}$ $\qquad$ $\frac{36}{40} \qquad \frac{35}{40}$ $\qquad$ $\frac{16}{24} \qquad \frac{15}{24}$

Give the correct sign, < or >, for each .

1. $\frac{1}{2}$ ⬤ $\frac{1}{3}$ 2. $\frac{3}{4}$ ⬤ $\frac{5}{6}$ 3. $\frac{1}{4}$ ⬤ $\frac{1}{5}$ 4. $\frac{7}{8}$ ⬤ $\frac{2}{3}$

5. $\frac{4}{5}$ ⬤ $\frac{3}{4}$ 6. $\frac{5}{6}$ ⬤ $\frac{2}{3}$ 7. $\frac{3}{10}$ ⬤ $\frac{1}{4}$ 8. $\frac{5}{7}$ ⬤ $\frac{2}{3}$

9. $\frac{1}{2}$ ⬤ $\frac{3}{8}$ 10. $\frac{5}{8}$ ⬤ $\frac{3}{4}$ 11. $\frac{5}{6}$ ⬤ $\frac{9}{10}$ 12. $\frac{7}{10}$ ⬤ $\frac{3}{4}$

13. $\frac{3}{5}$ ⬤ $\frac{63}{100}$ 14. $\frac{4}{5}$ ⬤ $\frac{7}{15}$ 15. $\frac{24}{25}$ ⬤ $\frac{83}{100}$ 16. $\frac{7}{12}$ ⬤ $\frac{13}{24}$

17. $\frac{5}{8}$ ⬤ $\frac{1}{2}$ 18. $\frac{1}{6}$ ⬤ $\frac{1}{8}$ 19. $\frac{3}{10}$ ⬤ $\frac{33}{100}$ 20. $\frac{1}{5}$ ⬤ $\frac{1}{4}$

21. $\frac{9}{16}$ ⬤ $\frac{7}{8}$ 22. $\frac{5}{6}$ ⬤ $\frac{2}{3}$ 23. $\frac{3}{8}$ ⬤ $\frac{2}{5}$ 24. $\frac{13}{20}$ ⬤ $\frac{5}{8}$

25. Which is the smallest number, $\frac{1}{4}$, $\frac{1}{3}$, or $\frac{2}{5}$?

26. Which is the largest number, $\frac{5}{8}$, $\frac{2}{3}$, or $\frac{3}{5}$?

☆ 27. Which of these numbers is less than one of the numbers but greater than the other?

$\frac{1}{3}$, $\frac{1}{4}$, $\frac{3}{8}$

☆ 28. Arrange these numbers in order from smallest to largest.

$\frac{2}{5}$, $\frac{1}{3}$, $\frac{1}{2}$, $\frac{1}{4}$, $\frac{3}{8}$, $\frac{3}{10}$

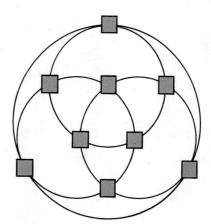

Place the numbers from 2 to 10 in the squares so that the sum of the numbers around any of the circles is the same.

Self-check

What part of each region is dark brown?

1.

2.

Give each missing numerator or denominator.

3. $\frac{1}{2} = \frac{\text{▨}}{8}$

4. $\frac{5}{6} = \frac{10}{\text{▨}}$

5. $\frac{2}{3} = \frac{\text{▨}}{12}$

6. $\frac{3}{4} = \frac{\text{▨}}{24}$

Give the lowest-terms fraction for each.

7. $\frac{10}{15}$ **8.** $\frac{6}{12}$ **9.** $\frac{12}{16}$ **10.** $\frac{70}{100}$ **11.** $\frac{24}{30}$

Solve the equations.   **12.** $\frac{3}{4} = \frac{n}{20}$ **13.** $\frac{2}{3} = \frac{8}{n}$

14. Write $3\frac{7}{10}$ as an improper fraction.   **15.** Write $\frac{27}{4}$ as a mixed numeral.

Give the correct sign, > or <, for each ⬤.

16. $\frac{2}{3}$ ⬤ $\frac{1}{4}$ **17.** $\frac{2}{5}$ ⬤ $\frac{2}{3}$.   **18.** $\frac{3}{4}$ ⬤ $\frac{7}{8}$

Answers for Self-check—page 199

Test

What part of each region is dark brown?

1.

2.

Give the missing numerator or denominator.

3. $\frac{1}{4} = \frac{\text{▨}}{8}$ 2

4. $\frac{4}{5} = \frac{12}{\text{▨}}$

5. $\frac{7}{8} = \frac{\text{▨}}{16}$

6. $\frac{1}{3} = \frac{\text{▨}}{15}$

Give the lowest-terms fraction for each.

7. $\frac{12}{24}$ **8.** $\frac{8}{12}$ **9.** $\frac{25}{100}$ **10.** $\frac{15}{18}$ **11.** $\frac{48}{64}$

Solve the equations.   **12.** $\frac{2}{5} = \frac{12}{n}$ **13.** $\frac{3}{8} = \frac{n}{24}$

14. Write $6\frac{3}{4}$ as an improper fraction.   **15.** Write $\frac{29}{10}$ as a mixed numeral.

Give the correct sign, > or <, for each ⬤.

16. $\frac{1}{3}$ ⬤ $\frac{3}{4}$ **17.** $\frac{4}{5}$ ⬤ $\frac{7}{8}$ **18.** $\frac{1}{2}$ ⬤ $\frac{7}{12}$

Break the Code

Here is the code.
Look at the example.

Secret code

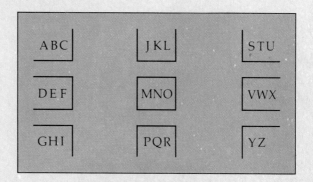

Example:

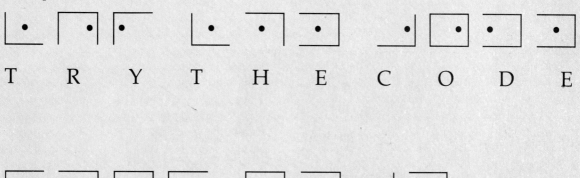

T   R   Y   T   H   E   C   O   D   E

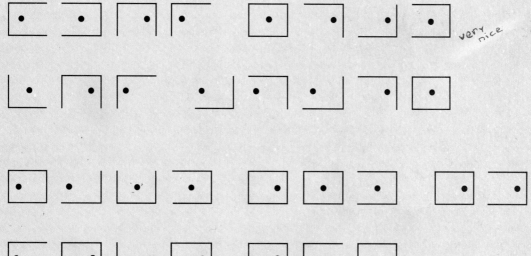

very nice

Adding and Subtracting Fractional Numbers

Getting started

Find the missing numbers.
Then use the code to find
the secret message.

$\frac{2}{15} + \frac{6}{15} = \frac{8}{15}$ ⟶ H

$\frac{5}{10} + \frac{2}{10} =$ ▓

$\frac{2}{3} + \frac{1}{3} =$ ▓

$\frac{2}{4} + \frac{1}{4} =$ ▓

$\frac{3}{10} + \frac{4}{10} =$ ▓

$\frac{1}{3} + \frac{1}{4} =$ ▓

$\frac{1}{5} + \frac{3}{5} =$ ▓

$\frac{2}{9} + \frac{4}{9} =$ ▓

$\frac{1}{2} + \frac{1}{4} =$ ▓

$\frac{4}{5} - \frac{1}{5} =$ ▓

$\frac{13}{10} - \frac{6}{10} =$ ▓

$\frac{7}{8} - \frac{3}{8} =$ ▓

C O D E	A	C	D	E	H	I	N	V	Y
	$\frac{7}{10}$	$\frac{6}{9}$	$\frac{3}{5}$	$\frac{3}{4}$	$\frac{8}{15}$	$\frac{4}{5}$	$\frac{7}{12}$	$\frac{3}{3}$	$\frac{4}{8}$

Find each sum. The pictures may help you.

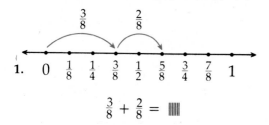

1. $\frac{3}{8} + \frac{2}{8} = $ ▦

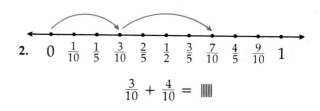

2. $\frac{3}{10} + \frac{4}{10} = $ ▦

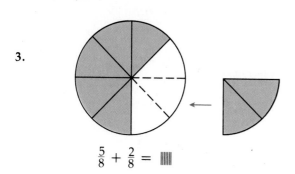

3. $\frac{5}{8} + \frac{2}{8} = $ ▦

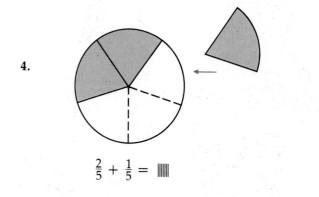

4. $\frac{2}{5} + \frac{1}{5} = $ ▦

Find each difference.

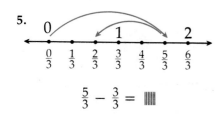

5. $\frac{5}{3} - \frac{3}{3} = $ ▦

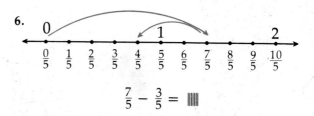

6. $\frac{7}{5} - \frac{3}{5} = $ ▦

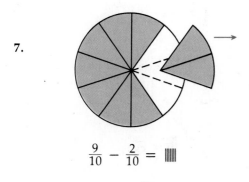

7. $\frac{9}{10} - \frac{2}{10} = $ ▦

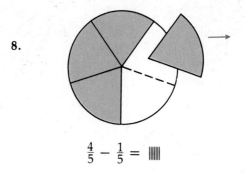

8. $\frac{4}{5} - \frac{1}{5} = $ ▦

9. Give a simple rule for finding sums and differences of two fractional numbers that have a common denominator.

Adding and subtracting with unlike denominators

Peas are planted in $\frac{1}{3}$ of the garden.
Corn is planted in $\frac{1}{2}$ of the garden.
How much of the garden is
planted in peas and corn?

Finding the answer

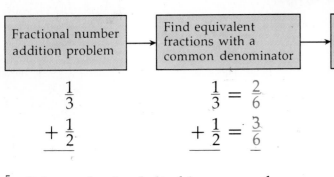

Fractional number addition problem	Find equivalent fractions with a common denominator	Add the fractions with the common denominator

$$\frac{1}{3}$$
$$+\frac{1}{2}$$

$$\frac{1}{3} = \frac{2}{6}$$
$$+\frac{1}{2} = \frac{3}{6}$$

$$\frac{2}{6}$$
$$+\frac{3}{6}$$
$$\frac{5}{6}$$

$\frac{5}{6}$ of the garden is planted in peas and corn.

Other examples

$$\frac{3}{8} = \frac{3}{8}$$
$$+\frac{3}{4} = \frac{6}{8}$$
$$\frac{9}{8} = 1\frac{1}{8}$$

$$\frac{7}{10} = \frac{7}{10}$$
$$+\frac{3}{5} = \frac{6}{10}$$
$$\frac{13}{10} = 1\frac{3}{10}$$

$$\frac{2}{3} = \frac{8}{12}$$
$$+\frac{1}{12} = \frac{1}{12}$$
$$\frac{9}{12} = \frac{3}{4}$$

Find the sums.

1. $\frac{1}{2}$
   $+\frac{3}{4}$

2. $\frac{3}{10}$
   $+\frac{2}{5}$

3. $\frac{4}{5}$
   $+\frac{1}{2}$

4. $\frac{5}{8}$
   $+\frac{1}{4}$

5. $\frac{2}{3}$
   $+\frac{1}{2}$

6. $\frac{1}{6}$
   $+\frac{1}{3}$

7. $\frac{3}{8}$
   $+\frac{1}{4}$

8. $\frac{17}{100}$
   $+\frac{3}{10}$

9. $\frac{3}{8}$
   $+\frac{5}{8}$

10. $\frac{4}{5}$
    $+\frac{3}{4}$

11. $\frac{1}{3}$
    $+\frac{3}{10}$

12. $\frac{3}{7}$
    $+\frac{1}{2}$

13. $\frac{7}{16}$
    $+\frac{3}{8}$

14. $\frac{1}{4}$
    $+\frac{5}{12}$

15. $\frac{13}{16}$
    $+\frac{1}{2}$

Find the differences.

Example:

$$\frac{3}{4} = \frac{15}{20}$$
$$-\frac{2}{5} = \frac{8}{20}$$
$$\overline{\phantom{-\frac{2}{5}=}\frac{7}{20}}$$

1. $\frac{1}{2}$
    $-\frac{1}{3}$

2. $\frac{4}{5}$
    $-\frac{1}{2}$

3. $\frac{9}{10}$
    $-\frac{3}{5}$

4. $\frac{9}{8}$
    $-\frac{3}{4}$

5. $\frac{5}{3}$
    $-\frac{1}{2}$

6. $\frac{1}{5}$
    $-\frac{1}{10}$

7. $\frac{7}{8}$
    $-\frac{1}{4}$

8. $\frac{7}{10}$
    $-\frac{1}{4}$

9. $\frac{3}{2}$
    $-\frac{1}{4}$

10. $\frac{2}{3}$
    $-\frac{1}{2}$

11. $\frac{5}{6}$
    $-\frac{3}{4}$

12. $\frac{73}{100}$
    $-\frac{7}{10}$

13. $\frac{4}{5}$
    $-\frac{3}{4}$

14. $\frac{7}{16}$
    $-\frac{1}{4}$

15. $\frac{7}{3}$
    $-\frac{3}{2}$

16. $\frac{11}{12}$
    $-\frac{2}{3}$

Find the sums.

17. $\frac{1}{2}$
    $\frac{1}{3}$
    $+\frac{1}{4}$

18. $\frac{1}{2}$
    $\frac{2}{5}$
    $+\frac{1}{10}$

19. $\frac{1}{4}$
    $\frac{3}{8}$
    $+\frac{3}{4}$

20. $\frac{1}{3}$
    $\frac{1}{2}$
    $+\frac{1}{6}$

21. $\frac{1}{2}$
    $\frac{7}{8}$
    $+\frac{5}{16}$

☆ 22. Paved $\frac{1}{3}$ of the walkway on Monday.
Paved $\frac{1}{2}$ of the walkway on Tuesday.
How much of the walkway is left
to be paved?

☆ 23. Mowed $\frac{2}{3}$ of the lawn.
Then mowed $\frac{1}{4}$ of the lawn.
How much more to mow?

More practice, page 388, Set A

Adding with mixed numerals

A plant store had $3\frac{1}{2}$ flats of pansies.
It had $2\frac{3}{4}$ flats of dwarf pansies.
How many flats in all?

Finding the answer

Mixed numeral addition problem	Rewrite the fractions using a common denominator	Add the fractions	Add the whole numbers Rename if necessary

$$3\frac{1}{2}$$
$$+\ 2\frac{3}{4}$$

$$3\frac{1}{2} = 3\frac{2}{4}$$
$$+\ 2\frac{3}{4} = 2\frac{3}{4}$$

$$3\frac{2}{4}$$
$$+\ 2\frac{3}{4}$$
$$\overline{\frac{5}{4}}$$

$$3\frac{2}{4}$$
$$+\ 2\frac{3}{4}$$
$$\overline{5\frac{5}{4} = 6\frac{1}{4}}$$

There were $6\frac{1}{4}$ flats in all.

Other examples

$$1\frac{1}{2} = 1\frac{3}{6}$$
$$+\ 8\frac{2}{3} = 8\frac{4}{6}$$
$$\overline{9\frac{7}{6} = 10\frac{1}{6}}$$

$$3\frac{9}{10} = 3\frac{18}{20}$$
$$+\ 8\frac{1}{4} = 8\frac{5}{20}$$
$$\overline{11\frac{23}{20} = 12\frac{3}{20}}$$

$$4\frac{7}{8}$$
$$+\ 3\frac{7}{8}$$
$$\overline{7\frac{14}{8} = 8\frac{6}{8} = 8\frac{3}{4}}$$

Add.

1. $2\frac{1}{2}$
$+\ 4\frac{3}{4}$

2. $7\frac{3}{5}$
$+\ 8\frac{1}{2}$

3. $6\frac{1}{3}$
$+\ 9\frac{1}{2}$

4. $10\frac{5}{8}$
$+\ 8\frac{3}{4}$

5. $2\frac{2}{3}$
$+\ 12\frac{1}{2}$

6. $10\frac{1}{5}$
$+\ 15\frac{7}{10}$

7. $21\frac{3}{4}$
$+\ 19\frac{3}{4}$

8. $33\frac{2}{5}$
$+\ 47\frac{3}{5}$

9. $26\frac{9}{10}$
$+\ 35\frac{1}{2}$

10. 12
$+\ 16\frac{3}{8}$

Find the sums.

1. $2\frac{3}{8}$
   $+ 4\frac{1}{4}$

2. $2\frac{1}{4}$
   $+ 5\frac{1}{2}$

3. $7\frac{1}{4}$
   $+ 2\frac{1}{6}$

4. $6\frac{3}{5}$
   $+ 7\frac{4}{5}$

5. $8\frac{7}{8}$
   $+ 1\frac{1}{2}$

6. $10\frac{5}{8}$
   $+ 7\frac{3}{4}$

7. $12\frac{7}{10}$
   $+ 17\frac{3}{10}$

8. $3\frac{5}{6}$
   $+ 8\frac{1}{2}$

9. $6\frac{5}{8}$
   $+ 7\frac{2}{3}$

10. $6\frac{7}{12}$
    $+ 7\frac{5}{6}$

11. $61\frac{1}{2}$
    $+ 91\frac{1}{8}$

12. $82\frac{3}{8}$
    $+ 72\frac{1}{4}$

13. $15\frac{7}{8}$
    $+ 27\frac{5}{6}$

14. $82\frac{2}{3}$
    $+ 36\frac{3}{4}$

15. $109\frac{7}{10}$
    $+ 274\frac{1}{2}$

16. $3\frac{1}{2}$
    $7\frac{1}{4}$
    $+ 6\frac{1}{8}$

17. $4\frac{1}{6}$
    $2\frac{1}{3}$
    $+ 8\frac{2}{3}$

18. $19\frac{4}{5}$
    $26\frac{1}{10}$
    $+ 35\frac{1}{4}$

19. $158\frac{1}{4}$
    $327\frac{3}{8}$
    $+ 962\frac{1}{2}$

20. $785\frac{5}{6}$
    $654\frac{1}{2}$
    $+ 327\frac{2}{3}$

21. $2\frac{2}{3}$ flats of white daisies
    $1\frac{1}{4}$ flats of yellow daisies
    How many flats of daisies
    in all?

22. $1\frac{7}{8}$ flats of white petunias
    $2\frac{3}{4}$ flats of red petunias
    How many flats of petunias
    in all?

It is estimated that each person makes about 2 kg of trash each day. How many kilograms of trash is your family responsible for in one year?

How much trash is created each year by your town or city?

More practice, page 388, Set B

Subtracting with mixed numerals

Canned fruit sale:
Had $12\frac{1}{2}$ cases to sell.
Sold all but $3\frac{3}{4}$ cases.
How many cases
were sold?

Finding the answer

Mixed numeral subtraction problem	→	Rewrite the fractions using a common denominator	→	Rename if necessary and subtract the fractions	→	Subtract the whole numbers Rename if necessary

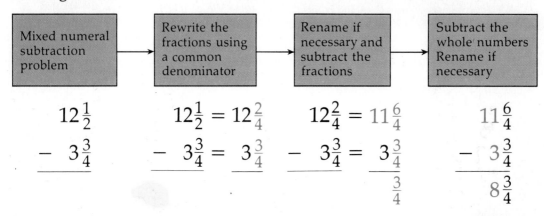

$$12\frac{1}{2}$$
$$-\ 3\frac{3}{4}$$

$$12\frac{1}{2} = 12\frac{2}{4}$$
$$-\ 3\frac{3}{4} = 3\frac{3}{4}$$

$$12\frac{2}{4} = 11\frac{6}{4}$$
$$-\ 3\frac{3}{4} = 3\frac{3}{4}$$
$$\frac{3}{4}$$

$$11\frac{6}{4}$$
$$-\ 3\frac{3}{4}$$
$$8\frac{3}{4}$$

$8\frac{3}{4}$ cases of canned fruit were sold.

Other examples

$$18\frac{2}{5} = 18\frac{4}{10} = 17\frac{14}{10}$$
$$-\ 9\frac{1}{2} = 9\frac{5}{10} = 9\frac{5}{10}$$
$$8\frac{9}{10}$$

$$10\ \ = 9\frac{3}{3}$$
$$-\ 6\frac{2}{3} = 6\frac{2}{3}$$
$$3\frac{1}{3}$$

Subtract.

1. $\quad 7\frac{1}{2}$
   $-3\frac{1}{4}$

2. $\quad 8\frac{7}{8}$
   $-5\frac{3}{4}$

3. $\quad 10\frac{1}{3}$
   $-\ 7\frac{2}{3}$

4. $\quad 12\frac{3}{5}$
   $-\ 9\frac{1}{2}$

5. $\quad 8$
   $-3\frac{1}{2}$

6. $\quad 15\frac{3}{4}$
   $-11\frac{3}{8}$

7. $\quad 16\frac{1}{4}$
   $-10\frac{1}{2}$

8. $\quad 8\frac{1}{3}$
   $-2\frac{1}{2}$

9. $\quad 23\frac{1}{6}$
   $-17\frac{2}{3}$

10. $\quad 12\frac{1}{8}$
    $-\ 3\frac{3}{4}$

Find the differences.

1. $7\frac{1}{2}$
   $-2\frac{3}{4}$

2. $9\frac{1}{2}$
   $-2\frac{3}{4}$

3. $8\frac{1}{8}$
   $-1\frac{3}{4}$

4. $6\frac{2}{3}$
   $-1\frac{7}{12}$

5. $7\frac{1}{4}$
   $-6\frac{5}{6}$

6. $8\frac{7}{9}$
   $-5\frac{5}{6}$

7. $4\frac{7}{10}$
   $-2\frac{11}{15}$

8. $7\frac{3}{5}$
   $-3\frac{9}{10}$

9. $26\frac{1}{2}$
   $-15\frac{1}{4}$

10. $47\frac{3}{4}$
    $-39\frac{2}{3}$

11. $83\frac{2}{3}$
    $-15\frac{3}{4}$

12. $91\frac{1}{2}$
    $-56\frac{1}{8}$

13. $65\frac{1}{8}$
    $-38\frac{1}{4}$

14. $27\frac{7}{10}$
    $-9\frac{4}{5}$

15. $96\frac{1}{2}$
    $-56\frac{9}{10}$

16. $79\frac{23}{100}$
    $-64\frac{7}{10}$

17. $123\frac{1}{2}$
    $-94\frac{3}{5}$

18. $271\frac{3}{4}$
    $-176\frac{7}{8}$

19. 500
    $-295\frac{1}{3}$

20. $897\frac{1}{2}$
    $-238\frac{1}{4}$

21. Had 10 cases of green beans.
    Sold all but $2\frac{1}{2}$ cases.
    How many cases were sold?

22. Had $8\frac{1}{3}$ cases of canned corn.
    Sold $2\frac{1}{2}$ cases. How many
    cases were left?

Claire counted 22 dogs
and birds in the park.
Altogether there were
68 legs on all the animals.
How many were birds?

More practice, page 389, Set A

Self-check

Add or subtract.

1. $\dfrac{3}{5}$
    $+\dfrac{1}{5}$

2. $\dfrac{7}{8}$
    $+\dfrac{5}{8}$

3. $\dfrac{3}{4}$
    $+\dfrac{1}{2}$

4. $\dfrac{2}{5}$
    $+\dfrac{9}{10}$

5. $1\dfrac{1}{2}$
    $+2\dfrac{1}{4}$

6. $3\dfrac{7}{8}$
    $+5\dfrac{1}{4}$

7. $16\dfrac{3}{10}$
    $+23\dfrac{1}{2}$

8. $29\dfrac{1}{3}$
    $+34\dfrac{2}{3}$

9. $50\dfrac{1}{2}$
    $+27\dfrac{2}{3}$

10. $83\dfrac{7}{10}$
    $+58\dfrac{3}{5}$

11. $\dfrac{7}{10}$
    $-\dfrac{3}{10}$

12. $\dfrac{73}{100}$
    $-\dfrac{29}{100}$

13. $\dfrac{9}{10}$
    $-\dfrac{1}{2}$

14. $\dfrac{3}{4}$
    $-\dfrac{1}{3}$

15. $7\dfrac{3}{4}$
    $-2\dfrac{1}{2}$

16. $8\dfrac{3}{8}$
    $-2\dfrac{3}{4}$

17. $16\dfrac{1}{2}$
    $-12\dfrac{7}{8}$

18. $26\dfrac{1}{5}$
    $-18\dfrac{3}{10}$

19. 57
    $-33\dfrac{1}{3}$

20. $40\dfrac{1}{2}$
    $-28\dfrac{4}{5}$

Answers for Self-check—page 209

Test

Add or subtract.

1. $\dfrac{3}{8}$
    $+\dfrac{7}{8}$

2. $\dfrac{1}{10}$
    $+\dfrac{5}{10}$

3. $\dfrac{1}{4}$
    $+\dfrac{3}{8}$

4. $\dfrac{1}{2}$
    $+\dfrac{1}{10}$

5. $1\dfrac{1}{3}$
    $+2\dfrac{1}{2}$

6. $4\dfrac{1}{4}$
    $+6\dfrac{1}{2}$

7. $8\dfrac{2}{5}$
    $+9\dfrac{1}{2}$

8. $16\dfrac{27}{100}$
    $+19\dfrac{7}{10}$

9. $44\dfrac{7}{16}$
    $+29\dfrac{3}{4}$

10. $133\dfrac{3}{4}$
    $+276\dfrac{5}{8}$

11. $\dfrac{7}{8}$
    $-\dfrac{3}{8}$

12. $\dfrac{1}{2}$
    $-\dfrac{1}{3}$

13. $\dfrac{7}{10}$
    $-\dfrac{2}{5}$

14. $\dfrac{2}{3}$
    $-\dfrac{1}{4}$

15. $6\dfrac{9}{10}$
    $-3\dfrac{1}{2}$

16. $21\dfrac{5}{}$
    $-17\dfrac{1}{4}$

17. $32\dfrac{1}{2}$
    $-26\dfrac{7}{8}$

18. $1\dfrac{1}{10}$
    $-\dfrac{59}{100}$

19. $75\dfrac{3}{8}$
    $-62\dfrac{3}{4}$

20. $269\dfrac{3}{10}$
    $-175\dfrac{4}{5}$

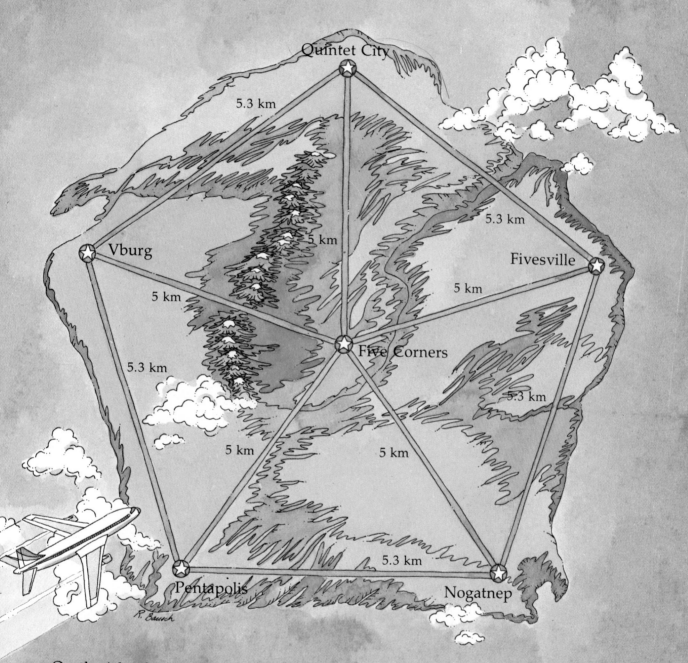

A Tour in Pentagonia

On the island of Pentagonia there are ten roads.
What is the shortest trip you could make traveling
each road at least once? (Two of the roads will
have to be traveled on twice.)

Multiplying Fractional Numbers

$\frac{1}{3}$ is shaded lightly.

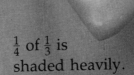

$\frac{1}{4}$ of $\frac{1}{3}$ is shaded heavily.

$\frac{1}{12}$ is shaded heavily.

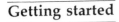

Getting started

Show how to shade
these parts of squares.

1. $\frac{1}{2}$ of $\frac{1}{3}$ 2. $\frac{1}{4}$ of $\frac{1}{4}$ 3. $\frac{1}{2}$ of $\frac{2}{3}$

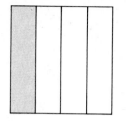

$\frac{1}{4}$ of the region
is shaded lightly.

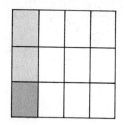

$\frac{1}{3}$ of $\frac{1}{4}$ is
shaded heavily.

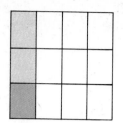

$\frac{1}{12}$ of the region
is shaded heavily.

We write:
$\frac{1}{3} \times \frac{1}{4} = \frac{1}{12}$

Study the figures. Then give the product.

1.

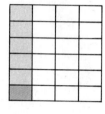

$\frac{1}{6}$ of $\frac{1}{4}$

$\frac{1}{6} \times \frac{1}{4} =$ ▥

2.

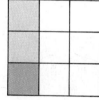

$\frac{1}{3}$ of $\frac{1}{3}$

$\frac{1}{3} \times \frac{1}{3} =$ ▥

3.

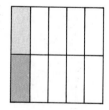

$\frac{1}{2}$ of $\frac{1}{5}$

$\frac{1}{2} \times \frac{1}{5} =$ ▥

4.

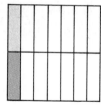

$\frac{1}{2}$ of $\frac{1}{7}$

$\frac{1}{2} \times \frac{1}{7} =$ ▥

5.

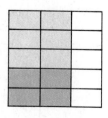

$\frac{2}{5}$ of $\frac{2}{3}$

$\frac{2}{5} \times \frac{2}{3} =$ ▥

6.

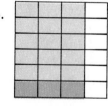

$\frac{1}{6}$ of $\frac{3}{4}$

$\frac{1}{6} \times \frac{3}{4} =$ ▥

Multiplying fractional numbers

$\frac{2}{3}$ of the students in Room 6 are on the basketball team. $\frac{4}{5}$ of these students practiced on Monday. What part of the students in Room 6 practiced on Monday?

Finding the answer

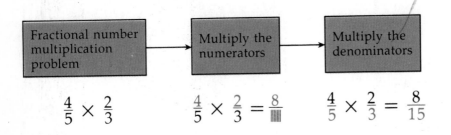

Fractional number multiplication problem	Multiply the numerators	Multiply the denominators
$\frac{4}{5} \times \frac{2}{3}$	$\frac{4}{5} \times \frac{2}{3} = \frac{8}{\text{▥}}$	$\frac{4}{5} \times \frac{2}{3} = \frac{8}{15}$

$\frac{8}{15}$ of the students in Room 6 practiced on Monday.

Other examples

$$\frac{3}{8} \times \frac{5}{2} = \frac{15}{16} \qquad \frac{3}{4} \times \frac{2}{3} = \frac{6}{12} = \frac{1}{2} \qquad \frac{3}{5} \times \frac{5}{3} = \frac{15}{15} = 1 \qquad \frac{1}{2} \times \frac{0}{10} = \frac{0}{20} = 0$$

Find the products.

1. $\frac{1}{2} \times \frac{2}{5}$ 2. $\frac{3}{4} \times \frac{3}{5}$ 3. $\frac{1}{10} \times \frac{3}{4}$ 4. $\frac{3}{8} \times \frac{1}{2}$ 5. $\frac{3}{2} \times \frac{3}{4}$

6. $\frac{2}{3} \times \frac{1}{2}$ 7. $\frac{5}{2} \times \frac{1}{5}$ 8. $\frac{9}{10} \times \frac{2}{3}$ 9. $\frac{7}{10} \times \frac{3}{10}$ 10. $\frac{5}{6} \times \frac{2}{5}$

11. $\frac{4}{3} \times \frac{3}{4}$ 12. $\frac{7}{8} \times \frac{2}{7}$ 13. $\frac{1}{2} \times \frac{5}{6}$ 14. $\frac{4}{5} \times \frac{2}{3}$ 15. $\frac{3}{5} \times \frac{3}{10}$

Find the products.

1. $\frac{1}{2} \times \frac{1}{8}$ 2. $\frac{2}{3} \times \frac{3}{8}$ 3. $\frac{1}{5} \times \frac{4}{3}$ 4. $\frac{5}{6} \times \frac{3}{10}$ 5. $\frac{1}{7} \times \frac{2}{3}$

6. $\frac{7}{8} \times \frac{2}{3}$ 7. $\frac{9}{10} \times \frac{1}{3}$ 8. $\frac{8}{3} \times \frac{3}{8}$ 9. $\frac{3}{4} \times \frac{1}{1}$ 10. $\frac{3}{8} \times \frac{3}{4}$

11. $\frac{2}{3} \times \frac{0}{2}$ 12. $\frac{4}{5} \times \frac{1}{2}$ 13. $\frac{2}{3} \times \frac{2}{3}$ 14. $\frac{4}{3} \times \frac{3}{5}$ 15. $\frac{3}{10} \times \frac{1}{10}$

16. $\frac{4}{5} \times \frac{3}{4}$ 17. $\frac{1}{2} \times \frac{1}{4}$ 18. $\frac{4}{10} \times \frac{3}{5}$ 19. $\frac{3}{4} \times \frac{5}{4}$ 20. $\frac{9}{16} \times \frac{4}{3}$

21. $\left(\frac{1}{3} \times \frac{2}{5}\right) \times \frac{1}{2}$ 22. $\left(\frac{2}{3} \times \frac{1}{2}\right) \times \frac{1}{2}$ 23. $\frac{1}{3} \times \left(\frac{2}{5} \times \frac{1}{2}\right)$

24. $\frac{2}{3} \times \left(\frac{1}{2} \times \frac{1}{2}\right)$ 25. $\left(\frac{1}{2} \times \frac{1}{3}\right) \times \frac{2}{5}$ 26. $\left(\frac{1}{2} \times \frac{1}{2}\right) \times \frac{2}{3}$

27. $\frac{1}{2} \times \left(\frac{2}{3} \times \frac{1}{2}\right)$ 28. $\frac{2}{3} \times \left(\frac{1}{2} \times \frac{1}{3}\right)$ 29. $\left(\frac{1}{2} \times \frac{2}{3}\right) \times \frac{1}{2}$

30. $\frac{2}{5}$ of the students in Room 12 have cameras. $\frac{1}{2}$ of these students joined a photo club. What part of the students in Room 12 joined a photo club?

31. $\frac{1}{8}$ of the students in Room 9 are in the school band. $\frac{1}{3}$ of those students play the trumpet. What part of the students in room 9 play the trumpet?

☆ 32. Draw a square. Color $\frac{1}{2}$ of the square yellow. Color $\frac{1}{4}$ of the yellow part blue. What part of the square is now green?

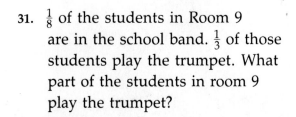

Area 2 cm²   ?

?

This square has an area of 2 cm². How long is each side? To solve the problem, you must find a number that gives a product of 2 when multiplied by itself. Try to find the length of one side of the square to the nearest thousandth of a centimeter. How close can you get to the answer?

Multiplying with mixed numerals

The distance around a circle
(the **circumference**) is about
$3\frac{1}{7}$ times the diameter of the circle.
What is the circumference of this can?

diameter
$2\frac{1}{2}$ units

Finding the answer

Mixed numeral multiplication problem	→	Write the mixed numerals as improper fractions	→	Multiply the improper fractions

$$3\frac{1}{7} \times 2\frac{1}{2} \qquad \frac{22}{7} \times \frac{5}{2} \qquad \frac{22}{7} \times \frac{5}{2} = \frac{110}{14} = 7\frac{6}{7}$$

The circumference of the can is about $7\frac{6}{7}$ units.

Other examples

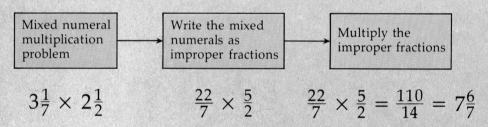

$$1\frac{3}{4} \times 1\frac{1}{2} = \frac{7}{4} \times \frac{3}{2} = \frac{21}{8} = 2\frac{5}{8} \qquad\qquad 2\frac{1}{2} \times 3\frac{2}{3} = \frac{5}{2} \times \frac{11}{3} = \frac{55}{6} = 9\frac{1}{6}$$

$$2\frac{1}{2} \times 4 = \frac{5}{2} \times \frac{4}{1} = \frac{20}{2} = 10 \qquad\qquad 8 \times \frac{3}{4} = \frac{8}{1} \times \frac{3}{4} = \frac{24}{4} = 6$$

Find the products.

1. $1\frac{1}{5} \times 1\frac{1}{2}$ 2. $2\frac{1}{5} \times 1\frac{1}{4}$ 3. $\frac{1}{2} \times 3\frac{1}{2}$ 4. $2\frac{2}{5} \times 3\frac{1}{2}$ 5. $6\frac{1}{2} \times 6$

6. $1\frac{2}{3} \times 9$ 7. $\frac{3}{4} \times 16$ 8. $3\frac{3}{4} \times 1\frac{1}{2}$ 9. $1\frac{1}{2} \times 1\frac{1}{2}$ 10. $3\frac{1}{6} \times 2\frac{2}{3}$

11. $\frac{3}{4} \times 5\frac{1}{3}$ 12. $1\frac{1}{10} \times 3\frac{1}{4}$ 13. $15 \times 1\frac{2}{3}$ 14. $\frac{9}{10} \times 3\frac{1}{3}$ 15. $4\frac{3}{4} \times 5\frac{1}{4}$

Multiply the diameter of each circle by $3\frac{1}{7}$ to find
the approximate circumference.

1.

$\frac{1}{2}$ unit

2.
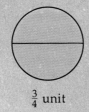
$\frac{3}{4}$ unit

3.
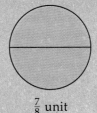
$\frac{7}{8}$ unit

4.
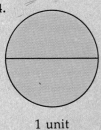
1 unit

5.
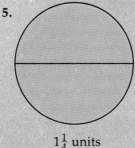
$1\frac{1}{4}$ units

6.
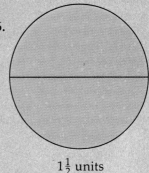
$1\frac{1}{2}$ units

Find the products.

7. $2\frac{1}{10} \times 1\frac{1}{3}$ **8.** $2\frac{1}{2} \times 4\frac{1}{2}$ **9.** $1\frac{3}{4} \times \frac{5}{8}$ **10.** $20 \times 2\frac{1}{4}$ **11.** $6 \times \frac{1}{2}$

12. $3\frac{1}{10} \times 15$ **13.** $1\frac{3}{8} \times 2\frac{1}{3}$ **14.** $2\frac{1}{4} \times 2\frac{1}{4}$ **15.** $1\frac{1}{5} \times 4\frac{1}{2}$ **16.** $1\frac{7}{8} \times \frac{2}{3}$

17. $2\frac{2}{5} \times 6\frac{1}{2}$ **18.** $2\frac{1}{10} \times 5\frac{3}{10}$ **19.** $6\frac{2}{3} \times 2\frac{1}{10}$ **20.** $5\frac{3}{8} \times \frac{4}{5}$ **21.** $18 \times 2\frac{2}{3}$

☆ **22.** Find some circular
objects. Measure their
diameters. Multiply by
$3\frac{1}{7}$ to find the approximate
circumferences.

First odd number
$$1 = 1$$
First 2 odd numbers
$$1 + 3 = 4$$
First 3 odd numbers
$$1 + 3 + 5 = 9$$
First 4 odd numbers
$$1 + 3 + 5 + 7 = 16$$
What is the sum of the first
100 odd numbers?

More practice, page 389, Set C

Reciprocals

A roll of material is $\frac{3}{4}$ unit wide.
Jan wants to cut a rectangular piece
that has an area of 1 square unit.
How long should the piece be?

Finding the answer

length × width = area

$$n \times \frac{3}{4} = 1$$

Since $\frac{4}{3} \times \frac{3}{4} = \frac{12}{12} = 1$

$$n = \frac{4}{3}$$

The piece of material
should be $\frac{4}{3}$ or $1\frac{1}{3}$ units long.

Two numbers whose product is 1 are **reciprocals** of each other.

$\frac{4}{3}$ is the reciprocal of $\frac{3}{4}$. $\frac{3}{4}$ is the reciprocal of $\frac{4}{3}$.

Other examples

What is the reciprocal of $2\frac{3}{4}$?

$2\frac{3}{4} = \frac{11}{4}$ $\frac{11}{4} \times \frac{4}{11} = 1$

$\frac{4}{11}$ is the reciprocal of $2\frac{3}{4}$.

What is the reciprocal of 5?

$5 = \frac{5}{1}$ $\frac{5}{1} \times \frac{1}{5} = 1$

$\frac{1}{5}$ is the reciprocal of 5.

Give the reciprocal of each number.

1. $\frac{1}{2}$
2. $\frac{4}{5}$
3. $\frac{2}{3}$
4. $\frac{3}{8}$
5. $\frac{9}{4}$

6. 9
7. $\frac{1}{10}$
8. $\frac{7}{8}$
9. $1\frac{1}{2}$
10. $2\frac{1}{3}$

11. Does zero have a reciprocal?   12. What number is equal to its reciprocal?

The area of each rectangle is 1 square unit. Find the length of *l*.

1.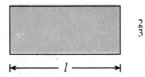
$\frac{1}{2}$
|←——— *l* ———→|

2.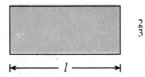
$\frac{2}{3}$
|←—— *l* ——→|

3.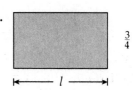
$\frac{3}{4}$
|←— *l* —→|

4.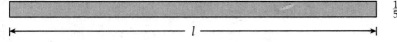
$\frac{1}{5}$
|←——————— *l* ———————→|

6.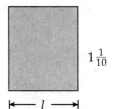
$1\frac{1}{10}$
|←— *l* —→|

5.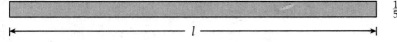
$\frac{3}{10}$
|←——— *l* ———→|

Give the reciprocal of each number.

7. $\frac{3}{5}$ **8.** $\frac{7}{4}$ **9.** 6   **10.** $\frac{1}{6}$ **11.** 1   **12.** $2\frac{1}{4}$

13. $\frac{9}{10}$ **14.** $3\frac{2}{5}$ **15.** $\frac{1}{100}$ **16.** $\frac{5}{6}$ **17.** $4\frac{1}{3}$ **18.** $12\frac{1}{2}$

19. $\frac{3}{100}$ **20.** $\frac{4}{3}$ **21.** $1\frac{1}{4}$ **22.** $\frac{9}{4}$ **23.** $\frac{10}{23}$ **24.** 3

Solve the equations.

25. $\frac{8}{5} \times \frac{5}{8} = n$ **28.** $5 \times \frac{1}{5} = n$

26. $\frac{5}{6} \times n = 1$ **29.** $\frac{1}{10} \times n = 1$

27. $n \times 2\frac{1}{2} = 1$ ☆ **30.** $7\frac{9}{13} \times \frac{13}{100} = n$

Think!

$a \times b = 1$
$9 \times a = b$

Two numbers are reciprocals of each other. One number is 9 times as large as the other. Find the two numbers.

Answers for Self-check **1.** $\frac{1}{10}$ **2.** $\frac{1}{24}$ **3.** $\frac{4}{15}$ **4.** $\frac{12}{50}$ or $\frac{6}{25}$ **5.** $\frac{8}{15}$ **6.** $\frac{14}{2}$ or 7   **7.** $\frac{36}{72}$ or $\frac{1}{2}$
8. $\frac{60}{2}$ or 30   **9.** $\frac{28}{3}$ or $9\frac{1}{3}$ **10.** $\frac{69}{4}$ or $17\frac{1}{4}$ **11.** $10\frac{2}{5}$ **12.** 5   **13.** $24\frac{3}{10}$ **14.** $8\frac{61}{100}$ **15.** $17\frac{2}{7}$ **16.** $\frac{8}{3}$ or $2\frac{2}{3}$
17. $\frac{1}{6}$ **18.** $\frac{3}{14}$ **19.** $\frac{5}{4}$ or $1\frac{1}{4}$ **20.** $\frac{8}{1}$ or 8

Self-check

Find the products.

1. $\frac{1}{2} \times \frac{1}{5}$ 2. $\frac{1}{8} \times \frac{1}{3}$ 3. $\frac{2}{5} \times \frac{2}{3}$ 4. $\frac{4}{5} \times \frac{3}{10}$ 5. $\frac{2}{3} \times \frac{4}{5}$

6. $3\frac{1}{2} \times 2$ 7. $1\frac{1}{8} \times \frac{4}{9}$ 8. $2\frac{1}{2} \times 12$ 9. $4\frac{2}{3} \times 2$ 10. $3 \times 5\frac{3}{4}$

11. $4\frac{1}{3} \times 2\frac{2}{5}$ 12. $1\frac{1}{2} \times 3\frac{1}{3}$ 13. $5\frac{2}{5} \times 4\frac{1}{2}$ 14. $2\frac{1}{10} \times 4\frac{1}{10}$

15. Find the circumference of the circle. $\left(\text{Multiply the diameter by } 3\frac{1}{7}.\right)$

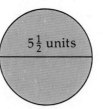

$5\frac{1}{2}$ units

Find the reciprocal of each number.

16. $\frac{3}{8}$ 17. 6   18. $4\frac{2}{3}$ 19. $\frac{4}{5}$ 20. $\frac{1}{8}$

Answers for Self-check—page 219

Test

Find the products.

1. $\frac{1}{3} \times \frac{1}{2}$ 2. $\frac{1}{4} \times \frac{1}{2}$ 3. $\frac{1}{5} \times \frac{2}{3}$ 4. $\frac{3}{8} \times \frac{1}{2}$ 5. $\frac{2}{3} \times \frac{3}{4}$

6. $2\frac{1}{4} \times 8$ 7. $1\frac{1}{3} \times \frac{3}{4}$ 8. $12 \times 2\frac{3}{4}$ 9. $4\frac{2}{3} \times 5$ 10. $6 \times 3\frac{1}{5}$

11. $4\frac{3}{4} \times 2\frac{1}{5}$ 12. $1\frac{2}{5} \times 5\frac{1}{3}$ 13. $6\frac{1}{4} \times 3\frac{2}{3}$ 14. $2\frac{7}{10} \times 3\frac{1}{2}$

15. Find the circumference of the circle. $\left(\text{Multiply the diameter by } 3\frac{1}{7}.\right)$

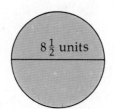

$8\frac{1}{2}$ units

Find the reciprocal of each number.

16. $\frac{1}{2}$ 17. 7   18. $2\frac{2}{3}$ 19. $\frac{3}{4}$ 20. $\frac{5}{11}$

The Chain Game

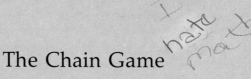

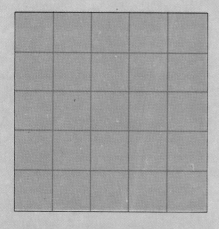

Playing Board: 5 by 5 square of graph paper

Players: 2

Rules:
Take turns writing the initial of your first name inside any empty square on the board. Try to initial squares that can be connected horizontally or vertically to form a chain. Your chain may not cross itself. Continue until all but one of the squares have been filled. Count one point for each initial in your chain. The player with the highest score (longest chain) is the winner.

Sample games:

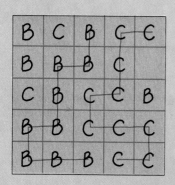

Score:

B 9, C 10

Score:

B 8, C 7

Dividing Fractional Numbers

Getting started

How many three fourths are there in $2\frac{1}{4}$?

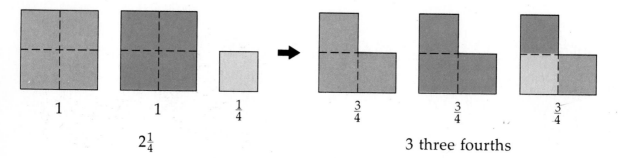

There are 3 three fourths in $2\frac{1}{4}$.

How many halves are there in $2\frac{1}{2}$?

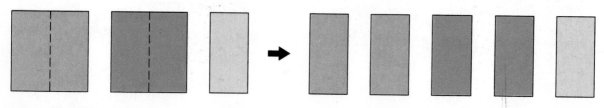

How many fourths are there in $1\frac{1}{2}$?

There are 6 fourths in $1\frac{1}{2}$.

We write: $1\frac{1}{2} \div \frac{1}{4} = 6$.

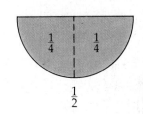

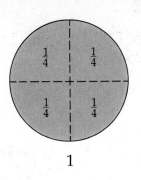

1                    $\frac{1}{2}$

You can check this division problem by multiplying. $6 \times \frac{1}{4} = \frac{6}{4} = 1\frac{1}{2}$

Use the pictures to help you solve each division problem.
Check by multiplying.

1.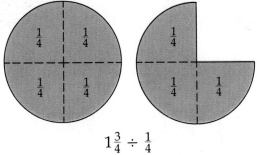

$1\frac{3}{4} \div \frac{1}{4}$

2.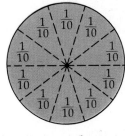

$1 \div \frac{1}{10}$

3.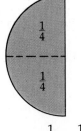

$\frac{1}{2} \div \frac{1}{4}$

4.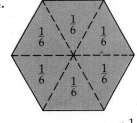

$1\frac{1}{2} \div \frac{1}{6}$

5.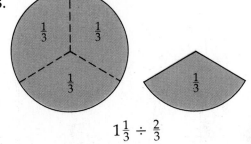

$1\frac{1}{3} \div \frac{2}{3}$

6.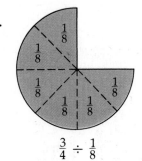

$\frac{3}{4} \div \frac{1}{8}$

Whole numbers and fractions in division

How many halves are there in 3?

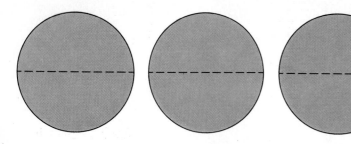

$$3 \div \frac{1}{2} = \frac{3}{1} \times \frac{2}{1} = 6$$

There are 6 halves in 3.

How many fourths are there in 2?

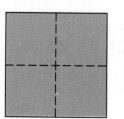 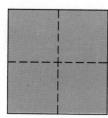

$$2 \div \frac{1}{4} = \frac{2}{1} \times \frac{4}{1} = 8$$

There are 8 fourths in 2.

1. How many thirds are there in 4?

   $4 \div \frac{1}{3} = $ ▓▓

2. How many sixths are there in 5?

   $5 \div \frac{1}{6} = $ ▓▓

3. How many tenths are there in 2?

   $2 \div \frac{1}{10} = $ ▓▓

4. How many eighths are there in 3?

   $3 \div \frac{1}{8} = $ ▓▓

Find the quotients.

5. $5 \div \frac{1}{2}$ 10

6. $4 \div \frac{1}{6}$

7. $8 \div \frac{1}{4}$

8. $10 \div \frac{1}{2}$

9. $12 \div \frac{1}{2}$

10. $1 \div \frac{1}{4}$

11. $7 \div \frac{1}{3}$

12. $5 \div \frac{1}{5}$

13. $2 \div \frac{1}{3}$

14. $3 \div \frac{1}{4}$

15. $9 \div \frac{1}{4}$

16. $4 \div \frac{1}{8}$

17. $3 \div \frac{1}{10}$

18. $8 \div \frac{1}{6}$

19. $15 \div \frac{1}{2}$

20. $20 \div \frac{1}{10}$

These 3 units are divided to make 4 regions of equal size.
How large is each region?

$$3 \div 4 = \frac{3}{1} \div \frac{4}{1}$$
$$= \frac{3}{1} \times \frac{1}{4} = \frac{3}{4}$$

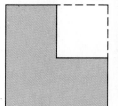 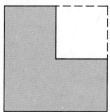 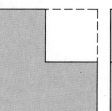 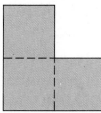

Each region is $\frac{3}{4}$ of a unit.

The quotient of two whole numbers can be written as a fraction.

$5 \div 8 = \frac{5}{8}$ $3 \div 6 = \frac{3}{6}$ or $\frac{1}{2}$ $8 \div 3 = \frac{8}{3}$ or $2\frac{2}{3}$

Find the quotients.

1. $7 \div 8$	2. $2 \div 5$	3. $9 \div 10$	4. $1 \div 3$
5. $4 \div 12$	6. $8 \div 16$	7. $6 \div 8$	8. $10 \div 15$
9. $5 \div 2$	10. $7 \div 4$	11. $10 \div 3$	12. $16 \div 5$
13. $3 \div 10$	14. $4 \div 3$	15. $6 \div 9$	16. $7 \div 28$
17. $25 \div 100$	18. $40 \div 6$	19. $15 \div 18$	20. $9 \div 5$
21. $1 \div 4$	22. $3 \div 9$	23. $100 \div 3$	24. $19 \div 20$

 A diamond this size has a mass of about $\frac{1}{3}$ carat.
One of the largest diamonds ever found, the
Cullinan diamond, had a mass of 3106 carats rough.
How many $\frac{1}{3}$ carat diamonds would it take to make
a diamond with a mass as great as the Cullinan's?

Dividing fractional numbers

A pitcher of orange juice is $\frac{9}{10}$ full.
One serving is $\frac{1}{5}$ of a pitcher. How many
servings of juice are there?

Finding the answer

Fractional number division problem	→	Find the reciprocal of the divisor	→	Multiply the dividend by the reciprocal of the divisor

$$\frac{9}{10} \div \frac{1}{5} \qquad \text{The reciprocal of } \frac{1}{5} \text{ is } \frac{5}{1}. \qquad \frac{9}{10} \times \frac{5}{1} = \frac{45}{10} = 4\frac{1}{2}$$

There are $4\frac{1}{2}$ servings of juice.

Other examples

$$\frac{2}{3} \div \frac{3}{4} = \frac{2}{3} \times \frac{4}{3} = \frac{8}{9} \qquad\qquad \frac{3}{4} \div \frac{3}{5} = \frac{3}{4} \times \frac{5}{3} = \frac{15}{12} = 1\frac{1}{4}$$

$$\frac{2}{3} \div 5 = \frac{2}{3} \div \frac{5}{1} = \frac{2}{3} \times \frac{1}{5} = \frac{2}{15} \qquad\qquad 4 \div \frac{3}{8} = \frac{4}{1} \times \frac{8}{3} = \frac{32}{3} = 10\frac{2}{3}$$

Find the quotients.

1. $\frac{2}{3} \div \frac{1}{2}$ 2. $\frac{1}{2} \div \frac{1}{4}$ 3. $\frac{1}{2} \div \frac{4}{5}$ 4. $\frac{3}{4} \div \frac{1}{10}$ 5. $\frac{3}{4} \div \frac{1}{2}$

6. $\frac{3}{5} \div \frac{3}{4}$ 7. $\frac{5}{6} \div \frac{2}{3}$ 8. $\frac{9}{10} \div \frac{2}{5}$ 9. $\frac{7}{8} \div \frac{1}{2}$ 10. $\frac{1}{3} \div \frac{2}{3}$

11. $\frac{1}{5} \div \frac{1}{2}$ 12. $\frac{3}{10} \div \frac{3}{4}$ 13. $\frac{3}{4} \div \frac{1}{8}$ 14. $\frac{3}{2} \div \frac{3}{4}$ 15. $\frac{3}{8} \div \frac{9}{10}$

Find the quotients.

1. $\frac{1}{2} \div \frac{1}{4}$ 2. $\frac{7}{8} \div \frac{1}{3}$ 3. $\frac{1}{2} \div \frac{5}{8}$ 4. $\frac{7}{10} \div \frac{3}{4}$ 5. $\frac{4}{5} \div \frac{2}{3}$

6. $\frac{1}{4} \div \frac{2}{5}$ 7. $\frac{3}{8} \div \frac{3}{4}$ 8. $\frac{7}{8} \div \frac{3}{4}$ 9. $\frac{5}{8} \div \frac{1}{3}$ 10. $4 \div \frac{1}{2}$

11. $9 \div \frac{3}{4}$ 12. $\frac{1}{2} \div 4$ 13. $\frac{2}{3} \div 5$ 14. $10 \div \frac{5}{6}$ 15. $1 \div \frac{3}{4}$

16. $2 \div 3$ 17. $\frac{5}{8} \div \frac{10}{3}$ 18. $\frac{3}{8} \div \frac{3}{8}$ 19. $\frac{5}{6} \div \frac{2}{3}$ 20. $\frac{9}{10} \div 3$

21. $\frac{1}{2} \div \frac{1}{10}$ 22. $\frac{7}{8} \div \frac{1}{4}$ 23. $\frac{3}{4} \div \frac{1}{2}$ 24. $\frac{1}{10} \div \frac{3}{10}$

25. $\frac{5}{8} \div \frac{3}{4}$ 26. $6 \div \frac{1}{3}$ 27. $\frac{2}{3} \div 4$ 28. $\frac{7}{10} \div \frac{2}{5}$

29. $10 \div \frac{2}{3}$ 30. $6 \div 9$ 31. $\frac{1}{15} \div \frac{1}{10}$ 32. $\frac{5}{8} \div \frac{5}{6}$

33. We have $\frac{3}{4}$ cup of blueberries. One serving is $\frac{3}{10}$ of a cup. How many servings of blueberries do we have?

34. There is $\frac{4}{5}$ of a whole cake on a plate. One serving is $\frac{1}{10}$ of a whole cake. How many servings can be made?

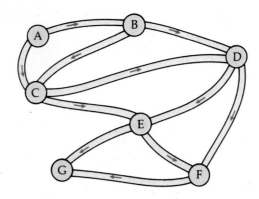

If you travel along each one-way street only in the direction shown by the arrow, how many different routes from A to G can you find?

More practice, page 390, Set B

Dividing with mixed numerals

A garden hose is leaking 1 ℓ of water every $\frac{3}{4}$ hour. How many liters of water will it leak in $3\frac{3}{4}$ hours?

Finding the answer

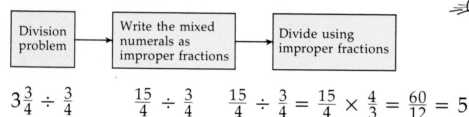

Division problem	→	Write the mixed numerals as improper fractions	→	Divide using improper fractions

$$3\frac{3}{4} \div \frac{3}{4} \qquad \frac{15}{4} \div \frac{3}{4} \qquad \frac{15}{4} \div \frac{3}{4} = \frac{15}{4} \times \frac{4}{3} = \frac{60}{12} = 5$$

The hose will leak 5 ℓ of water in $3\frac{3}{4}$ hours.

Other examples

$$2\frac{1}{2} \div 1\frac{1}{3} = \frac{5}{2} \div \frac{4}{3} = \frac{5}{2} \times \frac{3}{4} = \frac{15}{8} = 1\frac{7}{8}$$

$$8 \div 3\frac{1}{5} = \frac{8}{1} \div \frac{16}{5} = \frac{8}{1} \times \frac{5}{16} = \frac{40}{16} = 2\frac{1}{2}$$

$$7\frac{1}{4} \div 3 = \frac{29}{4} \div \frac{3}{1} = \frac{29}{4} \times \frac{1}{3} = \frac{29}{12} = 2\frac{5}{12}$$

Find the quotients.

1. $1\frac{1}{2} \div \frac{3}{4}$ 2. $3\frac{1}{4} \div \frac{1}{2}$ 3. $\frac{4}{5} \div 2\frac{2}{3}$ 4. $3\frac{1}{2} \div 2\frac{1}{4}$

5. $2\frac{1}{3} \div 1\frac{1}{5}$ 6. $\frac{9}{10} \div 1\frac{1}{4}$ 7. $1\frac{3}{8} \div 4\frac{1}{3}$ 8. $\frac{1}{6} \div 3\frac{1}{2}$

9. $10 \div 2\frac{1}{2}$ 10. $6 \div 1\frac{1}{3}$ 11. $9 \div 10$ 12. $2\frac{2}{3} \div 1\frac{1}{4}$

Divide.

1. $2\frac{1}{3} \div \frac{1}{3}$ 2. $5\frac{1}{4} \div 2\frac{1}{2}$ 3. $12 \div 1\frac{1}{2}$

4. $\frac{1}{2} \div 2\frac{1}{2}$ 5. $\frac{3}{4} \div 2\frac{1}{3}$ 6. $1\frac{1}{8} \div 3$ 7. $2\frac{1}{10} \div 1\frac{1}{5}$

8. $4 \div 1\frac{1}{3}$ 9. $3\frac{2}{3} \div 2$ 10. $10 \div 1\frac{1}{4}$

11. $4\frac{1}{2} \div 2\frac{7}{10}$ 12. $2\frac{2}{5} \div 1\frac{1}{3}$ 13. $9 \div 2\frac{1}{4}$

14. $2\frac{2}{3} \div 8$ 15. $3\frac{1}{3} \div 1\frac{2}{3}$ 16. $1 \div 2\frac{1}{2}$ 17. $5 \div 8$

18. $2\frac{4}{5} \div \frac{7}{8}$ 19. $100 \div 33\frac{1}{3}$ 20. $16\frac{1}{2} \div 4\frac{3}{4}$ 21. $6\frac{1}{2} \div 1\frac{1}{4}$

22. A faucet is leaking $1\ \ell$ of water every $2\frac{1}{2}$ hours. How many liters will it leak in $3\frac{3}{4}$ hours?

How many different nine-digit numerals can you form using each of the digits 1 through 9 exactly once? Take a guess.

You can find the answer by multiplying:

$1 \times 2 \times 3 \times 4 \times 5 \times 6 \times 7 \times 8 \times 9$

What is this product?

23. Diameter of paper cup: 7 cm
Circumference of paper cup: 22 cm
Divide the circumference by the diameter. Give the answer as a mixed numeral.

Answers for Self-check 1. 6 2. 12 3. 12 4. $3\frac{1}{3}$ 5. 8 6. 2 7. 4 8. $1\frac{3}{4}$ 9. $1\frac{1}{8}$ 10. 3 11. $1\frac{1}{2}$
12. $10\frac{5}{6}$ 13. $1\frac{3}{7}$ 14. $2\frac{4}{15}$ 15. $\frac{1}{4}$ 16. $2\frac{3}{8}$ 17. $\frac{2}{15}$

More practice, page 390, Set C

Self-check

1. How many halves in 3?

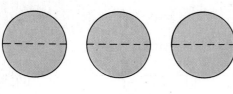

$$3 \div \tfrac{1}{2}$$

2. How many sixths in 2?

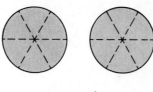

$$2 \div \tfrac{1}{6}$$

Find the quotients.

3. $3 \div \tfrac{1}{4}$ **4.** $\tfrac{2}{3} \div \tfrac{1}{5}$ **5.** $6 \div \tfrac{3}{4}$ **6.** $\tfrac{3}{5} \div \tfrac{3}{10}$ **7.** $\tfrac{1}{2} \div \tfrac{1}{8}$

8. $\tfrac{7}{8} \div \tfrac{1}{2}$ **9.** $\tfrac{3}{8} \div \tfrac{1}{3}$ **10.** $1\tfrac{1}{2} \div \tfrac{1}{2}$ **11.** $2\tfrac{1}{4} \div \tfrac{3}{2}$ **12.** $4\tfrac{1}{3} \div \tfrac{2}{5}$

13. $2\tfrac{1}{2} \div 1\tfrac{3}{4}$ **14.** $3\tfrac{2}{5} \div 1\tfrac{1}{2}$ **15.** $\tfrac{3}{8} \div 1\tfrac{1}{2}$ **16.** $4\tfrac{3}{4} \div 2$ **17.** $\tfrac{4}{5} \div 6$

Answers for Self-check—page 229

Test

1. How many thirds in 4?

$$4 \div \tfrac{1}{3}$$

2. How many eighths in 3?

$$3 \div \tfrac{1}{8}$$

Find the quotients.

3. $4 \div \tfrac{1}{2}$ **4.** $\tfrac{7}{8} \div \tfrac{1}{2}$ **5.** $6 \div \tfrac{2}{3}$ **6.** $\tfrac{1}{4} \div \tfrac{1}{8}$ **7.** $\tfrac{9}{10} \div \tfrac{3}{5}$

8. $\tfrac{3}{4} \div \tfrac{2}{5}$ **9.** $\tfrac{7}{10} \div \tfrac{1}{3}$ **10.** $2\tfrac{1}{3} \div \tfrac{4}{3}$ **11.** $3\tfrac{1}{2} \div \tfrac{2}{3}$ **12.** $1\tfrac{2}{3} \div \tfrac{1}{2}$

13. $4\tfrac{2}{3} \div 1\tfrac{3}{4}$ **14.** $2\tfrac{1}{5} \div 1\tfrac{3}{10}$ **15.** $\tfrac{4}{5} \div 1\tfrac{1}{3}$ **16.** $3\tfrac{1}{5} \div 4$ **17.** $\tfrac{2}{3} \div 4$

Tangrams

The tangram puzzle is made of 7 pieces that form a square. These pieces can be placed side by side to form many other shapes.

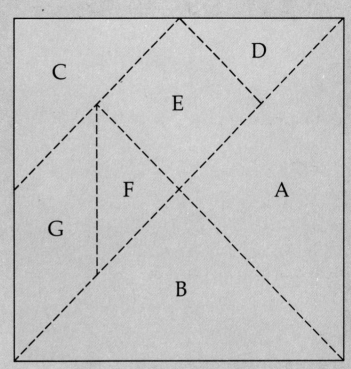

Copy or trace these tangram pieces.

Cut along the dotted lines.

Try to make these figures with the tangram pieces.

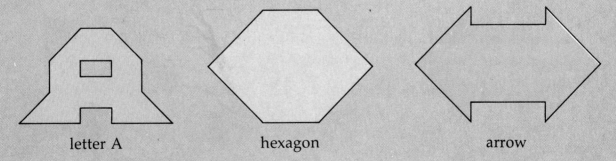

letter A   hexagon   arrow

Make some other tangram figures. Trace them onto cards. Ask your classmates to solve your tangram puzzle cards.

Space Geometry

Getting started

The appearance of an object changes according to how it is viewed.
Space figures are 3-dimensional,
but they can be shown on a flat,
or 2-dimensional, surface.

Graph paper is often helpful
when drawing space figures.

Draw a copy of this cube on graph paper.
The dashed lines show hidden edges.

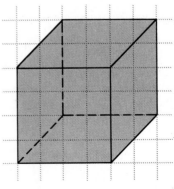

Copy each polyhedron on graph paper.

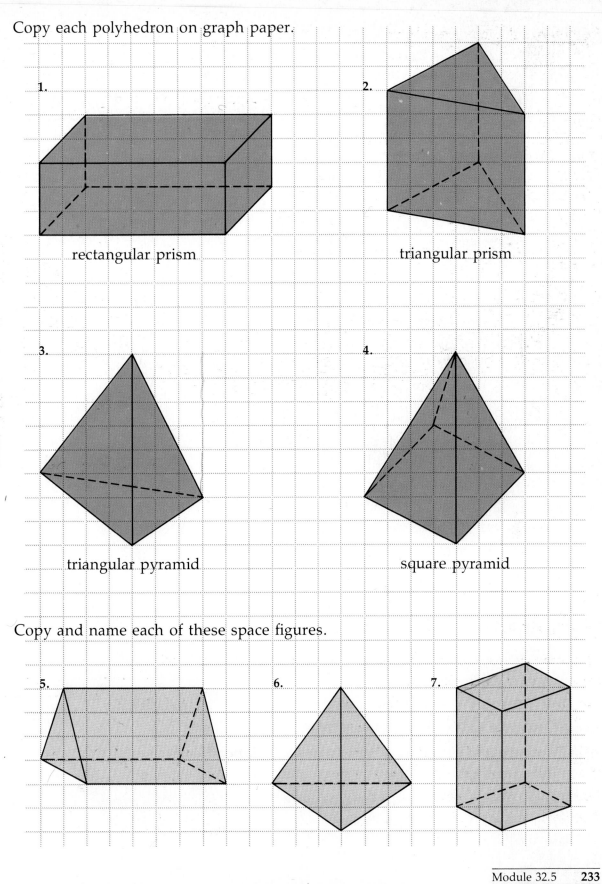

1.

rectangular prism

2.

triangular prism

3.

triangular pyramid

4.

square pyramid

Copy and name each of these space figures.

5.

6.

7.

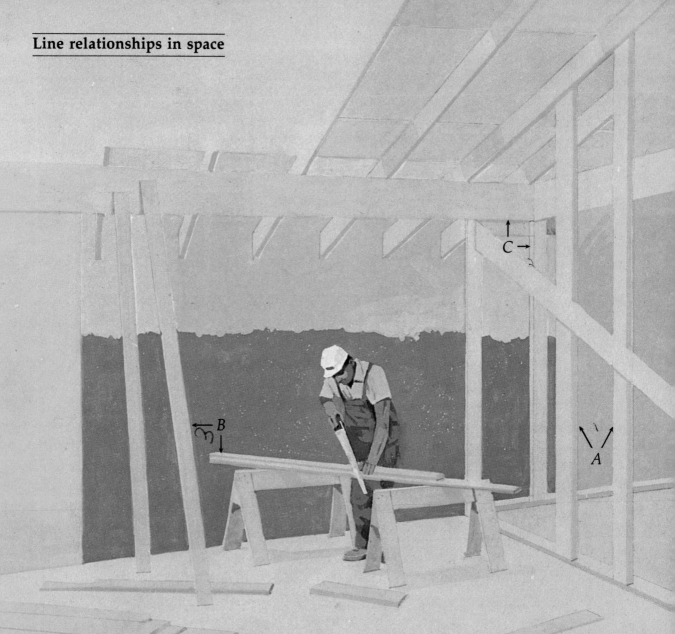

The boards suggest some special relations
between lines.

1. Two lines in the same plane that do not intersect are **parallel**.
   Which pair of boards suggests parallel lines, *A*, *B*, or *C*?

2. Two lines that intersect at right angles are **perpendicular**.
   Which pair of boards suggests perpendicular lines?

3. Two lines that do not intersect and are not parallel are **skew lines**.
   Skew lines are never in the same plane. Which pair of boards
   suggests skew lines?

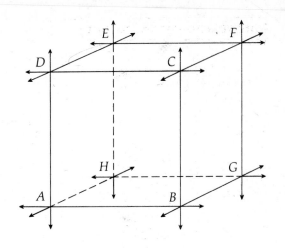

$\overleftrightarrow{AB}$ and $\overleftrightarrow{DC}$ are in the same plane and do not intersect.

We say: Line AB is parallel to line DC.

We write: $\overleftrightarrow{AB} \parallel \overleftrightarrow{DC}$

Which pairs of lines are parallel?

1. $\overleftrightarrow{CF}$ and $\overleftrightarrow{EF}$

2. $\overleftrightarrow{EF}$ and $\overleftrightarrow{AB}$

3. $\overleftrightarrow{CB}$ and $\overleftrightarrow{FG}$

4. $\overleftrightarrow{ED}$ and $\overleftrightarrow{BC}$

5. $\overleftrightarrow{AD}$ and $\overleftrightarrow{BC}$

6. $\overleftrightarrow{AD}$ and $\overleftrightarrow{EF}$

$\overleftrightarrow{CB}$ and $\overleftrightarrow{CD}$ intersect at right angles.

We say: Line CB is perpendicular to line CD.

We write: $\overleftrightarrow{CB} \perp \overleftrightarrow{CD}$

Which pairs of lines are perpendicular?

7. $\overleftrightarrow{AD}$ and $\overleftrightarrow{AB}$

8. $\overleftrightarrow{DE}$ and $\overleftrightarrow{BG}$

9. $\overleftrightarrow{CF}$ and $\overleftrightarrow{EF}$

10. $\overleftrightarrow{BC}$ and $\overleftrightarrow{AH}$

11. $\overleftrightarrow{FG}$ and $\overleftrightarrow{BG}$

12. $\overleftrightarrow{EF}$ and $\overleftrightarrow{EH}$

$\overleftrightarrow{EF}$ and $\overleftrightarrow{BC}$ do not intersect and are not parallel. $\overleftrightarrow{EF}$ and $\overleftrightarrow{BC}$ are skew lines.

Which pairs of lines are skew lines?

13. $\overleftrightarrow{AB}$ and $\overleftrightarrow{FG}$

14. $\overleftrightarrow{CF}$ and $\overleftrightarrow{BG}$

15. $\overleftrightarrow{AD}$ and $\overleftrightarrow{BG}$

Polyhedrons

Each of these patterns can be folded to make a space figure.

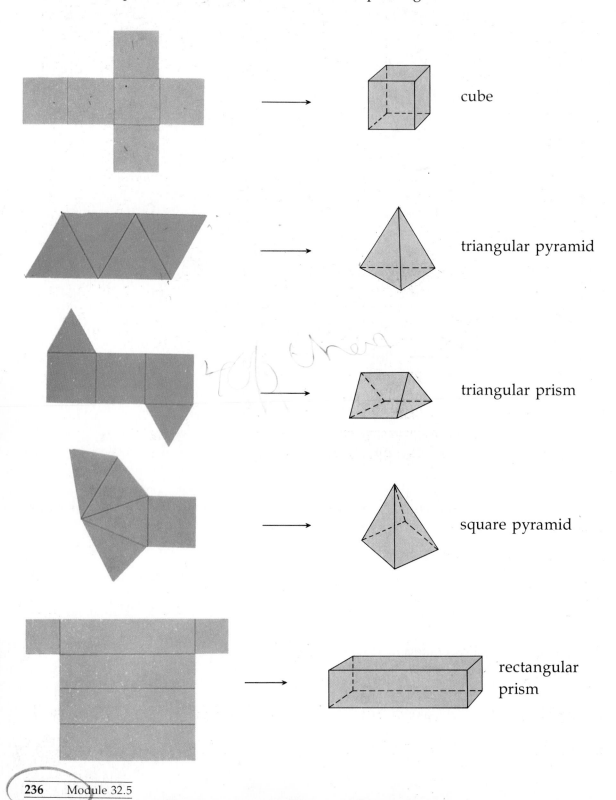

cube

triangular pyramid

triangular prism

square pyramid

rectangular prism

Copy the table and give the missing numbers.

	Name	Number of faces	Number of vertices	Number of edges
1.	rectangular prism	6	8	12
2.	triangular pyramid	4	4	6
3.	square pyramid	5	5	8
4.	triangular prism	5	6	9

5. For each space figure, add the number of faces
   and the number of vertices. Then subtract the number of edges.
   What do you notice about the differences you found?

Practicing your skills

Find the products and quotients.

1.	348 × 76	**2.**	408 × 92	**3.**	845 × 85	**4.**	679 × 78	**5.**	527 × 48
6.	95.2 × 6.8	**7.**	651 × 0.29	**8.**	70.3 × 0.16	**9.**	8.41 × 0.9	**10.**	2.08 × 0.04

11. $42\overline{)7893}$ **12.** $57\overline{)6018}$ **13.** $39\overline{)2406}$ **14.** $81\overline{)5664}$

15. $0.8\overline{)7.24}$ **16.** $5.9\overline{)46.02}$ **17.** $3.5\overline{)74.9}$ **18.** $6.7\overline{)50.25}$

✪ Cross sections

These figures show how you can think of cutting
space figures to get cross sections.

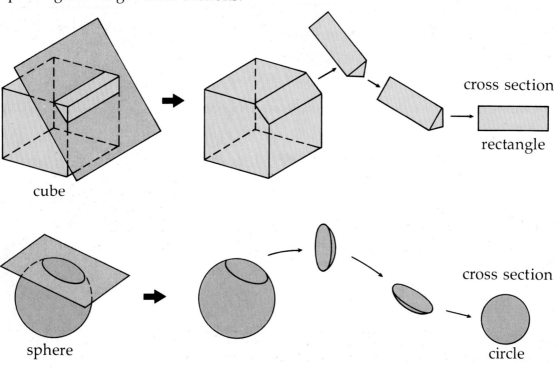

cube

cross section

rectangle

sphere

cross section

circle

Draw the cross sections.
Name as many of the cross section figures as you can.

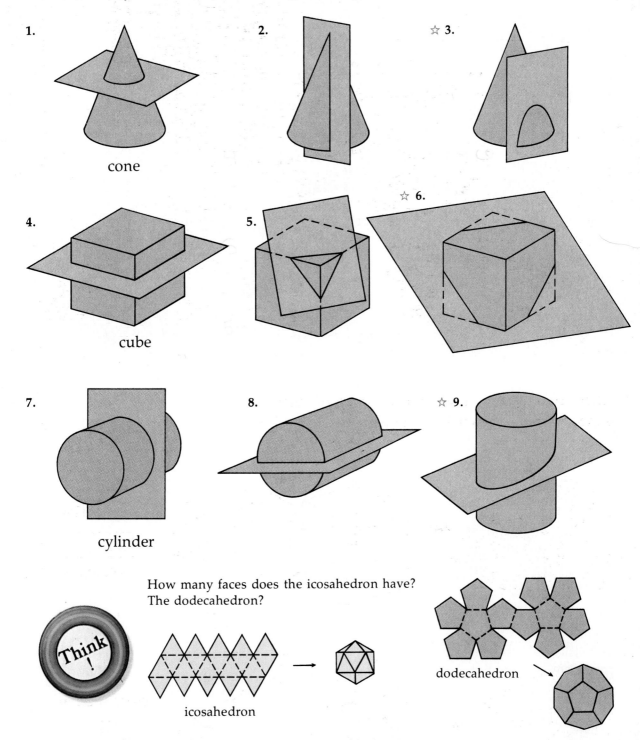

1.

cone

2.

☆ **3.**

4.

cube

5.

☆ **6.**

7.

cylinder

8.

☆ **9.**

How many faces does the icosahedron have?
The dodecahedron?

Think!

icosahedron

dodecahedron

Answers for Self-check 1. **B** and **C** 2. **A** and **C** 3. **A** and **C** 4. 5 vertices, 5 faces, 8 edges
5. 8 vertices, 6 faces, 12 edges 6. 6 vertices, 5 faces, 9 edges 7. **B**

Self-check

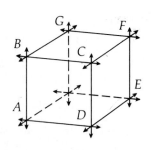

1. Which pairs of lines are parallel?

   A $\overleftrightarrow{BC}$ and $\overleftrightarrow{DE}$ B $\overleftrightarrow{EF}$ and $\overleftrightarrow{DC}$ C $\overleftrightarrow{BG}$ and $\overleftrightarrow{CF}$

2. Which pairs of lines are perpendicular?   A $\overleftrightarrow{FG}$ and $\overleftrightarrow{BG}$ B $\overleftrightarrow{CD}$ and $\overleftrightarrow{FG}$ C $\overleftrightarrow{AD}$ and $\overleftrightarrow{DE}$

3. Which pairs of lines are skew lines?   A $\overleftrightarrow{BC}$ and $\overleftrightarrow{DE}$ B $\overleftrightarrow{AB}$ and $\overleftrightarrow{BG}$ C $\overleftrightarrow{CD}$ and $\overleftrightarrow{FG}$

Give the number of vertices, faces, and edges for each figure.

4.   5.   6.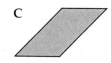

7. Which figure shows this cross section?

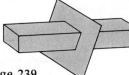   A   B   C

Test

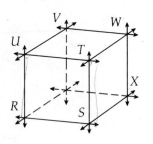

1. Which pairs of lines are parallel?

   A $\overleftrightarrow{RU}$ and $\overleftrightarrow{ST}$ B $\overleftrightarrow{UV}$ and $\overleftrightarrow{WX}$ C $\overleftrightarrow{SX}$ and $\overleftrightarrow{TW}$

2. Which pairs of lines are perpendicular?   A $\overleftrightarrow{RU}$ and $\overleftrightarrow{ST}$ B $\overleftrightarrow{UV}$ and $\overleftrightarrow{VW}$ C $\overleftrightarrow{TW}$ and $\overleftrightarrow{WX}$

3. Which pairs of lines are skew lines?   A $\overleftrightarrow{TW}$ and $\overleftrightarrow{XW}$ B $\overleftrightarrow{TU}$ and $\overleftrightarrow{XW}$ C $\overleftrightarrow{ST}$ and $\overleftrightarrow{VW}$

Give the number of vertices, faces, and edges for each figure.   4.   5. 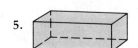   6.

7. Which figure shows this cross section?

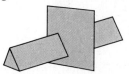   A   B   C

240   Module 32.5

Put-Together Puzzlers

1. Trace and cut out the four pieces below. Can you rearrange them to form the T-shaped figure?

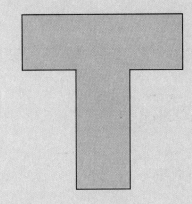

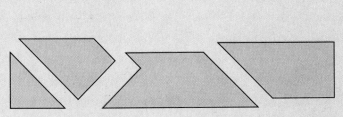

2. Trace and cut out four of these figures. Can you put them together to form a square?

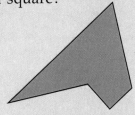

3. Draw a figure like this on your graph paper and cut it out.

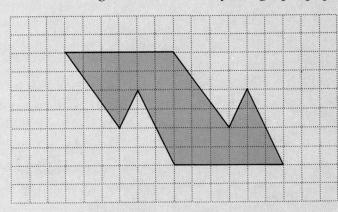

Make one straight cut so that the two parts can be placed together to form a square.

Level 32 review

Give each missing numerator or denominator.

1. $\frac{2}{3} = \frac{▉}{12}$ 2. $\frac{7}{8} = \frac{14}{▉}$ 3. $\frac{1}{6} = \frac{▉}{24}$ 4. $\frac{4}{5} = \frac{▉}{100}$ 5. $\frac{3}{4} = \frac{15}{▉}$

Find the lowest-terms fraction for each.

6. $\frac{20}{30}$ 7. $\frac{14}{16}$ 8. $\frac{12}{18}$ 9. $\frac{6}{24}$ 10. $\frac{75}{100}$

Write as mixed numerals.

11. $\frac{13}{3}$ 12. $\frac{26}{5}$ 13. $\frac{43}{8}$ 14. $\frac{13}{10}$ 15. $\frac{11}{4}$

Solve each equation.

16. $\frac{1}{3} = \frac{n}{9}$ 17. $\frac{2}{5} = \frac{40}{n}$ 18. $\frac{5}{8} = \frac{n}{24}$ 19. $\frac{1}{4} = \frac{25}{n}$ 20. $\frac{5}{6} = \frac{n}{30}$

Add.

21. $\frac{3}{8}$ $+\frac{1}{8}$ 22. $\frac{2}{5}$ $+\frac{3}{10}$ 23. $\frac{1}{3}$ $+\frac{3}{4}$ 24. $3\frac{7}{8}$ $+1\frac{1}{4}$ 25. $2\frac{4}{5}$ $+5\frac{1}{4}$

Subtract.

26. $\frac{4}{5}$ $-\frac{2}{5}$ 27. $\frac{9}{10}$ $-\frac{1}{4}$ 28. $6\frac{3}{4}$ $-2\frac{2}{3}$ 29. $5\frac{3}{10}$ $-1\frac{4}{5}$ 30. $8\frac{1}{2}$ $-2\frac{3}{4}$

Find the products.

31. $\frac{1}{5} \times \frac{2}{3}$ 32. $\frac{3}{10} \times \frac{1}{4}$ 33. $\frac{1}{3} \times \frac{4}{5}$ 34. $\frac{7}{8} \times \frac{2}{3}$ 35. $\frac{3}{5} \times \frac{5}{6}$

36. $2\frac{1}{2} \times \frac{1}{3}$ 37. $\frac{3}{4} \times 1\frac{2}{5}$ 38. $3\frac{1}{4} \times 2\frac{1}{2}$ 39. $1\frac{1}{2} \times 3\frac{1}{3}$ 40. $4\frac{3}{8} \times 2\frac{2}{5}$

Find the quotients.

41. $\frac{1}{3} \div \frac{1}{2}$ 42. $\frac{3}{4} \div \frac{1}{4}$ 43. $\frac{7}{8} \div \frac{2}{3}$ 44. $\frac{1}{2} \div \frac{4}{5}$ 45. $\frac{1}{5} \div \frac{1}{10}$

46. $4\frac{1}{2} \div \frac{2}{3}$ 47. $2\frac{2}{5} \div 1\frac{1}{3}$ 48. $3\frac{1}{2} \div 1\frac{1}{4}$ 49. $\frac{1}{4} \div 3$ 50. $\frac{2}{5} \div 2$

Fractions and Decimals
Ratio
Percent
Using Your Skills
Coordinate Geometry

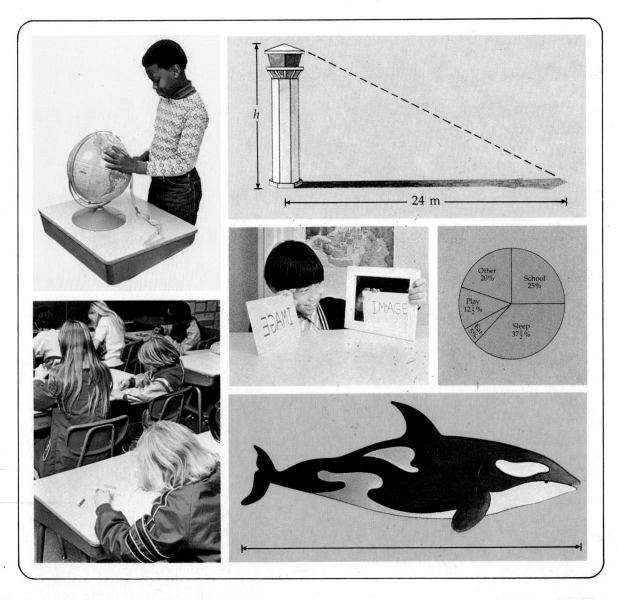

Fractions and Decimals

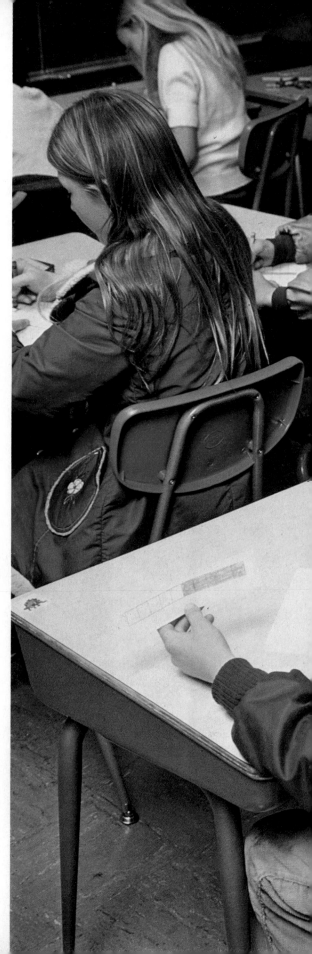

The fractions $\frac{1}{2}$ or $\frac{5}{10}$ can be shown as tenths on a 10-strip.

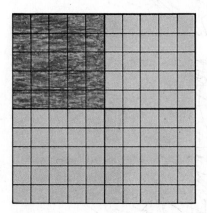

0.5

The fractions $\frac{1}{4}$ or $\frac{25}{100}$ can be shown as hundredths on a 100-square.

0.25

Which of the fractions below can be shown on a 10-strip by coloring whole squares?

$\frac{1}{5}$ $\frac{1}{3}$ $\frac{1}{10}$ $\frac{3}{4}$

Which can be shown on a hundred-square?

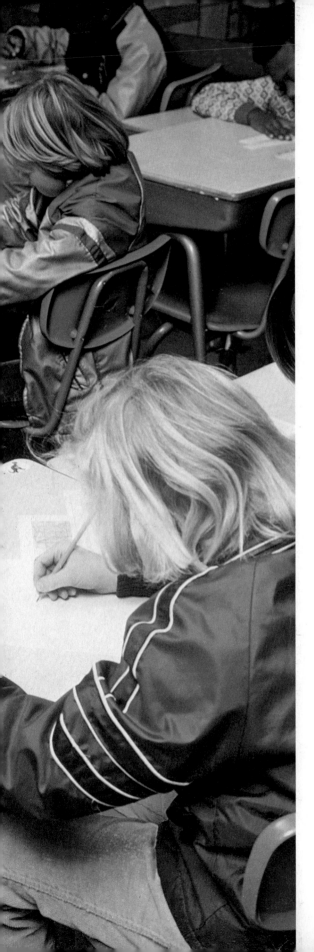

Give the number of tenths.
Then give the decimal.

1. 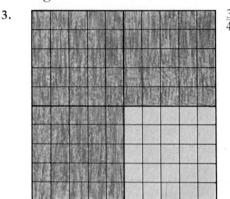 $\dfrac{3}{5} = \dfrac{\text{IIIII}}{10} = \text{IIIII}$

2. $\dfrac{2}{5} = \dfrac{\text{IIIII}}{10} = \text{IIIII}$

Give the number of hundredths.
Then give the decimal.

3. 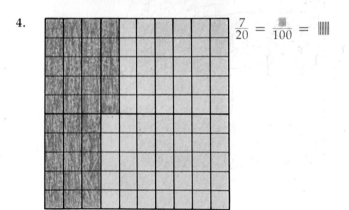 $\dfrac{3}{4} = \dfrac{\text{IIIII}}{100} = \text{IIIII}$

4. $\dfrac{7}{20} = \dfrac{\text{IIIII}}{100} = \text{IIIII}$

Give the number of thousandths.
Then give the decimal.

5. $\dfrac{3}{8} = \dfrac{3 \times 125}{8 \times 125} = \dfrac{\text{IIIII}}{1000} = \text{IIIII}$

6. $\dfrac{9}{40} = \dfrac{9 \times 25}{40 \times 25} = \dfrac{\text{IIIII}}{1000} = \text{IIIII}$

From fractions to decimals

Only $\frac{1}{8}$ of an iceberg
is above the surface
of the water. What is
the decimal for the part
of an iceberg above the water?

Finding the answer

Fraction	Divide the numerator by the denominator	Decimal

$\frac{1}{8}$ $\begin{array}{r} 0.1\,2\,5 \\ 8\overline{)1.0^20^40} \end{array}$ 0.125

The decimal for $\frac{1}{8}$ is 0.125.

Other examples

$\frac{1}{4} \longrightarrow \begin{array}{r} 0.25 \\ 4\overline{)1.00} \end{array} \rightarrow 0.25$ $\frac{3}{16} \longrightarrow \begin{array}{r} 0.1875 \\ 16\overline{)3.0000} \end{array} \rightarrow 0.1875$ $\frac{8}{5} \longrightarrow \begin{array}{r} 1.6 \\ 5\overline{)8.0} \end{array} \rightarrow 1.6$

Write a decimal for each fraction.

1. 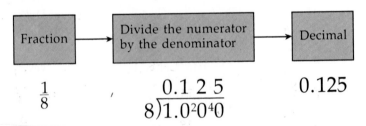 $\frac{1}{2}$ 2. $\frac{1}{5}$ 3. $\frac{1}{20}$ 4. $\frac{3}{4}$ 5. $\frac{3}{10}$

6. $\frac{2}{5}$ 7. $\frac{5}{8}$ 8. $\frac{12}{10}$ 9. $\frac{3}{8}$ 10. $\frac{5}{4}$

4 places

Write a decimal for each fraction.

1. $\frac{3}{5}$	**2.** $\frac{1}{16}$	**3.** $\frac{6}{10}$	**4.** $\frac{3}{2}$	**5.** $\frac{9}{8}$
6. $\frac{7}{16}$	**7.** $\frac{7}{4}$	**8.** $\frac{6}{5}$	**9.** $\frac{9}{16}$	**10.** $\frac{1}{25}$
11. $\frac{11}{8}$	**12.** $\frac{3}{20}$	**13.** $\frac{9}{5}$	**14.** $\frac{8}{25}$	**15.** $\frac{15}{8}$
16. $\frac{9}{50}$	**17.** $\frac{28}{25}$	**18.** $\frac{13}{8}$	**19.** $\frac{19}{16}$	**20.** $\frac{27}{20}$

21. Copy the table and give the missing numbers.

Fractions to Decimals	
$\frac{1}{2}$ = ▒	$\frac{1}{10}$ = ▒
$\frac{1}{4}$ = ▒	$\frac{1}{16}$ = ▒
$\frac{1}{5}$ = ▒	$\frac{1}{20}$ = ▒
$\frac{1}{8}$ = ▒	$\frac{1}{25}$ = ▒

22. About $\frac{7}{8}$ of an iceberg is below the water's surface. Give this fraction as a decimal.

Find the decimal (to 7 decimal places) for each of these fractions.

$\frac{1}{7}$ $\frac{2}{7}$ $\frac{3}{7}$ $\frac{4}{7}$ $\frac{5}{7}$ $\frac{6}{7}$

Do you see a pattern in the digits of these decimals?

More practice, page 391, Set A

Writing fractions as mixed decimals

The table shows that the mixed
decimal for $\frac{3}{8}$ is $0.37\frac{1}{2}$. What
is the mixed decimal for $\frac{5}{8}$?

Fractions to Decimals	
$\frac{1}{2} = 0.50$	$\frac{3}{8} = 0.37\frac{1}{2}$
$\frac{1}{4} = 0.25$	$\frac{5}{8} =$ ▓▓▓

Finding the answer

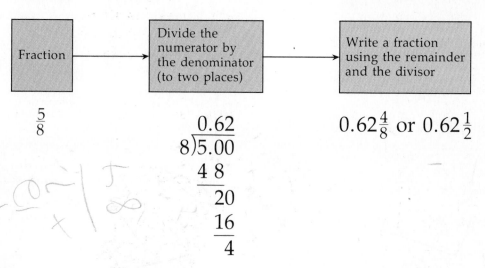

| Fraction | → | Divide the numerator by the denominator (to two places) | → | Write a fraction using the remainder and the divisor |

$\frac{5}{8}$

$$\begin{array}{r} 0.62 \\ 8\overline{)5.00} \\ 4\ 8 \\ \hline 20 \\ 16 \\ \hline 4 \end{array}$$

$0.62\frac{4}{8}$ or $0.62\frac{1}{2}$

The mixed decimal for $\frac{5}{8}$ is $0.62\frac{1}{2}$.

Other examples

$\frac{4}{3} \rightarrow$
$$\begin{array}{r} 1.33 \\ 3\overline{)4.00} \\ 3 \\ \hline 1\ 0 \\ 9 \\ \hline 10 \\ 9 \\ \hline 1 \end{array}$$
$\rightarrow 1.33\frac{1}{3}$

$\frac{5}{6} \rightarrow$
$$\begin{array}{r} 0.83 \\ 6\overline{)5.00} \\ 4\ 8 \\ \hline 20 \\ 18 \\ \hline 2 \end{array}$$
$\rightarrow 0.83\frac{2}{6}$ or $0.83\frac{1}{3}$

Write a mixed decimal for each fraction.

1. $\frac{3}{8}$ 2. $\frac{2}{3}$ 3. $\frac{1}{6}$ 4. $\frac{7}{12}$ 5. $\frac{9}{16}$ 6. $\frac{7}{8}$

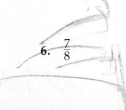

Write a mixed decimal for each fraction.

1. $\frac{1}{8}$ 2. $\frac{5}{6}$ 3. $\frac{2}{9}$ 4. $\frac{9}{8}$ 5. $\frac{5}{12}$

6. $\frac{5}{16}$ 7. $\frac{7}{16}$ 8. $\frac{5}{3}$ 9. $\frac{11}{6}$ 10. $\frac{15}{16}$

11. $\frac{7}{6}$ 12. $\frac{4}{15}$ 13. $\frac{2}{7}$ 14. $\frac{5}{11}$ 15. $\frac{5}{9}$

16. Copy and complete this table.

Fractions to Decimals	
$\frac{1}{2}$ = ▟▙▙	$\frac{2}{3}$ = ▟▙▙
$\frac{1}{3}$ = ▟▙▙	$\frac{3}{4}$ = ▟▙▙
$\frac{1}{4}$ = ▟▙▙	$\frac{2}{5}$ = ▟▙▙
$\frac{1}{5}$ = ▟▙▙	$\frac{3}{5}$ = ▟▙▙
$\frac{1}{6}$ = ▟▙▙	$\frac{4}{5}$ = ▟▙▙
$\frac{1}{8}$ = ▟▙▙	$\frac{5}{6}$ = ▟▙▙
$\frac{1}{10}$ = ▟▙▙	$\frac{3}{8}$ = ▟▙▙
$\frac{1}{12}$ = ▟▙▙	$\frac{5}{8}$ = ▟▙▙
$\frac{1}{16}$ = ▟▙▙	$\frac{7}{8}$ = ▟▙▙

17. Write a mixed decimal for each of these fractions. Then write the fractions in order from smallest to largest.

$$\frac{2}{3}, \frac{13}{16}, \frac{7}{8}, \frac{11}{12}, \frac{5}{6}$$

How many minutes will you have lived when you are exactly 12 years old? Guess first. Then figure it out. Use 365 days in 1 year.

Practicing your skills

Multiply or divide.

1. $\frac{1}{5} \times \frac{2}{3}$ 2. $\frac{3}{4} \times \frac{1}{6}$ 3. $\frac{5}{6} \times \frac{2}{5}$ 4. $\frac{3}{2} \times \frac{5}{8}$ 5. $\frac{2}{7} \times 6$

6. $\frac{3}{4} \div \frac{1}{2}$ 7. $\frac{9}{10} \div \frac{3}{5}$ 8. $4 \div \frac{2}{3}$ 9. $\frac{2}{3} \div \frac{1}{6}$ 10. $\frac{5}{8} \div \frac{3}{4}$

More practice, page 391, Set B

From decimals to fractions

About 0.25 of the earth's surface
is land. What fraction of the
earth's surface is land?

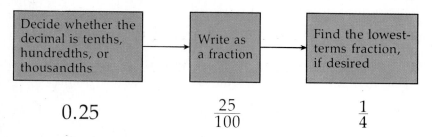

Finding the answer

Decide whether the decimal is tenths, hundredths, or thousandths	→	Write as a fraction	→	Find the lowest-terms fraction, if desired

$$0.25 \qquad\qquad \frac{25}{100} \qquad\qquad \frac{1}{4}$$

About $\frac{1}{4}$ of the earth's surface is land.

Other examples

$$0.3 = \frac{3}{10} \qquad\qquad 0.75 = \frac{75}{100} \text{ or } \frac{3}{4} \qquad\qquad 6.377 = 6\frac{377}{1000}$$

Write a lowest-terms fraction or a mixed numeral for each decimal.

1. 0.25   2. 4.7   3. 8.25   4. 0.05

5. 0.005   6. 0.9   7. 0.125   8. 0.875

9. 0.500   10. 1.35   11. 9.75   12. 0.375

Give the lowest-terms fraction for each decimal in the table.

decimal	0.10	0.125	0.2	0.25	0.5	0.4	0.75
fraction	▦	▦	▦	▦	▦	▦	▦
	1.	2.	3.	4.	5.	6.	7.

Sometimes a decimal describes a thing better than a fraction does. At other times, a fraction seems better. Write a fraction or mixed numeral for each decimal.

8. 0.375 of a cup

9. 0.40 of a candy bar

10. 0.875 of a day

11. 2.250 squares of tile

12. 3.125 hours

13. 4.75 pizzas

Write a decimal for each fraction or mixed numeral.

14. $3\frac{1}{2}$ cakes

15. $\frac{4}{5}$ of a dollar

16. $\frac{5}{8}$ of a box of nails

17. $\frac{1}{20}$ of a person's salary

18. $2\frac{1}{4}$ minutes

19. $\frac{1}{25}$ of the population

20. About 0.2 of the earth's atmosphere is oxygen. What fraction of the earth's atmosphere is oxygen?

Think !

Pat has enough pennies, nickels, dimes, and quarters to give each of her friends a total of 25¢ in a different way. What is the largest number of friends she could have?

21. About 0.05 of the mass of the earth's crust is iron. What fraction of the mass is iron?

	P	N	D	Q
1st friend	25	0	0	0
2nd friend	20	1	0	0

Answers for Self-check 1. 0.5 2. 0.05 3. 0.75 4. 0.375 5. 0.8 6. 0.12$\frac{1}{2}$ 7. 0.62$\frac{1}{2}$ 8. 0.06$\frac{1}{4}$
9. 0.33$\frac{1}{3}$ 10. 0.16$\frac{2}{3}$ 11. $\frac{1}{4}$ 12. $\frac{1}{8}$ 13. 2$\frac{3}{8}$ 14. $\frac{5}{8}$ 15. $\frac{1}{20}$ 16. 1$\frac{3}{4}$ 17. $\frac{3}{5}$ 18. 3$\frac{2}{5}$

More practice, page 391, Set C

Self-check

Write a decimal for each fraction.

1. $\frac{1}{2}$ 2. $\frac{1}{20}$ 3. $\frac{3}{4}$ 4. $\frac{3}{8}$ 5. $\frac{4}{5}$

Write a mixed decimal for each fraction.

6. $\frac{1}{8}$ 7. $\frac{5}{8}$ 8. $\frac{1}{16}$ 9. $\frac{1}{3}$ 10. $\frac{1}{6}$

Write the lowest-terms fraction or mixed numeral for each decimal.

11. 0.25   12. 0.125   13. 2.375   14. 0.625

15. 0.05   16. 1.75   17. 0.6   18. 3.4

Answers for Self-check—page 251

Test

Write a decimal for each fraction.

1. $\frac{1}{5}$ 2. $\frac{1}{8}$ 3. $\frac{1}{4}$ 4. $\frac{5}{8}$ 5. $\frac{1}{16}$

Write a mixed decimal for each fraction.

6. $\frac{2}{3}$ 7. $\frac{1}{6}$ 8. $\frac{3}{8}$ 9. $\frac{5}{6}$ 10. $\frac{1}{8}$

Write the lowest-terms fraction or mixed numeral for each decimal.

11. 0.75   12. 0.875   13. 3.125   14. 1.4

15. 0.50   16. 0.6   17. 5.8   18. 3.25

Pentominoes

Pentominoes are figures that can be made with five squares.
Each square shares at least one side with another square.
Here are the twelve pentominoes.

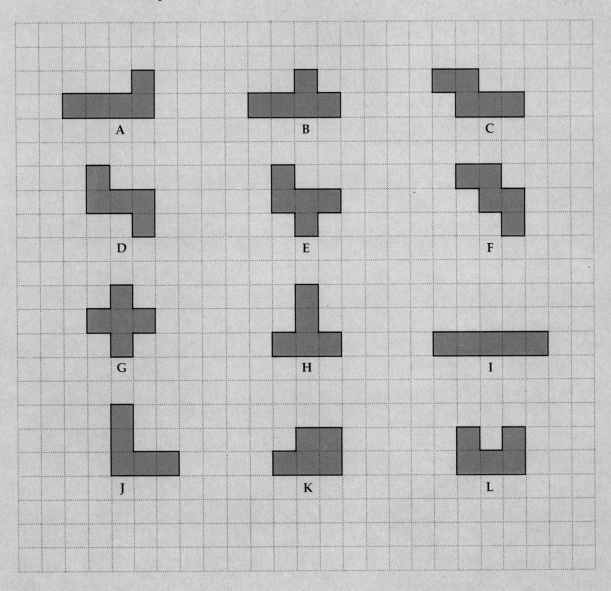

1. Which pentominoes have just 1 line of symmetry?

2. Which have 2 lines of symmetry?

3. Find three patterns that can be folded to make an open-top box.

Ratio

Band Instruments	
Oboes	✏
Tubas	🎺 🎺
French horns	📯 📯 📯
Saxophones	🎷 🎷 🎷 🎷
Flutes	／ ／ ／ ／
Trombones	／ ／ ／ ／ ／ ／
Drums	◯ ◯ ◯ ◯ ◯ ◯ ◯ ◯
Trumpets	🎺 🎺 🎺 🎺 🎺 🎺 🎺 🎺 🎺
Clarinets	／ ／ ／ ／ ／ ／ ／ ／ ／ ／

Getting started

The graph shows the number of each kind of musical instrument played by a school band.

The band has
1 oboe
to
2 tubas.

The band has
2 tubas
to
4 saxophones.

2 to 4 is the same as 1 to 2.

Find another pair of instruments that can be compared as 1 to 2.

The band has
3 French horns
to
1 oboe.

The band has
6 trombones
to
2 tubas.

  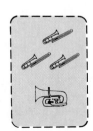

3 to 1 is the same as 6 to 2.

Find another pair of instruments that can be compared as 3 to 1.

We see:	We say:	We write:

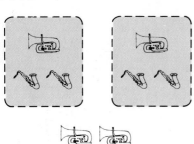

The **ratio** of the number of tubas to the number of saxophones is 1 to 2.

$\frac{1}{2}$

The ratio of the number of tubas to the number of saxophones is 2 to 4.

$\frac{2}{4}$

$\frac{1}{2}$ and $\frac{2}{4}$ are **equal ratios**.   We write: $\frac{1}{2} = \frac{2}{4}$

Complete the description of the two ratios.
Then give an equation that shows the equal ratios.

Example:

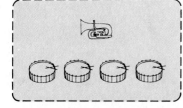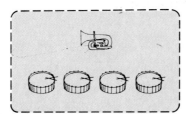

1 to 2
5 to 10

$\frac{1}{2} = \frac{5}{10}$

1.

1 to 4
||||| to |||||

$\frac{|||||}{|||||} = \frac{|||||}{|||||}$

2.

3 to 1
||||| to |||||

$\frac{|||||}{|||||} = \frac{|||||}{|||||}$

3.

2 to 3
||||| to |||||

$\frac{|||||}{|||||} = \frac{|||||}{|||||}$

Using ratio tables

Trip to Fun World:
Driving speed—2 km each 3 minutes

The **ratio table** below shows other
distances that could be driven
in longer periods of time.

	⟨2 × 2⟩	⟨2 × 3⟩	⟨2 × 4⟩	⟨2 × 5⟩
km	2	4	6	8	10
min	3	6	9	12	15
	⟨3 × 2⟩	⟨3 × 3⟩	⟨3 × 4⟩	⟨3 × 5⟩

The equivalent fractions $\frac{2}{3}$, $\frac{4}{6}$, $\frac{6}{9}$, $\frac{8}{12}$, and $\frac{10}{15}$
are equal ratios. They all compare the number
of kilometers with the number of minutes.

Copy and complete each table of equal ratios.

1.

Each minute
20 people enter
the park.

minutes	1	2	3	4	5
people	20	▨	▨	▨	▨

40

2.

8 rides
cost $3.

rides	8	16	24	32	40
dollars	3	▨	▨	▨	▨

3.

The flying saucer
spins 3 times
in 13 seconds.

spins	3	6	9	12	15
seconds	13	▨	▨	▨	▨

Solve the problems. Copy and complete as much
of each ratio table as you need.

1. On a map of the park, 1 cm shows
    a distance of 100 m. How far is it
    from the ferris wheel to Pirate Island?

cm	1				
m	100				

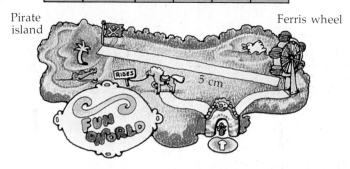

Pirate island   Ferris wheel

5 cm

2.  2 T-shirts cost $5.
   How much would
   8 shirts cost?

shirts	2				
dollars	5				

3.  3 space shows take
   2 hours. How many can
   be shown in 10 hours?

shows ~~seconds~~	3				
hours	2				

4. 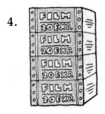 1 roll of film takes
   20 pictures. How many
   pictures will 4 rolls
   take?

rolls of film	1				
pictures	20				

5.  3 helium balloons cost
   75 cents. How much
   would 12 balloons cost?

balloons	3				
cents	75				

Equal ratios problems

A distance of 2 cm on the globe
represents 833 km. The distance from
Chicago to Paris on the globe is 16 cm.
About how many kilometers is it from
Chicago to Paris?

Finding the answer

When the ratios are equal, the cross products are equal.

Write an equation with equal ratios	→	Find the cross products	→	Divide to find n

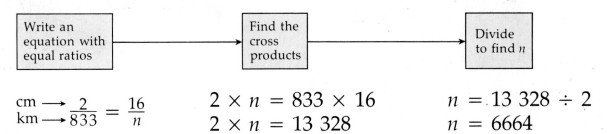

cm $\longrightarrow \dfrac{2}{833} = \dfrac{16}{n}$ $\longleftarrow$ km

$2 \times n = 833 \times 16$
$2 \times n = 13\ 328$

$n = 13\ 328 \div 2$
$n = 6664$

It is about 6664 km from Chicago to Paris.

Other examples

$\dfrac{3}{5} = \dfrac{n}{200}$

$5 \times n = 3 \times 200$
$n = 600 \div 5$
$n = 120$

$\dfrac{n}{12} = \dfrac{10}{30}$

$30 \times n = 12 \times 10$
$n = 120 \div 30$
$n = 4$

$\dfrac{15}{n} = \dfrac{75}{60}$

$75 \times n = 15 \times 60$
$n = 900 \div 75$
$n = 12$

Find the number for n.

1. $\dfrac{2}{5} = \dfrac{n}{30}$

2. $\dfrac{3}{10} = \dfrac{24}{n}$

3. $\dfrac{5}{n} = \dfrac{23}{69}$

4. $\dfrac{1}{7} = \dfrac{28}{n}$

5. $\dfrac{n}{17} = \dfrac{9}{51}$

6. $\dfrac{4}{n} = \dfrac{32}{24}$

7. $\dfrac{3}{8} = \dfrac{n}{56}$

8. $\dfrac{3}{7} = \dfrac{21}{n}$

Solve.

1 cm on the map represents 95 km
on the road. Solve the equations
to find the actual distances.

Sacramento

San
Francisco

Las
Vegas

San Luis
Obispo

Los Angeles

San Diego

1. San Francisco to San Luis Obispo

   Map distance: 2.5 cm

   $$\text{cm} \rightarrow \frac{1}{95} = \frac{2.5}{n} \begin{array}{l} \leftarrow \text{map distance} \\ \leftarrow \text{actual distance} \end{array}$$
   $\text{km} \rightarrow$

2. San Luis Obispo to Los Angeles

   Map distance: 2 cm $\frac{1}{95} = \frac{2}{n}$

3. Sacramento to Las Vegas

   Map distance: 5 cm $\frac{1}{95} = \frac{5}{n}$

4. Los Angeles to San Diego

   Map distance: 1.5 cm $\frac{1}{95} = \frac{1.5}{n}$

Write and solve an equation for each problem.

5. The electric cars used in the early 1900's
   could go about 32 km in 1 hour. At that
   rate, how far could they go in 5 hours?

6. The first steam-powered car could travel
   only 5 km each hour. How many hours
   would it take that car to travel 120 km?

☆ 7. The diameter of the earth at the equator
   is about 40 000 km. Use a string to find this
   distance in centimeters on a globe. Then use
   the information to find the scale: 1 cm = ▓ km.
   Now use the string to estimate the distance
   between some pairs of cities.

Time yourself to find
out how many words
you can read in 1 minute.
Estimate the number of
words on a page. About
how long would it take
you to read a book with
365 pages?

More practice, page 392, Set A

Equal ratios in similar triangles

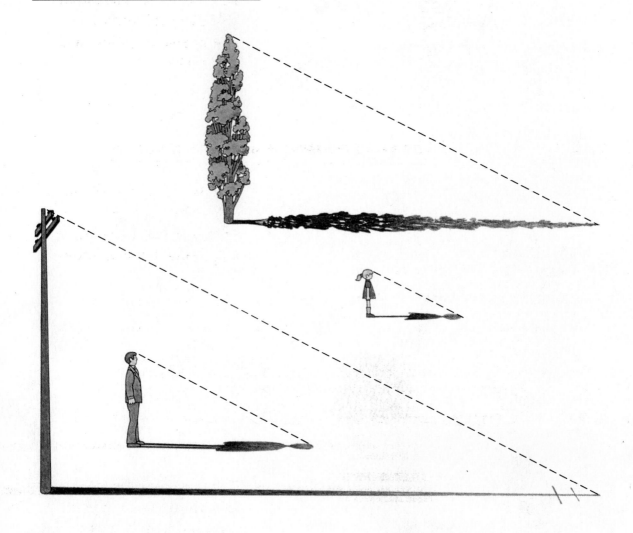

The objects and their shadows suggest
similar triangles. The ratios of the
corresponding sides of similar triangles
are equal.

Solve the problems.

1. The girl is 1 m tall.
   Her shadow is 2 m long.
   The man is 2 m tall.
   How long is his shadow?

2. The telephone pole is
   6 m tall. How long is
   the telephone pole's
   shadow?

3. The tree's shadow is 8 m long. How tall is the tree?

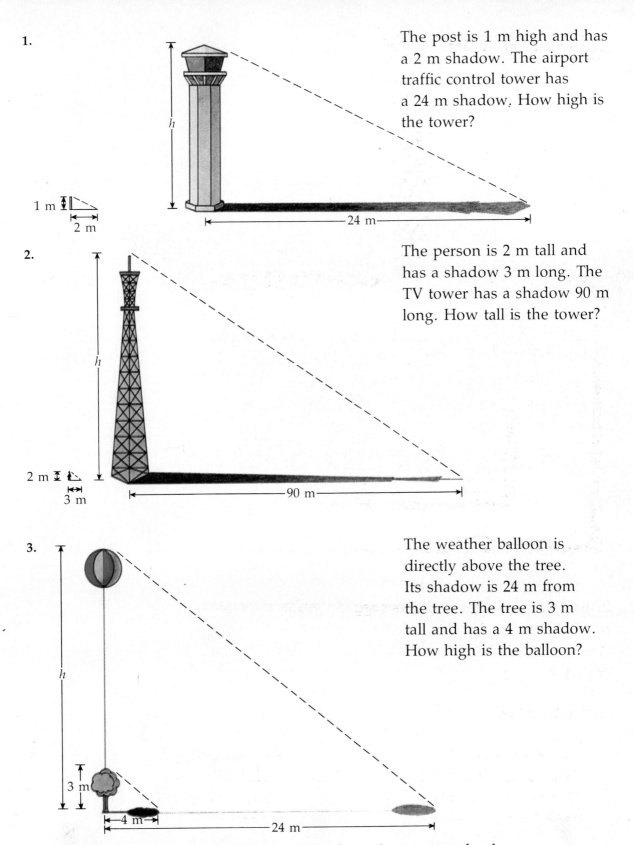

1. The post is 1 m high and has a 2 m shadow. The airport traffic control tower has a 24 m shadow. How high is the tower?

1 m

2 m

24 m

2. The person is 2 m tall and has a shadow 3 m long. The TV tower has a shadow 90 m long. How tall is the tower?

h

2 m

3 m

90 m

3. The weather balloon is directly above the tree. Its shadow is 24 m from the tree. The tree is 3 m tall and has a 4 m shadow. How high is the balloon?

h

3 m

4 m

24 m

★ **4.** Use equal ratios to find the height of a flagpole at your school.

⊛ The number π—an important ratio

The ratio of the circumference (C) of a circle to the diameter (d) of that circle is an important ratio.

A ring has a circumference of 6.27 cm and a diameter of 2 cm. What is the decimal for this ratio $\left(\frac{C}{d}\right)$ to the nearest hundredth?

Finding the answer

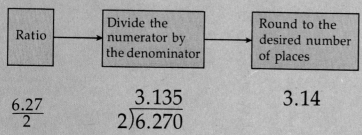

$$\frac{6.27}{2} \qquad \begin{array}{r} 3.135 \\ 2\overline{)6.270} \end{array} \qquad 3.14$$

The decimal for the ratio $\frac{C}{d}$ is about 3.14.

Find the ratio $\frac{C}{d}$ as a decimal to the nearest hundredth for each object.

	Object	Circumference C (cm)	Diameter d (cm)	$\frac{C}{d}$ (as a decimal)
1.	bracelet	22	7	▨
2.	record	94.3	30	▨
3.	rim of a bowl	59.7	19	▨
4.	bike wheel	207	66	▨

The circumference of each circle is given. Measure the diameter to the nearest centimeter and find $\frac{C}{d}$ to the nearest hundredth.

1.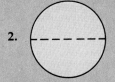

C = 3.14 cm

2.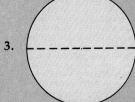

C = 6.28 cm

3.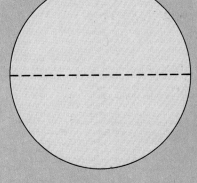

C = 9.42 cm

4.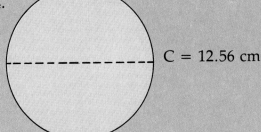

C = 12.56 cm

5.

C = 15.7 cm

6.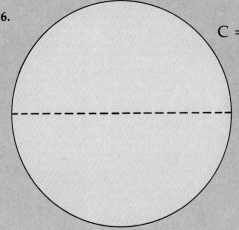

C = 18.85 cm

$$\frac{C}{d} = \pi \qquad \text{(the Greek letter pi, pronounced ''pie'')}$$

The decimal for the number π has been computed to over 500 000 decimal places.

$$\pi = 3.141592653589 \ldots$$

☆ **7.** Measure the circumference and diameter of several circular objects and find $\frac{C}{d}$. Is $\frac{C}{d}$ close to π for your measurements?

A rope 50 meters long was needed to encircle one of the world's largest trees. What was the diameter of a cross section of the tree trunk?

Answers for Self-check   **1.**

tickets	2	4	6	8	10
dollars	5	10	15	20	25

2. $25   **3.** 92   **4.** $4.32   **5.** 6 m   **6.** 3.14

Self-check

1. Copy and complete this table of equal ratios.

tickets	2	4	▦	▦	▦
dollars	5	10	▦	▦	▦

2. Use the table above to find the cost of 10 tickets.

3. Find the number for n. $\frac{4}{23} = \frac{16}{n}$

4. 1 ℓ of milk costs $0.36. How much for 12 ℓ?

5.

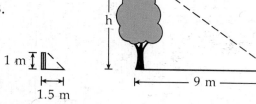

A 1 m post has a 1.5 m shadow. How tall is a tree that has a 9 m shadow?

6. Give the ratio $\frac{C}{d}$ for this circle as a decimal to the nearest hundredth.

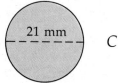

21 mm $C = 66$ mm

Answers for Self-check—page 263

Test

1. Copy and complete this table of equal ratios.

cans of orange juice	1	2	▦	▦	▦
cans of water	3	6	▦	▦	▦

2. How many cans of water are needed for 4 cans of juice?

3. A car travels 250 km in 5 hours. At that rate, how far does it travel in 8 hours? $\frac{250}{5} = \frac{n}{8}$

4. If 2 candy bars cost $0.25, how much would 12 candy bars cost?

5.

8 m

12 m h 3 m

The 8 m post has a 12 m shadow. How tall is the post that has a 3 m shadow?

6. Give the ratio $\frac{C}{d}$ for a circle with diameter 7 cm and circumference 22 cm as a decimal to the nearest hundredth.

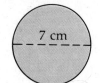

7 cm $C = 22$ cm

Folds and Cuts

Fold a square piece of paper three times,
the last time along the diagonal.
Then cut off a corner.

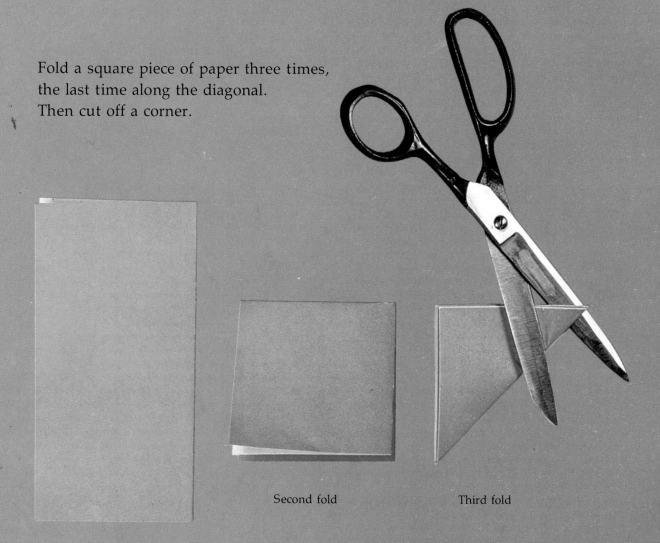

First fold

Second fold

Third fold

Can you cut off a corner so that when
you unfold the cut-off piece it is a square?
An octagon? A four-pointed star?

Try to make some other interesting shapes
by folding and cutting.

Percent

Getting started

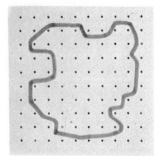

Estimate how many of the 100 dots in each square are inside the loop. Then count to check your estimate.

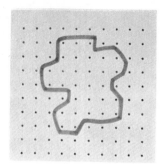

When we want to compare a number with 100, we often use percent.
Percent means per hundred.

We see:

We write:

ratio	fraction	decimal	percent
50 to 100	$\frac{50}{100}$	0.50	50%

We read: fifty percent

Write the missing ratio, fraction, decimal, or percent.

1.

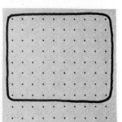

ratio	fraction	decimal	percent
25 to 100	$\frac{25}{100}$	0.25	▓

2.

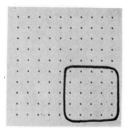

ratio	fraction	decimal	percent
80 to 100	▓	▓	▓

3.

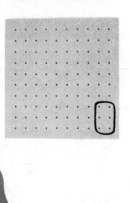

ratio	fraction	decimal	percent
▓ to 100	▓	▓	6%

Write each decimal as a percent.

4. 0.45   **5.** 0.28   **6.** 0.33

7. 0.99   **8.** 0.05   **9.** 0.75

Writing fractions and decimals as percents

A poll showed that $\frac{3}{4}$ of the students think the class president is doing a good job. What percent of the students think the class president is doing a good job?

Finding the answer

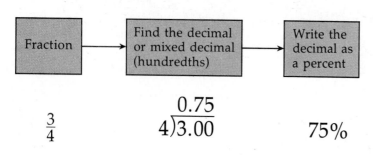

| Fraction | → | Find the decimal or mixed decimal (hundredths) | → | Write the decimal as a percent |

$$\frac{3}{4} \qquad \begin{array}{r} 0.75 \\ 4\overline{)3.00} \end{array} \qquad 75\%$$

75% of the students think the class president is doing a good job.

Other examples

$$\frac{2}{5} \longrightarrow \begin{array}{r} 0.40 \\ 5\overline{)2.00} \end{array} \longrightarrow 40\%$$

$$\frac{4}{3} \longrightarrow \begin{array}{r} 1.33\frac{1}{3} \\ 3\overline{)4.00} \end{array} \longrightarrow 133\frac{1}{3}\%$$

$$\frac{1}{16} \longrightarrow \begin{array}{r} 0.06\frac{4}{16} \\ 16\overline{)1.00} \end{array} \longrightarrow 0.06\frac{1}{4} \longrightarrow 6\frac{1}{4}\%$$

Write a percent for each fraction.

1. $\frac{1}{2}$ 2. $\frac{1}{4}$ 3. $\frac{1}{5}$ 4. $\frac{1}{10}$ 5. $\frac{1}{20}$ 6. $\frac{3}{25}$

7. $\frac{3}{50}$ 8. $\frac{3}{5}$ 9. $\frac{7}{10}$ 10. $\frac{7}{20}$ 11. $\frac{4}{5}$ 12. $\frac{7}{25}$

Write a percent for each fraction.

1. $\frac{5}{8}$ 2. $\frac{1}{6}$ 3. $\frac{3}{8}$ 4. $\frac{5}{6}$ 5. $\frac{1}{3}$ 6. $\frac{2}{3}$

7. $\frac{7}{8}$ 8. $\frac{15}{24}$ 9. $\frac{17}{25}$ 10. $\frac{1}{12}$ 11. $\frac{3}{16}$ 12. $\frac{6}{8}$

13. $\frac{4}{8}$ 14. $\frac{6}{5}$ 15. $\frac{7}{4}$ 16. $\frac{5}{3}$ 17. $\frac{21}{34}$ 18. $\frac{9}{8}$

19. Copy the table. Give the missing decimals and percents.

Fraction	Decimal	Percent
$\frac{1}{10}$	0.10	▨
$\frac{1}{8}$	▨	$12\frac{1}{2}\%$
$\frac{1}{6}$	$0.16\frac{2}{3}$	▨
$\frac{1}{5}$	▨	▨
$\frac{1}{4}$	▨	▨
$\frac{1}{3}$	▨	▨
$\frac{1}{2}$	▨	▨

20. 16 of the 25 students in a class ride a bus to school. What percent of the students ride a bus to school?

☆ 21. Choose a question that interests you and take a poll of your class. Use percent to report the results.

Each page of a book has 100 rows with 50 dots in each row. The book contains 1 million dots. How many pages are there in the book?

More practice, page 392, Set B

Writing percents as decimals and fractions

Greenland is the world's largest island. It is about 25% of the size of the United States (not including Alaska and Hawaii). What fraction of the size of the United States is Greenland?

Finding the answer

Write the percent as a decimal	Write the decimal as a fraction	Write the fraction in lowest terms (if desired)

$$25\% = 0.25 \qquad\qquad \frac{25}{100} \qquad\qquad \frac{1}{4}$$

Greenland is about $\frac{1}{4}$ the size of the United States.

Other examples

$$5\% = 0.05 = \frac{5}{100} = \frac{1}{20}$$

$$12\tfrac{1}{2}\% = 0.12\tfrac{1}{2} = 0.125 = \frac{125}{1000} = \frac{1}{8}$$

$$125\% = 1.25 = \frac{125}{100} = \frac{5}{4} \text{ or } 1\tfrac{1}{4}$$

Write a decimal and a lowest-terms fraction for each percent.

1. 10% 2. 50% 3. 20% 4. 75% 5. 80%

6. 15% 7. 40% 8. 90% 9. 60% 10. 45%

Write a decimal and a lowest-terms fraction for each percent.

1. 4%
2. 2%
3. 6%
4. 8%
5. 7%

6. $37\frac{1}{2}$%
7. $62\frac{1}{2}$%
8. $87\frac{1}{2}$%
9. $22\frac{1}{2}$%
10. $27\frac{1}{2}$%

11. 110%
12. 120%
13. 175%
14. 105%
15. 145%

16. 30%
17. $24\frac{1}{2}$%
18. 70%
19. 5%
20. 150%

21. Baffin Island is about 30% of the size of Greenland. Write this percent as a decimal and as a lowest-terms fraction.

22. Australia is about 350% of the size of Greenland. Write this percent as a decimal and as a lowest-terms fraction.

It takes the planet Mercury 88 of our days to travel around the sun; therefore, a "year" on Mercury is 88 of our days. If a person is 10 years old, what is his age in Mercury years? Use 365 days for a year on the earth.

Practicing your skills

Add, subtract, multiply, or divide.

1. 3719
+ 8387

2. 5014
− 3766

3. 2.19
+ 0.87

4. 8.45
− 5.76

5. $\frac{2}{3}$
$+ \frac{1}{4}$

6. $\frac{5}{6}$
$- \frac{3}{8}$

7. 735
× 64

8. 3.59
× 6.8

9. $\frac{3}{5} \times \frac{2}{3}$

10. $\frac{7}{8} \times 3$

11. $8\overline{)2592}$
12. $36\overline{)2097}$
13. $\frac{3}{4} \div \frac{1}{4}$
14. $\frac{1}{2} \div \frac{4}{5}$
15. $3 \div \frac{1}{6}$

More practice, page 392, Set C

Finding a percent of a number

About 16% of all the trees that are cut down are used to make paper. Out of every 150 trees that are cut down, about how many are used to make paper?

Finding the answer

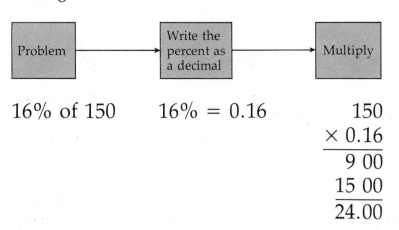

Problem	→	Write the percent as a decimal	→	Multiply

16% of 150   16% = 0.16

$$\begin{array}{r} 150 \\ \times\ 0.16 \\ \hline 9\ 00 \\ 15\ 00 \\ \hline 24.00 \end{array}$$

About 24 of the trees are used to make paper.

Other examples

25% of 280

$0.25 \times 280 = 70$

$12\frac{1}{2}\%$ of 336

$0.125 \times 336 = 42$

110% of 500

$1.10 \times 500 = 550$

Find the products.

1. 10% of 90
2. 75% of 240
3. 60% of 300
4. 15% of 500

5. $37\frac{1}{2}\%$ of 72
6. 40% of 45
7. 25% of 824
8. 1% of 1080

9. 6% of 650
10. 50% of 945
11. $12\frac{1}{2}\%$ of 96
12. 125% of 48

Solve.

1. 12% of 75

2. 5% of 1200

3. 20% of 125

4. 8% of 450

5. 150% of 300

6. $87\frac{1}{2}$% of 200

7. 11% of 250

8. $12\frac{1}{2}$% of 500

9. 120% of 1000

10. 50% of 1450

11. 4% of 2500

12. $5\frac{1}{2}$% of 600

13. About 10% of all the trees that are cut down are used as fuel. Out of every 750 trees that are cut down, about how many are used as fuel?

14. The lumber and building industries use about 62% of all the trees that are cut down. Out of every 400 trees that are cut down, about how many are used by the lumber and building industries?

☆ 15. About 67% of a person's body mass is water. About how many kilograms of your mass is water?

The average person's eye blinks about 25 times a minute. If a person is awake 15 hours a day, how many times does the person's eye blink in a year?

More practice, page 393, Set A

✪ Shortcuts with percent

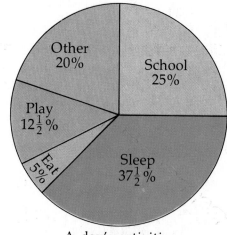

A student spends about 25% of a day in school. About how many hours is the student in school?

Play $12\frac{1}{2}$%

Other 20%

School 25%

Eat 5%

Sleep $37\frac{1}{2}$%

A day's activities
(24 hours)

Finding the answer

25% of 24

You could use this method:

$$\begin{array}{r} 24 \\ \times\ 0.25 \\ \hline 1\ 20 \\ 4\ 80 \\ \hline 6.00 \end{array}$$

Here is a shortcut:

25% of 24

$$\frac{1}{4} \times 24 = \frac{24}{4} = 6$$

The student is in school about 6 hours.

Other examples

50% of 140

$$\frac{1}{2} \times 140 = \frac{140}{2} = 70$$

10% of 90

$$\frac{1}{10} \times 90 = \frac{90}{10} = 9$$

$33\frac{1}{3}$% of 150

$$\frac{1}{3} \times 150 = \frac{150}{3} = 50$$

Solve.

1. 25% of 12

2. 50% of 28

3. 10% of 160

4. 50% of 84

5. 25% of 28

6. $33\frac{1}{3}$% of 15

7. 10% of 70

8. $33\frac{1}{3}$% of 24

9. 50% of 124

10. 25% of 48

11. 10% of 610

12. 25% of 36

13. $33\frac{1}{3}$% of 18

14. 50% of 480

15. 10% of 780

Solve.

Examples: 20% of 45

$$\frac{1}{5} \times 45 = \frac{45}{5} = 9$$

5% of 40

$$\frac{1}{20} \times 40 = \frac{40}{20} = 2$$

1. 20% of 25
2. 20% of 500
3. 20% of 95
4. 50% of 16
5. 25% of 8
6. 10% of 120
7. 25% of 64
8. 50% of 6842
9. $33\frac{1}{3}$% of 39
10. 10% of 3800
11. 20% of 150
12. 50% of 12 860
13. $33\frac{1}{3}$% of 9000
14. 20% of 125
15. 5% of 200

Solve these problems about the information shown on the circle graph.

16. How many students prefer ice cream?

17. How many prefer cake?

18. How many prefer cake or other desserts?

19. How many prefer pie or ice cream?

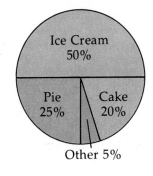

Favorite Desserts of 120 Students

☆ 20. 24 students were asked to name their favorite kind of TV show. According to the graph, how many students liked each kind?

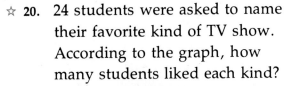
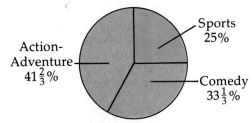

Here are the seven pieces of the tangram puzzle put together to form a square.

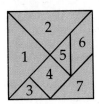

☆ 21. Conduct a poll of 24 students. Compare the results of your poll with the results shown above.

Find the percent of the large square that is covered by each piece.

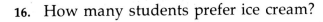

Answers for Self-check 1. 25% 2. 10% 3. 20% 4. $37\frac{1}{2}$% 5. $66\frac{2}{3}$% 6. 120% 7. $\frac{2}{5}$ 8. $\frac{3}{4}$ 9. $\frac{1}{8}$
10. $\frac{5}{4}$ or $1\frac{1}{4}$ 11. $\frac{1}{25}$ 12. 12 13. 18 14. 42 15. 11.34 kg

More practice, page 393, Set B

Self-check

Write a percent for each fraction.

1. $\frac{1}{4}$
2. $\frac{1}{10}$
3. $\frac{1}{5}$
4. $\frac{3}{8}$
5. $\frac{2}{3}$
6. $\frac{6}{5}$

Write each percent as a lowest-terms fraction.

7. 40%
8. 75%
9. $12\frac{1}{2}\%$
10. 125%
11. 4%

Solve.

12. 30% of 40
13. 15% of 120
14. 175% of 24

15. About 18% of the body mass is bone. What is the mass of bone for a person with a body mass of 63 kg?

Answers for Self-check—page 275

Test

Write a percent for each fraction.

1. $\frac{1}{8}$
2. $\frac{1}{2}$
3. $\frac{1}{3}$
4. $\frac{4}{5}$
5. $\frac{3}{4}$
6. $\frac{9}{6}$

Write each percent as a lowest-terms fraction.

7. 60%
8. $37\frac{1}{2}\%$
9. 25%
10. 5%
11. 110%

Solve.

12. 35% of 635
13. 6% of 580
14. 145% of 64

15. There are 25 students in a class.
24% of the students wear glasses.
How many of the students wear glasses?

The Tower of Hanoi Puzzle

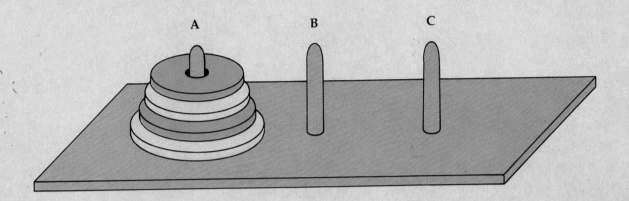

Move the four discs from peg A to one of the other pegs.

Rules:
1. You can only move a top disc, and only one disc at a time.
2. You cannot place a larger disc on top of a smaller one.

To solve the puzzle you might stack four different-sized cardboard discs (or use a quarter, nickel, penny, and dime), from largest to smallest, on square A.

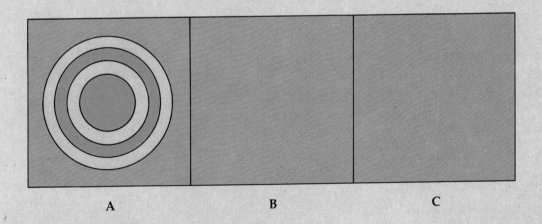

Following the rules of the game, how many moves do you need to move all of the discs to square B or square C?

Using Your Skills

Facts about Our Class

Ratio of boys to girls: 3 to 5

Ratio of left-handers to right-handers: 1 to 6

25% of the students wear glasses.

$87\frac{1}{2}$% of the students are 12 years old.

75% of the students take a bus to school.

$33\frac{1}{3}$% of the students were born in our city.

Getting started

1. There are 9 boys in the class. How many girls are there? How many students are there in all?

2. How many students in the class are 12 years old?

3. What other problems can you solve?

One way to see if your answer makes sense is to compare it with an estimate of the answer.

Estimate to see if these answers make sense. If the answer is wrong, give the correct answer.

1. A school has 250 students. 18% of them are left-handed. How many are left-handed? (Answer: 45)

   Estimate hint: 18% is almost 20% or $\frac{1}{5}$.

2. On Saturday night, 240 people attended the school play. 35% of them were students. How many students attended?

(Answer: 60)
Estimate hint: 35% is a little more than $33\frac{1}{3}\%$ or $\frac{1}{3}$.

3. A class has 25 students. 12% of the students ride a bicycle to school. How many ride a bicycle? (Answer: 6)

4. The school lunchroom has 150 chairs. 32% of them are empty. How many of the chairs are empty? (Answer: 48)

Ratio—fact and fantasy

Fact: The ratio of a mouse's mass to the mass of food it eats each day is 2 to 1.

Fantasy: What if this ratio were the same for humans?

1. How many kilograms of food would a person whose mass is 72 kg eat each day?

$$\text{body mass} \longrightarrow \frac{2}{1} = \frac{72}{n} \longleftarrow \text{food mass}$$

2. How many kilograms of food would you eat each day?

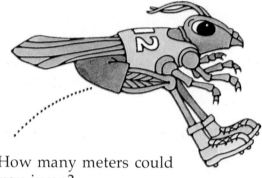

Fact: The ratio of a grasshopper's length to the distance it can jump is 1 to 20.

Fantasy: What if this ratio were the same for humans?

3. How many meters could a person 1.7 m tall jump?

$$\text{height or length} \longrightarrow \frac{1}{20} = \frac{1.7}{n} \longleftarrow \text{distance jumped}$$

4. How many meters could you jump?

Fact: The ratio of a cat's mass to its number of heartbeats per minute is 3 to 40.

Fantasy: What if this ratio were the same for humans?

5. How many heartbeats per minute would this be for a 66 kg person?

$$\text{body mass} \longrightarrow \frac{3}{40} = \frac{66}{n} \longleftarrow \text{heartbeats}$$

6. How many heartbeats per minute would this be for you?

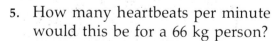

Fact: The ratio of an ant's mass to the mass it can lift is 1 to 50.

Fantasy: What if this ratio were the same for humans?

7. How many kilograms could a person whose mass is 70 kg lift?

8. How many kilograms could you lift?

Fact: The ratio of the mass a bee can pull on wheels to its body mass is 300 to 1.

Fantasy: What if this ratio were the same for humans?

9. How many kilograms could a person whose mass is 76 kg pull?

10. How many kilograms could you pull?

Fact: The ratio of a fly's mass when dry to its mass when wet is 1 to 2.

Fantasy: What if this ratio were the same for humans?

11. What would be the mass of a 56 kg person when wet?

12. What would be your mass when wet?

✪ Scale drawings

In these drawings, 2 cm represents 1 m. We write: Scale: 2 cm = 1 m

Measure to the nearest tenth of a centimeter.
Then use equal ratios to find the height or length
of each animal.

Example: Dolphin

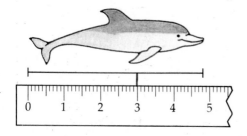

$$\begin{matrix} \text{cm} \\ \text{m} \end{matrix} \quad \frac{2}{1} = \frac{4.8}{n}$$

$2 \times n = 4.8 \qquad n = 2.4$

1. Sea otter

2. Emperor penguin

3. Leatherback turtle

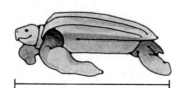

4. Sea lion

5. Salt water crocodile

6. Killer whale

This map is drawn to scale. Scale: 1 cm = 25 m

Measure the dot-to-dot distances on the map
(to the nearest tenth of a centimeter).
Then use equal ratios to find the actual distances.

1. How far must you walk to get from the entrance to the turtles?

$$\begin{array}{c} \text{cm} \longrightarrow \\ \text{m} \longrightarrow \end{array} \frac{1}{25} = \frac{5.5}{n} \qquad n = \text{▥}$$

2. How far is it from the turtles straight to the sea lions?

How far is it from

3. the sea lions to the dolphins?

4. the walrus to the killer whale?

5. the penguins to the polar bears?

6. the dolphins to the crocodiles?

7. How far is it from the entrance to the otters, if you visit each attraction?

Finding interest

Banks and savings companies pay their customers **interest** on the money deposited in savings accounts. If a bank pays 5% per year interest, how much interest would it pay on $145 deposited in an account for one year?

Finding the answer

Rate of interest × Amount of savings = Interest

$\quad$ 5% $\qquad$ × $\qquad$ $145 $\qquad$ = $\quad$ n

$$\begin{array}{r} \$\ 145 \\ \times\ 0.05 \\ \hline \$\ 7.25 \end{array}$$

The interest on $145 for one year at a rate of 5% per year is $7.25.

Find the interest for one year on the following amounts.

1. Amount of savings: $500
   Rate of interest: 4%
   Interest: ▧

2. Amount of savings: $250
   Rate of interest: 4.5%
   Interest: ▧

3. Amount of savings: $2000
   Rate of interest: 5%
   Interest: ▧

4. Amount of savings: $3500
   Rate of interest: 6%
   Interest: ▧

When you borrow money, you have to pay interest.

Find the interest for one year on the following amounts.

Example: Amount borrowed: $100

Rate of interest: 12%

Interest: ▓

$ 100
× 0.12
$12.00

1. Amount borrowed: $1000

   Rate of interest: 8%

   Interest: ▓

2. Amount borrowed: $50

   Rate of interest: 14%

   Interest: ▓

3. Amount borrowed: $25 000

   Rate of interest: 7%

   Interest: ▓

4. Amount borrowed: $375

   Rate of interest: 12%

   Interest: ▓

5. Amount borrowed: $500

   Rate of interest: 9%

   Interest: ▓

6. Amount borrowed: $150

   Rate of interest: 12%

   Interest: ▓

7. Amount borrowed: $1200

   Rate of interest: 12.5%

   Interest: ▓

8. Amount borrowed: $625

   Rate of interest: 8.4%

   Interest: ▓

Solve.

☆ 9. A person borrowed $3000 for six months. The interest rate was 12% per year. What was the amount of interest for six months?

☆ 10. Find the interest rate a local bank pays on savings and the rate they charge for loans. Make up and solve some problems using these rates.

Astronauts get to the moon and back i. a few days. Suppose you could drive there at 95 km per hour. If you made no stops, how long would it take to get there and back? (Use a one-way distance of 400 000 km.)

Finding discounts and sale prices

REGULAR PRICE
$65.⁰⁰

How much discount (amount off) would you get if you bought this clock radio on sale?

What would the sale price of the clock radio be?

SALE
20% OFF

Finding the answer

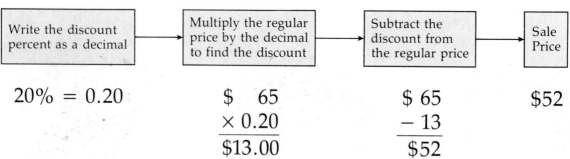

Write the discount percent as a decimal	Multiply the regular price by the decimal to find the discount	Subtract the discount from the regular price	Sale Price

$$20\% = 0.20$$

$$\begin{array}{r} \$ \ 65 \\ \times \ 0.20 \\ \hline \$13.00 \end{array}$$

$$\begin{array}{r} \$ \ 65 \\ - \ 13 \\ \hline \$52 \end{array}$$

$52

The discount would be $13. The sale price would be $52.

Other examples

Price $40, discount 10%

$40 × 0.10 = $4 ⟵ discount

$40 − $4 = $36 ⟵ sale price

Price $125, discount 15%

$125 × 0.15 = $18.75 ⟵ discount

$125 − $18.75 = $106.25 ⟵ sale price

Find the discount and sale price.

1. hair dryer: $24—25% off

2. wrist watch: $35—20% off

3. movie camera: $150—20% off

4. digital clock: $20—15% off

5. guitar: $40—40% off

6. bicycle speedometer: $12—25% off

Find the sale price of each item.

1.

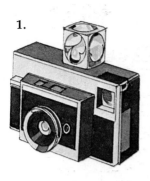

Regular price: $20
Sale price: 25% off

4.

Regular price: $24
Sale price: 15% off

7.

Regular price: $12
Sale price: 10% off

2.

Regular price: $18
Sale price: 15% off

5.

Regular price: $44
Sale price: 25% off

8.

Regular price: $25
Sale price: 20% off

3.

Regular price: $16
Sale price: 5% off

6.

Regular price: $195
Sale price: 30% off

9.

Regular price: $85.50
Sale price: 20% off

1. A baseball player went to bat 420 times during the season. 30% of the times he went to bat he got a hit. How many hits did he get?

2. The weather forecaster says there is a 10% chance of rain on Monday, a 50% chance of rain on Tuesday, and an 80% chance of rain on Wednesday.
On which day is it least likely to rain?
On which day is it most likely to rain?

3. Each serving of a cereal gives you 8% of the protein you need each day. You need about 65 g of protein a day. How many grams of protein do you get from a serving of cereal?

4. 10% of each can of punch is pure grape juice. How many milliliters of pure grape juice are there in a 1000 ml can?

5. A school has 340 students. 15% of the students made the honor roll. How many students made the honor roll?

6. A student spelled 18 out of 20 words on a spelling test correctly. What percent of the words did the student spell correctly?

7. The tennis team's star player won 75% of the matches she played last season. If she played 28 matches, how many did she win?

8. A greeting card company lets the people who sell the cards keep 6% of the money they take in on sales. How much could a person keep from sales of $72?

9. A sales clerk must add 5% sales tax to the cost of the items sold. How much tax should the clerk add on an item that costs $8.80?

10. Whole milk contains about 4% butterfat. How many milliliters of butterfat are there in 900 ml of milk?

11. A bank pays 6% per year interest on savings accounts. How much does it pay on a deposit of $75 left in an account for a year?

12. A family bought a TV set for $350. They paid 25% of the cost when they bought it. How much money was that?

⊛Estimation—percent of error

A student estimated the length of the classroom
to be 9 m. When she measured it, she found
that the length was 10 m. What was the percent
of error of the student's estimate?

Finding the answer

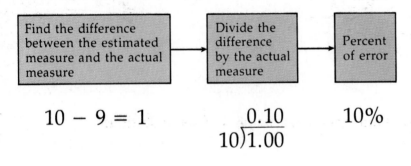

Find the difference between the estimated measure and the actual measure	Divide the difference by the actual measure	Percent of error

$$10 - 9 = 1 \qquad \begin{array}{r} 0.10 \\ 10\overline{)1.00} \end{array} \qquad 10\%$$

The percent of error was 10%.

Another example

Estimated measure: 7 m $8 - 7 = 1$ $\begin{array}{r} 0.125 \\ 8\overline{)1.000} \end{array}$ ⟶ 0.13 ⟶ 13%
Actual measure: 8 m   (nearest hundredth)

Copy and complete this table.

	Distance	Estimated measure	Actual measure	Difference	Percent of error
1.	Length of room	9 m	11 m	▦	▦
2.	Width of room	6 m	7 m	▦	▦
3.	Length of longest hallway in school	55 m	46 m	▦	▦
4.	Outside length of school building	70 m	75 m	▦	▦
5.	Outside width of school building	23 m	30 m	▦	▦

This table shows the estimated and measured heights of some students. Copy and complete the table.

	Estimated height (cm)	Measured height (cm)	Difference	Percent of error
1.	146	153	▦	▦
2.	135	145	▦	▦
3.	150	148	▦	▦
4.	164	159	▦	▦
5.	151	158	▦	▦

☆ 6. Make a table like the one above and estimate the heights of several of your classmates. Then measure to find the actual heights and complete the table.

☆ 7. Make a table like the one on page 290 and estimate the distances for your school building. Then measure the distances and complete the table. (Sometimes you can use floor or ceiling tiles, bricks, or sections of sidewalk to help you estimate distances. Or, if you know the approximate length of your usual step, you can step off the distances and estimate.)

Answers for Self-check   1. 15   2. 36 000 cm   3. 66   4. $12   5. 27.5 m   6. 5%

Self-check

1. The ratio of girls to boys in a class was 5 to 4. There were 12 boys. How many girls were there?

2. The ratio of a flea's length to the distance it can jump is 1 to 200. If this ratio were true for humans, how far could a person 180 cm tall jump?

3. A school has 440 students. 15% of them are absent. How many students are absent?

4. The regular price of a pair of skates is $16. They are on sale at 25% off. What is the sale price?

5. Scale: 1 cm = 5 m

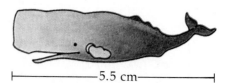

|—————5.5 cm—————|

How long is the actual whale?

☆ 6. Estimated height: 148 cm
Measured height: 156 cm
What is the percent of error of the estimate?

Answers for Self-check—page 291

Test

1. The ratio of men to women at a party is 6 to 7. There are 21 women at the party. How many men are at the party?

2. Suppose the ratio of a person's mass to the amount of food the person needs each day is 2 to 95. How many kilograms of food does a person whose mass is 72 kg need each day?

3. A bank pays 5% per year interest on savings. How much interest does it pay per year on $240?

4. The regular price of a tennis racket is $18. It is on sale at 15% off. What is the sale price?

5. Scale: 1 cm = 10 m

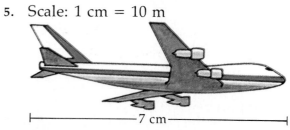

|—————7 cm—————|

How long is the actual jet?

☆ 6. Estimated length of a classroom: 15 m
Measured length of the classroom: 12 m
What is the percent of error of the estimate?

Toothpick Puzzles

1.

Remove 4 toothpicks to leave 5 congruent squares.

2.

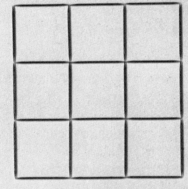

Remove 8 toothpicks to leave 1 large square and 1 smaller square.

3.

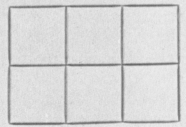

Remove 5 toothpicks to leave 3 congruent squares.

4.

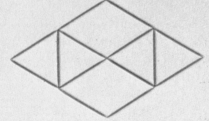

Remove 4 toothpicks, leaving exactly 4 equilateral triangles.

5. This figure has square faces and can be made with 12 toothpicks.

Can you use 6 toothpicks to make a space figure that has triangular faces?
(Use glue or modeling clay to stick the toothpicks together.)

Coordinate Geometry

Getting started

To find the answer to the riddle, match the letters on the grid with the number pairs below.

What did the triangle say to the rhombus after the rhombus straightened up?

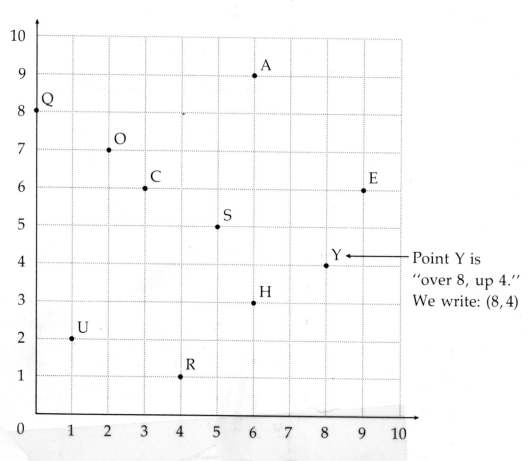

Point Y is "over 8, up 4." We write: (8, 4)

Answer:

Y			A	R	E				
(8,4)	(2,7)	(1,2)	(6,9)	(4,1)	(9,6)	(5,5)	(1,2)	(3,6)	(6,3)

A	F	U	C	K	E	R
(6,9)	(5,5)	(0,8)	(1,2)	(6,9)	(4,1)	(9,6)

The **coordinates** of point A are $\left(2, 5\frac{1}{2}\right)$.

Give the coordinates of each of these points.

1. B 2. C 3. D

4. E 5. F 6. G

7. H 8. I 9. J

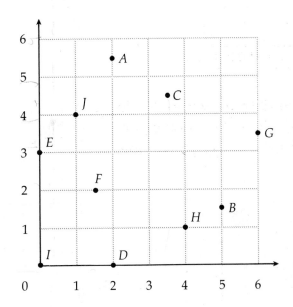

First number

Give the letter for each pair of coordinates.

10. $(1,3)$ 11. $(3,4)$

12. $(2,3)$ 13. $(5,3)$

14. $(1,1)$ 15. $(4,0)$

16. $(0,0)$ 17. $(3,3)$

18. $(2,0)$ 19. $(0,2)$

20. $(1,4)$ 21. $(0,5)$

22. $(2,5)$ 23. $(4,4)$

24. $(2,2)$ 25. $(3,1)$

26. $(4,1)$ 27. $(5,5)$

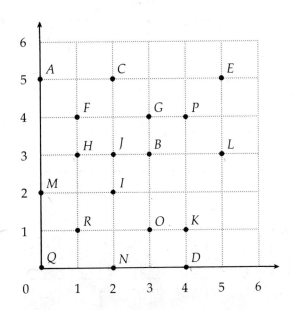

Graphing geometric figures

When the points with the coordinates below are graphed and connected in order, a hexagon is formed.

(3,4), (3,7), (6,9), (9,7), (9,4), (6,2), (3,4)

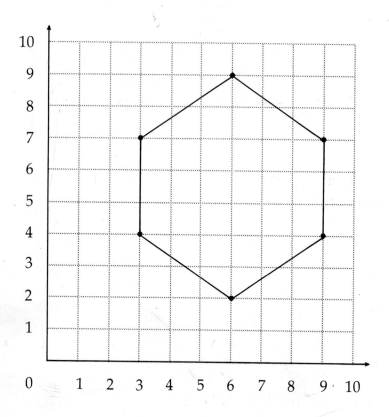

Graph each set of points and connect them, in order, to form a geometric figure.

1. (1,3), (3,8), (5,2), (1,3)

2. (7,5), (5,9), (1,7), (3,3), (7,5)

3. (1,1), (1,3), (6,3), (6,1), (1,1)

4. (5,2), (9,6), (7,8), (3,4), (5,2)

5. (7,8), (6,5), (1,5), (2,8), (7,8)

6. (2,5), (5,7), (8,5), (7,2), (3,2), (2,5)

7. (3,9), (6,9), (8,7), (8,4), (6,2), (3,2), (1,4), (1,7), (3,9)

8. (4,7), (5,9), (7,9), (5,6), (7,3), (5,3), (4,5), (3,3), (1,3), (3,6), (1,9), (3,9), (4,7)

The coordinates for the points at the corners of the rectangle are (2,4), (2,7), (8,7), and (8,4).

The rectangle is 6 units long and 3 units wide.

Perimeter = 3 + 6 + 3 + 6 = 18 units
Area = 3 × 6 = 18 square units

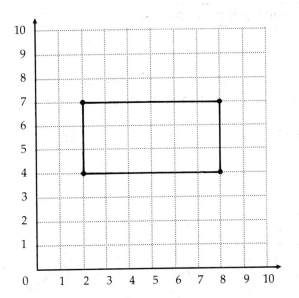

Graph and connect the points in the order given. Then give the perimeter and area of the figure.

1. (1,1), (1,6), (3,6), (3,1), (1,1)

2. (9,9), (9,3), (5,3), (5,9), (9,9)

3. (2,8), (8,8), (8,2), (2,2), (2,8)

4. (0,0), (0,5), (9,5), (9,0), (0,0)

5. (1,2), (1,6), (3,6), (3,4), (6,4), (6,2), (1,2)

6. (4,5), (4,9), (10,9), (10,5), (8,5), (8,7), (6,7), (6,5), (4,5)

Graph each figure. Find its area.

☆ 7. (1,1), (2,4), (5,3), (4,1), (1,1)

☆ 8. (5,2), (9,4), (7,8), (3,6), (5,2)

☆ 9. Invent a figure and give the coordinates, in order, to a classmate. Ask your classmate to graph the figure.

The four corners of a rectangle have these coordinates.
(27,32), (69,32), (69,58), (27,58)
How many units is the perimeter?
How many square units is the area?

Translating figures

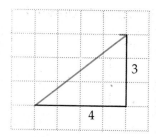

A student made a "point slider" to "slide" each point of rectangle *ABCD* to a new position. Each point was moved "right 4, up 3." The red arrow shows the distance and direction of the slide.

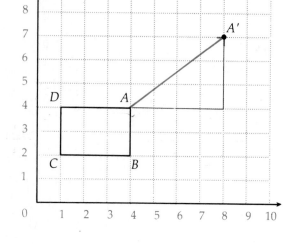

The slide is also called a **translation**. Rectangle *A'B'C'D'* is the **slide image** or **translation image** of rectangle *ABCD*.

On your graph paper, draw rectangle *ABCD* in the position shown here.

Then show the translation image of *ABCD* after each of these translations.

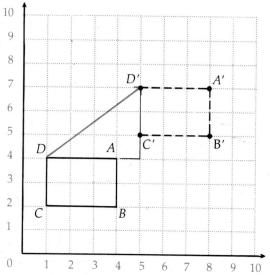

1.

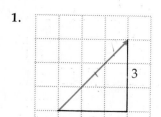

"right 3, up 3"

2.

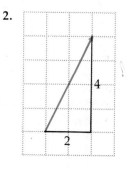

"right 2, up 4"

3.

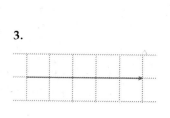

"right 5"

4.

"up 4"

Copy each figure on graph paper.
Draw the translation image of each figure.

1. "right 2, up 3"

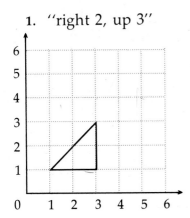

2. "left 3, up 3"

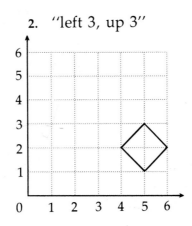

3. "right 4, down 2"

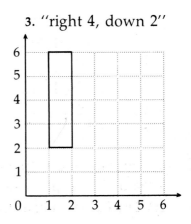

4. "right 2, up 2"

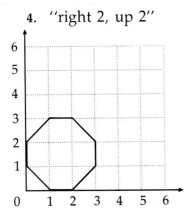

5. "down 4"

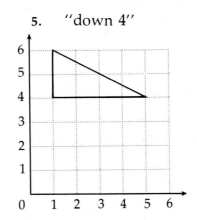

6. "right 3"

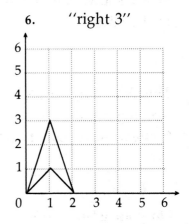

★ **7.** Triangle *A'B'C'* is a translation image of triangle *ABC*. What translation was used?

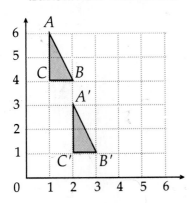

Think!

Give the shortest path along the blue lines to point *C* in the maze by writing, in order, the coordinates of the points where you turn.

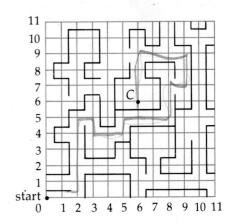

Module 33.5   **299**

A mirror shows a **reflection image**. Suppose the dotted line in each drawing is a mirror. Is the picture on the right a reflection image of the picture on the left?

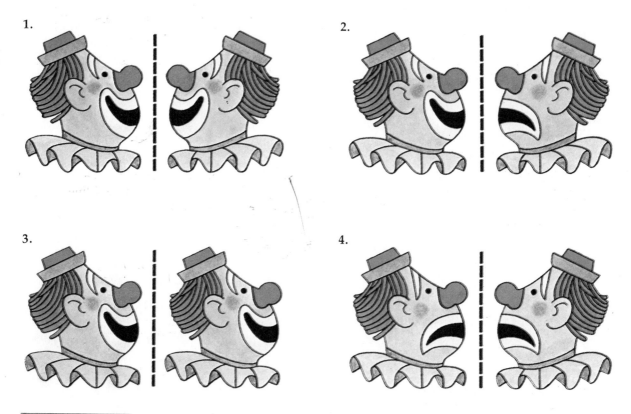

1.

2.

3.

4.

Suppose the dotted line on the grid is a mirror.
Copy each figure. Then show its reflection image.

Example:

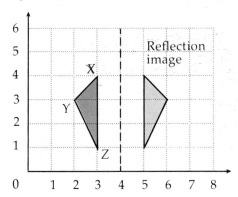

1.

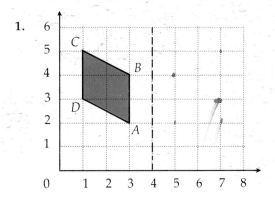

2.

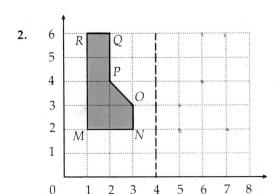

3.

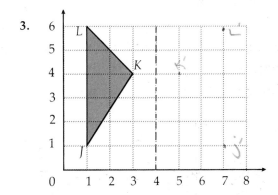

☆ 4. Give the coordinates
of the reflection image
of each figure in
problems 1, 2, and 3.

Is this subtraction
problem correct? Put a
mirror on the dotted line
to check it.

☆ 5. Use a mirror to find out
what this message says.

ⵌⴰⵜⴰⴱ ⵇⵓⴱⵜⵜ ⵡⵜⴰⴱⵓ ?

Write a "mirror message" and
ask a classmate to read it.

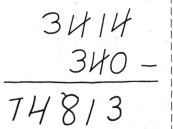

Each pair of coordinates for points A, B, and C
was multiplied by 3. Then the new coordinates
were used to draw the larger triangle.

Point	Coordinates	× 3
A	(1, 1)	(3, 3)
B	(2, 1)	(6, 3)
C	(2, 3)	(6, 9)

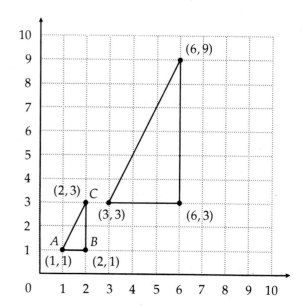

The two triangles have the same shape,
but not the same size.

They are **similar triangles**.

Multiply the coordinates for
points X, Y, and Z by 2.

1. X: (2, 2)

2. Y: (4, 2)

3. Z: (1, 3)

4. Mark the points for the
   new coordinates on
   graph paper and draw
   the triangle for these points.

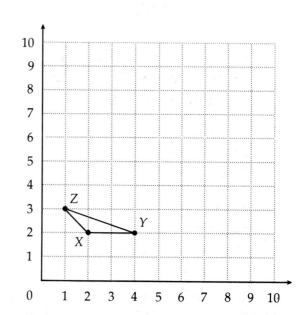

5. Are the two triangles similar?

Copy each figure on graph paper. Then graph a similar
figure by multiplying each of the coordinates by the number given.

1.

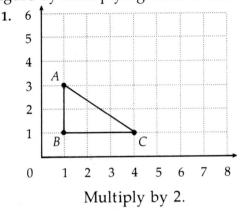

Multiply by 2.

2.

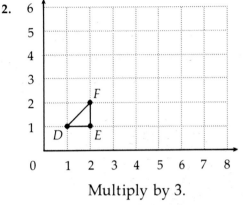

Multiply by 3.

3.

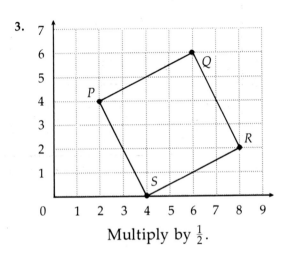

Multiply by $\frac{1}{2}$.

4.

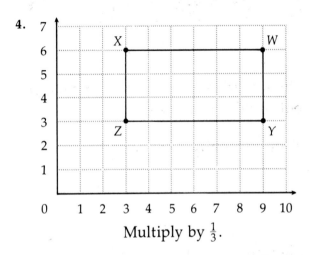

Multiply by $\frac{1}{3}$.

☆ **5.** Draw a figure like this one
on graph paper. Then make a
larger figure that is similar.

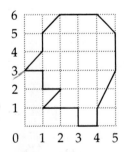

☆ **6.** Trace a favorite cartoon character
or picture on a small grid. Use
a larger grid to make a larger,
similar picture.

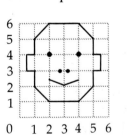
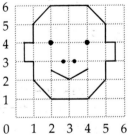

Answers for Self-check 1. (1,3) 2. (1,1) 3. (5,1) 4. (5,3) 5. (3,5) 6. Coordinates of the
reflection image are (0,3), (1,4), (3,0), (1,0). 7. Perimeter—18 units; area—20 square units
8. Coordinates of the translation image are (5,4), (6,5), (7,4), (7,6), (5,6). 9. Coordinates of the
similar figure are (4,6), (6,4), (4,2), (2,4).

Self-check

Give the coordinates of each point.

1. A
2. B
3. C
4. D
5. E

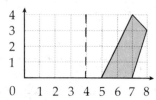

6. Suppose the dotted line is a mirror. Draw the reflection image of the figure on graph paper.

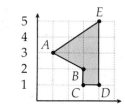

Answers for Self-check—page 303

7. Give the perimeter and the area of the figure formed when these points are graphed and connected in order. (2, 1), (2, 6), (6, 6), (6, 1), (2, 1)

8. Use graph paper to show the translation image for a "right 4, up 3" translation of the figure shown.

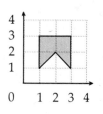

9. Multiply the coordinates by 2. Graph the similar figure on your graph paper.

Test

Give the coordinates of each point.

1. A
2. B
3. C
4. D
5. E

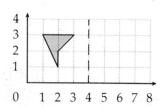

6. Suppose the dotted line is a mirror. Draw the reflection image of the figure on graph paper.

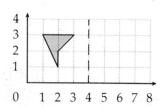

7. Give the perimeter and the area of the figure formed when these points are graphed and connected in order. (1, 2), (4, 2), (4, 5), (1, 5), (1, 2)

8. Use graph paper to show the translation image for a "left 2, down 3" translation.

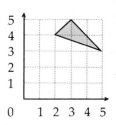

9. Multiply the coordinates by 3. Graph the similar figure on your graph paper.

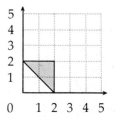

Using Pick's Rule

Pick's Rule

1. Count the nails on the edges of the figure.

2. Divide by 2.

3. Add the number of nails inside the figure.

4. Subtract 1.

You can find the area of any polygon on a geoboard or dot paper by using Pick's Rule. What is the area of this hexagon?

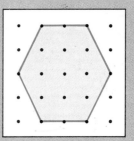

What is the area of each of these polygons?

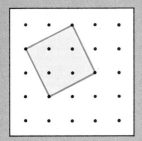
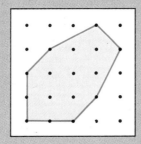
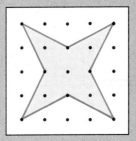

Make some figures of your own on the geoboard or dot paper. Find their areas using Pick's Rule. Check your answers by counting squares or parts of squares.

Level 33 review

Write a decimal for each fraction.

1. $\frac{1}{4}$ **2.** $\frac{1}{2}$ **3.** $\frac{3}{5}$ **4.** $\frac{5}{8}$ **5.** $\frac{3}{20}$ **6.** $\frac{7}{10}$

Write a mixed decimal for each fraction.

7. $\frac{1}{3}$ **8.** $\frac{7}{8}$ **9.** $\frac{1}{6}$ **10.** $\frac{5}{12}$ **11.** $\frac{2}{3}$ **12.** $\frac{1}{16}$

Write the lowest-terms fraction or mixed numeral for each decimal.

13. 0.3   **14.** 2.75   **15.** 0.5   **16.** 1.25   **17.** 0.375

18. Copy and complete this table of equal ratios.

cups of flour	2	4			
cups of milk	3	6			

Find the number for n.

19. $\frac{3}{5} = \frac{n}{20}$ **20.** $\frac{7}{2} = \frac{56}{n}$ **21.** $\frac{n}{4} = \frac{8}{32}$ **22.** $\frac{12}{n} = \frac{54}{9}$

23. A tree 5 m tall has a 15 m shadow. How tall is a tree that has a 12 m shadow?

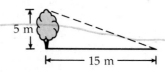 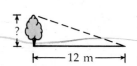

Write a percent for each fraction.

24. $\frac{3}{4}$ **25.** $\frac{9}{10}$ **26.** $\frac{3}{20}$ **27.** $\frac{1}{2}$ **28.** $\frac{2}{5}$ **29.** $\frac{1}{3}$

Write a decimal and a lowest-terms fraction for each percent.

30. 25%   **31.** 80%   **32.** $37\frac{1}{2}$%   **33.** 50%   **34.** 40%

Solve.

35. 10% of 200   **36.** 25% of 320   **37.** 90% of 450   **38.** $33\frac{1}{3}$% of 180

Level **34**

Integers
Probability
Statistics
Large Numbers
Volume

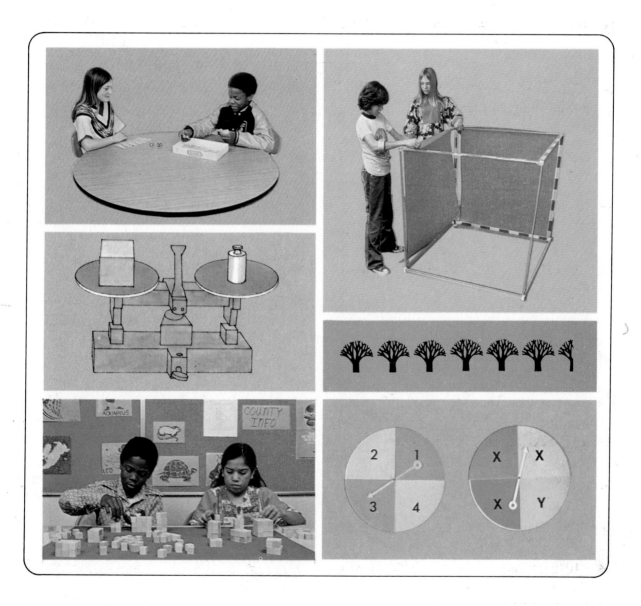

Integers

Getting started

Rules for playing Break the Bank:

1. Two players and the bank start with six dollars each.

Player 1

BANK

Player 2

2. Each player takes a turn tossing a red cube and a green cube. The player then **pays the bank** or **draws out of the bank** according to the toss.

	Toss A		Toss B	
	Pay	Draw	Pay	Draw
Examples:	5	3	2	5

Pay in 2.   Draw out 3.

3. When either player or the bank runs out of money, each player scores the amount of money he or she has at that time.

How much would you pay in or draw out for each of these tosses?

1.

2.

3.

4.

5.

6.

How much money would you be ahead or behind after 3 tosses?

	First toss	Second toss	Third toss

7. → → →

8. → → →

9.  → → →

10. → → →

Positive and negative integers

Integers are numbers that are used to describe things that are the opposite of each other.

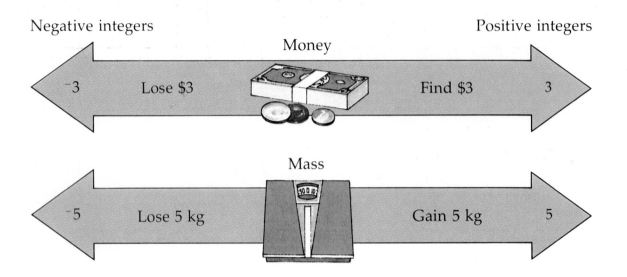

Negative integers
Positive integers

Money

$^-3$ Lose $3   Find $3   3

Mass

$^-5$ Lose 5 kg   Gain 5 kg   5

Give the missing negative integer.

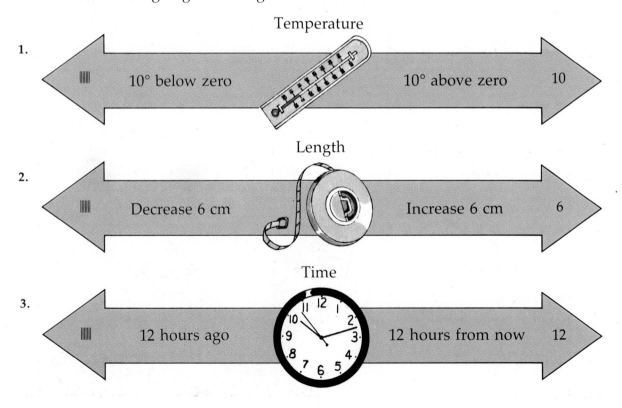

Temperature

1.   10° below zero   10° above zero   10

Length

2.   Decrease 6 cm   Increase 6 cm   6

Time

3.   12 hours ago   12 hours from now   12

1. Study the number line. Then give the missing integers.

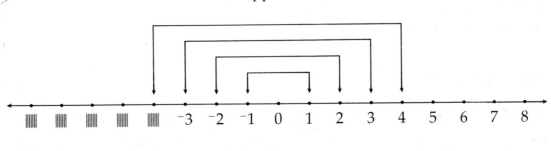

opposites

negative integers   zero   positive integers

Give the missing integer.

2. opposites
    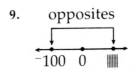
    ▓ 0 2

3. opposites
    ⁻4 0 ▓

4. opposites
    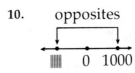
    ▓ 0 7

5. opposites
    ⁻8 0 ▓

6. opposites
    ▓ 0 17

7. opposites
    ⁻1 0 ▓

8. opposites
    ▓ 0 59

9. opposites
    ⁻100 0 ▓

10. opposites
    ▓ 0 1000

Give the opposite and the integer.

Example: Answer:
Find $5, 5   Lose $5, ⁻5

11. Lose 7 kg, ⁻7

12. 6° above zero, 6

13. Decrease 15 cm, ⁻15

14. 18 km west, ⁻18

15. Spend $10, ⁻10

16. Gain 2 kg, 2

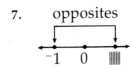

Here are 5 rows of a triangle.
Find the pattern and give the
numbers in the next 3 rows.

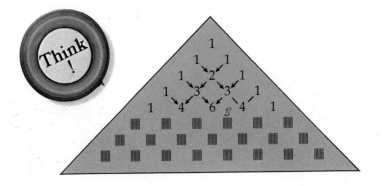

Addition of integers

These examples may help you understand adding integers.

Receive $5   Pay out $2   Ahead $3   Receive $3   Pay out $4   Behind $1

    5   +   ⁻2   =   3   3   +   ⁻4   =   ⁻1

Find the sums.

1.

Receive $6   Pay out $4   Result?

    6   +   ⁻4   =   n

2.

Receive $1   Pay out $3   Result?

    1   +   ⁻3   =   n

3.

Pay out $4   Receive $6   Result?

    ⁻4   +   6   =   n

4.

Pay out $5   Receive $1   Result?

    ⁻5   +   1   =   n

5.

Receive $3   Pay out $3   Result?

    3   +   ⁻3   =   n

6.

Pay out $4   Pay out $3   Result?

    ⁻4   +   ⁻3   =   n

7.

Receive $2   Pay out $6   Result?

    2   +   ⁻6   =   n

8.

Receive $2   Receive $4   Result?

    2   +   4   =   n

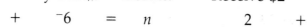

Find the sums.

1.

$$6 + {}^-2 = n$$

2.

$${}^-5 + 4 = n$$

3.

$${}^-2 + {}^-3 = n$$

4.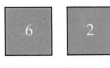

$$3 + {}^-6 = n$$

5.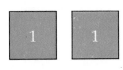

$${}^-1 + 1 = n$$

6.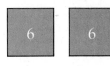

$${}^-6 + {}^-6 = n$$

7.

$$4 + {}^-4 = n$$

8.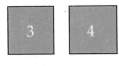

$$3 + 4 = n$$

9.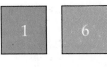

$${}^-1 + 6 = n$$

10.

$$5 + {}^-2 = n$$

11.

$${}^-2 + {}^-2 = n$$

12.

$$4 + {}^-1 = n$$

Find the sums.

13. $7 + {}^-3$ 14. $\;{}^-6 + 1$

15. ${}^-4 + 9$ 16. $\;{}^-3 + 8$

17. ${}^-6 + {}^-3$ 18. $\;{}^-7 + {}^-1$

19. $5 + {}^-5$ 20. $\;{}^-2 + 2$

21. $6 + 0$ 22. $\;0 + {}^-5$

23. ${}^-6 + 0$ 24. $\;{}^-4 + {}^-4$

25. ${}^-8 + {}^-7$ 26. $\;{}^-12 + 5$

27. $7 + {}^-15$ 28. $\;{}^-17 + 8$

29. ${}^-8 + {}^-9$ 30. $\;16 + {}^-9$

Which cereal costs less per gram?

350 g   480 g

67¢   86¢

More practice, page 394, Set A

As with whole numbers, you can think of subtracting integers as finding one of the addends.

$$
\begin{array}{ccc}
A & A & S \\
5 + 3 & = & 8
\end{array}
\qquad
\begin{array}{ccc}
A & A & S \\
6 + \,^-2 & = & 4
\end{array}
$$

$$
\begin{array}{ccc}
S & A & A \\
8 - 3 & = & 5
\end{array}
\qquad
\begin{array}{ccc}
S & A & A \\
4 - \,^-2 & = & 6
\end{array}
$$

Find the differences.

1.
$$
\begin{array}{ccc}
A & A & S \\
^-2 + 5 & = & 3
\end{array}
$$
$$
\begin{array}{ccc}
S & A & A \\
3 - 5 & = & n
\end{array}
$$

2.
$$
\begin{array}{ccc}
A & A & S \\
^-2 + \,^-3 & = & ^-5
\end{array}
$$
$$
\begin{array}{ccc}
S & A & A \\
^-5 - \,^-2 & = & n
\end{array}
$$

3.
$$
\begin{array}{ccc}
A & A & S \\
7 + \,^-3 & = & 4
\end{array}
$$
$$
\begin{array}{ccc}
S & A & A \\
4 - \,^-3 & = & n
\end{array}
$$

4.
$$
\begin{array}{ccc}
A & A & S \\
4 + \,^-6 & = & ^-2
\end{array}
$$
$$
\begin{array}{ccc}
S & A & A \\
^-2 - 4 & = & n
\end{array}
$$

5.
$$
\begin{array}{ccc}
A & A & S \\
^-5 + \,^-2 & = & ^-7
\end{array}
$$
$$
\begin{array}{ccc}
S & A & A \\
^-7 - \,^-2 & = & n
\end{array}
$$

6.
$$
\begin{array}{ccc}
A & A & S \\
^-1 + 8 & = & 7
\end{array}
$$
$$
\begin{array}{ccc}
S & A & A \\
7 - \,^-1 & = & n
\end{array}
$$

Find the sums and differences.

7.
$4 + \,^-9 = n$
$^-9 + 4 = n$
$^-5 - \,^-9 = n$
$^-5 - 4 = n$

8.
$^-8 + 1 = n$
$1 + \,^-8 = n$
$^-7 - 1 = n$
$^-7 - \,^-8 = n$

9.
$^-3 + \,^-6 = n$
$^-6 + \,^-3 = n$
$^-9 - \,^-6 = n$
$^-9 - \,^-3 = n$

10.
$9 + \,^-4 = n$
$^-4 + 9 = n$
$5 - \,^-4 = n$
$5 - 9 = n$

11.
$^-9 + 6 = n$
$6 + \,^-9 = n$
$^-3 - 6 = n$
$^-3 - \,^-9 = n$

12.
$^-1 + 7 = n$
$7 + \,^-1 = n$
$6 - 7 = n$
$6 - \,^-1 = n$

Find the missing addends and differences.

1. $n + {}^-8 = {}^-5$
$^-5 - {}^-8 = n$

2. $n + {}^-6 = {}^-7$
$^-7 - {}^-6 = n$

3. $n + {}^-3 = 1$
$1 - {}^-3 = n$

4. $n + 3 = {}^-5$
$^-5 - 3 = n$

5. $n + 6 = 0$
$0 - 6 = n$

6. $n + 9 = 6$
$6 - 9 = n$

7. $n + 0 = {}^-5$
$^-5 - 0 = n$

8. $n + {}^-2 = 4$
$4 - {}^-2 = n$

9. $n + {}^-3 = {}^-9$
$^-9 - {}^-3 = n$

Find the differences. Thinking of addends and a sum may help you.

10. S   A   A
$2 - {}^-4 = n$

11. S   A   A
$^-3 - 5 = n$

12. S   A   A
$^-1 - {}^-3 = n$

13. S   A   A
$4 - {}^-2 = n$

14. S   A   A
$^-2 - 7 = n$

15. S   A   A
$7 - {}^-5 = n$

16. S   A   A
$^-7 - 4 = n$

17. S   A   A
$3 - 9 = n$

18. S   A   A
$^-4 - {}^-3 = n$

19. S   A   A
$5 - {}^-3 = n$

20. S   A   A
$2 - 8 = n$

21. S   A   A
$6 - {}^-1 = n$

22. S   A   A
$4 - 9 = n$

23. S   A   A
$^-7 - {}^-7 = n$

24. S   A   A
$5 - {}^-2 = n$

Think!

Copy and complete this magic square.

3	$^-2$	$^-1$
$^-4$	▓	▓
▓	▓	$^-3$

Self-check

Give the missing integers.

1. Lose 3 kg, ⁻3
   Gain 3 kg, ▦

2. opposites
   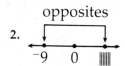
   ▦   0   6

3.
   ⁻4 ⁻3 ▦ ⁻1 0 1 2 3 4

Find the sums.

4. | 3 | | 5 |

   Receive $3   Pay out $5   Result?
      3   +   ⁻5   = n

5. | 5 | | 2 |
   $5 + {}^-2 = n$

6. $12 + {}^-5 = n$

Find the differences.

7. $7 + {}^-3 = 4$
   ${}^-3 + 7 = 4$
   $4 - {}^-3 = n$

8. S   A   A
   ${}^-3 - 4 = n$

Answers for Self-check—page 315

Test

Give the missing integers.

1. 7° above zero, 7
   7° below zero, ▦

2. opposites

   ⁻9   0   ▦

3.
   ⁻4 ▦ ⁻2 ⁻1 0 1 2 3 4

Find the sums.

4. | 6 | | 2 |

   Receive $6   Pay out $2   Result?
      6   +   ⁻2   = n

5. | 3 | | 6 |
   $3 + {}^-6 = n$

6. ${}^-11 + 7 = n$

Find the differences.

7. ${}^-8 + 2 = {}^-6$
   $2 + {}^-8 = {}^-6$
   ${}^-6 - 2 = n$

8. S   A   A
   $2 - 5 = n$

For fun

A Nomograph for Integers

The red line shows that $4 + {}^-9 = {}^-5$ or ${}^-5 - {}^-9 = 4$.
The blue line shows that ${}^-2 + 8 = 6$ or $6 - 8 = {}^-2$.

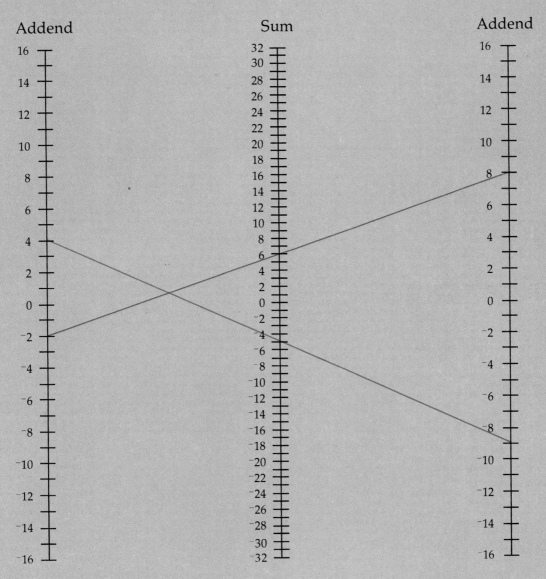

Addend   Sum   Addend

Use a ruler to help you find these sums and differences.

1. ${}^-7 + 4$ 2. $6 + {}^-11$ 3. ${}^-8 + {}^-9$ 4. $3 + {}^-14$ 5. ${}^-12 + 8$

6. $10 - {}^-2$ 7. $6 - 9$ 8. $8 - {}^-4$ 9. ${}^-7 - {}^-5$ 10. ${}^-3 - 12$

Probability

Getting started

You start out for a walk at River Road and Park Drive. You are going to walk 4 blocks. At each corner, you will flip a coin to decide which way to go.

 Heads: Go north one block.

 Tails: Go east one block.

If you toss 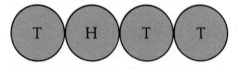 , you will end up at the gas station. Where would you end up after each series of tosses?

1.

2.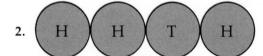

3.

4.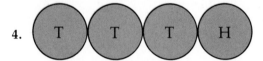

5. What tosses would you need to get to the pizza parlor?

6. Can you get to the drugstore in your 4 block walk?

7. Would you ever end up at the hardware store after walking 4 blocks if you use the coin rules?

8. Where do you think you are most likely to end your walk?

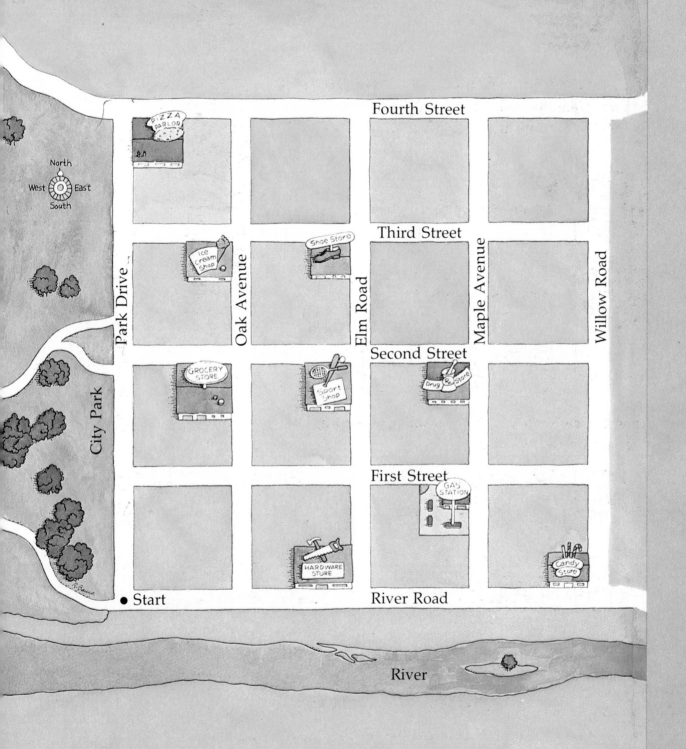

Outcomes

If you do this,	what are all the possible outcomes?	Are all the possible outcomes equally likely? If not, which is most likely?
Experiment	**Possible outcomes**	**Equally likely or not**
Toss a coin.	Heads Tails	Equally likely
Spin the pointer.	1, 2, or 3	3 is most likely.

Give the missing information in each row.

1. Toss a cube with sides numbered 1–6.	1 2 3 4 5 ?	?
2. Draw 1 marble without looking.	red ?	?
3. Spin the pointer.	?	?

Answer the question for each experiment.

1. Toss a cube with the letters **A, B, C, D, E, F** on the faces.

About how many times would you expect to get **A** in 60 tosses?

2. Spin a spinner like this one.

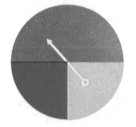

About how many times would you expect to land on red in 50 spins?

3. Draw a marble without looking. Replace it after each draw and shake the box.

About how many blue marbles would you expect to draw in 40 turns?

4. Draw a card without looking. Replace it after each draw and shuffle.

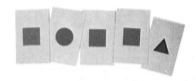

About how many circles would you expect to draw in 25 turns?

5. Which of the experiments above have equally likely outcomes?

Trace the letter **E** and cut along the dotted lines. Then put the pieces together so that they exactly cover a tracing of the square.

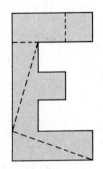

Experiment	Equally likely outcomes	Chances	Probability
Toss a penny.	Heads Tails	There is 1 chance out of 2 of getting heads.	The probability of getting heads is $\frac{1}{2}$.
Spin the pointer.	1, 2, 3	There are 2 chances out of 3 of getting an odd number.	The probability of getting an odd number is $\frac{2}{3}$.

Give the missing information in each row.

	Equally likely outcomes	Chances	Probability
1. Draw a card without looking.	1 2 3 4	There is 1 chance out of ▨ of getting a 3.	The probability of getting a 3 is ▨.
2. Toss a cube that has one of the letters **A, B, C, D, E, F** on each face.	A B C D E F	There are 2 chances out of ▨ of getting a vowel (**A** or **E**).	The probability of getting a vowel is ▨.
3. Toss a cube with sides numbered 1-6.	1 2 3 4 5 6	There are ▨ chances out of 6 of getting an odd number.	The probability of getting an odd number is ▨.

Suppose you draw one of these
cards without looking.

1. What are the possible outcomes?

2. What are the chances of getting
   an odd number?

3. What is the probability of
   getting an odd number?

4. What is the probability of getting
   an even number?

Suppose you draw a marble without looking.

5. What are the possible outcomes?

6. Do you have a better chance
   of getting a red marble or
   a blue marble?

7. What is the probability of
   getting a red marble?

Suppose you spin the pointer.

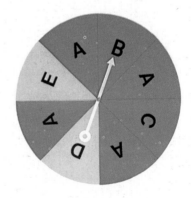

8. What letter do you think
   you will get most often
   in 10 spins?

What is the probability that

9. you will get an **A**?

10. you will get a **B**?

11. you will get yellow?

12. you will get green?

One airline gives an award
to people who have traveled
over 800 000 km by air.
Estimate how many days these
people have spent in the air.
Use 952 km/h as the average
speed for jet travel.

1. According to the weather report, there are 2 chances out of 10 that it will rain tomorrow. What is the probability of rain? Do you think it is more likely to rain or not to rain?

2. The seed company says that 90 out of 100 (or 9 out of 10) of the seeds will grow. If you plant just one seed, what is the probability that it will grow? Do you think it is more likely to grow or not to grow?

3. A basketball player
   made 80 of his first
   100 free throws.
   Using these numbers,
   what is the probability
   he will make his next
   free throw?
   Is he more likely to
   make it or miss it?

4. One estimate states that
   1 out of every 9 people
   is left-handed.
   What is the probability
   that the arrow is pointing
   at a left-handed person?
   Is that person more likely
   to be left-handed or
   right-handed?

Answers for Self-check   1. 1, 2, 3, 4   2. Yes   3. $\frac{1}{2}$ 4. $\frac{2}{3}$

Self-check

Spin the pointer.

1. What are the possible outcomes?

2. Are the outcomes equally likely?

Toss a coin.

3. What is the probability of getting heads?

Draw one card without looking.

4. What is the probability of getting an odd number?

Answers for Self-check—page 325

Test

Draw one bead without looking.

1. What are the possible outcomes?

2. Are the outcomes equally likely?

Toss a number cube.

3. What is the probability of getting a 2?

Spin the pointer.

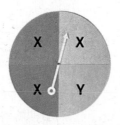

4. What is the probability of getting an **X**?

Right Angle Paths

Rules:

Place the toothpicks end to end.
Always make a right angle.
No squares are allowed.
Different positions of the same figure do not count.

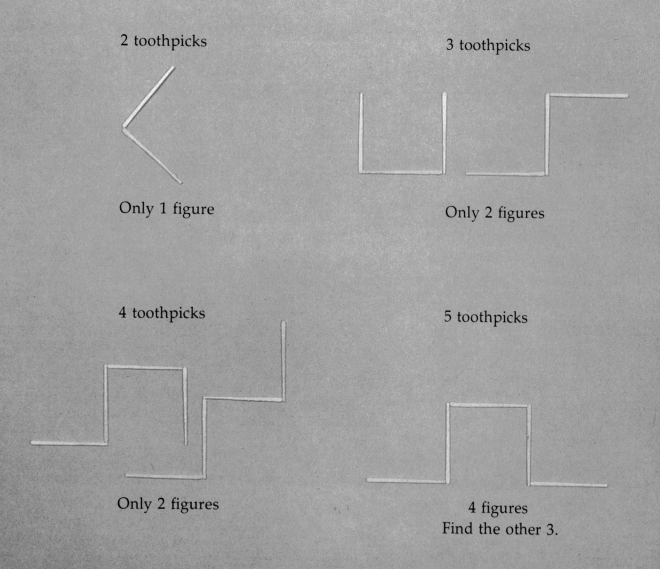

2 toothpicks

Only 1 figure

3 toothpicks

Only 2 figures

4 toothpicks

Only 2 figures

5 toothpicks

4 figures
Find the other 3.

How many different paths can you make with 6 toothpicks?

Statistics

Time to get to school

Minutes

Over 30	II
25-29	IIII II
20-24	IIII
15-19	IIII III
10-14	IIII IIII IIII II
5-9	IIII IIII IIII
0-4	IIII III

Tony

Getting started

One student took a survey to find out how long different students take to get to school. He recorded his findings on a tally sheet.

1. If you had been included in the survey, where would the mark for you be?

2. Which amount of time is taken by the greatest number of students?

3. Which amount of time is taken by the smallest number of students?

4. Can you tell if anyone takes 15 minutes to get to school?

☆ 5. Take a survey of your class. Use one of the ideas below or choose one of your own.

    A Shoe size   **B** Number of pets   **C** Favorite color   **D** Hobby

Presenting data—bar graphs

The class took a vote on what kind of food to have at their spring picnic. The bar graph shows how the students voted.

Favorite
Picnic Food

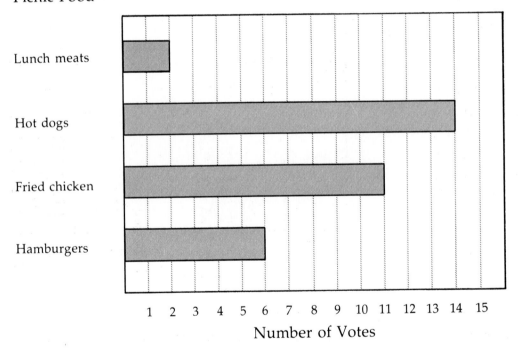

1. What picnic food received the most votes?

2. The class decided to have two of the picnic foods listed above. What should they be?

3. How many students voted in all?

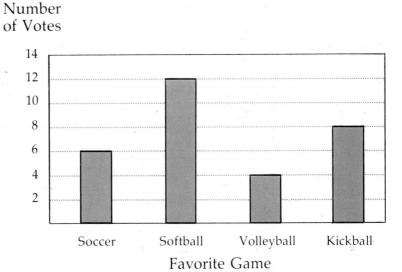

The student in charge of games for the picnic polled the class to find out their favorite game. The bar graph shows the results of the poll.

1. Which game was most popular? How many students chose it?

2. If the class plays two games, what do you think they will be?

☆ 3. Choose one of the ideas below and poll your class. Make a bar graph to show the results of your poll.

A Favorite food   B Best place for a picnic   C Favorite drink   D Favorite game

Presenting data—line graphs

This line graph shows the changes in pulse rate of an astronaut from just before until just after blast-off.

Pulse
Rate

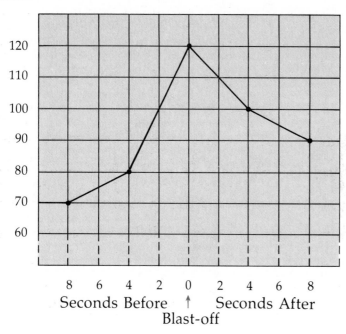

8   6   4   2   0   2   4   6   8

Seconds Before ↑ Seconds After

Blast-off

1. When was the astronaut's pulse rate the highest? What was the rate then?

2. What was the pulse rate 4 seconds after blast-off?

3. What was the difference in pulse rate 8 seconds before and 8 seconds after blast-off?

4. What would you estimate the pulse rate was 6 seconds after blast-off?

5. How much higher was the pulse rate at blast-off than at 8 seconds before blast-off?

A student made this graph
to show how fast his pulse
rate slowed down when he
stopped after running for
5 minutes.

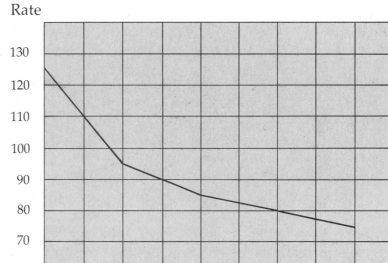

Pulse Rate

Number of Seconds after Stopping

1. What was the student's fastest pulse rate?

2. When was the student's pulse rate about 85?

3. Estimate the pulse rate after the student has rested for 20 minutes.

☆ 4. Make a line graph for one of these ideas.

   A Outside temperature each hour from 9:00 A.M. to 3:00 P.M.

   B High temperature each day, Monday through Friday

   C The number of cars (or trucks) that pass your school in a 2-minute
      period at 9:00, 10:00, 11:00, 12:00, 1:00, 2:00, and 3:00

Presenting data—picture graphs

The school science club took a winter
field trip to the city park. They kept a
record of the kinds and numbers of
birds they saw. The picture graph
below shows their findings.

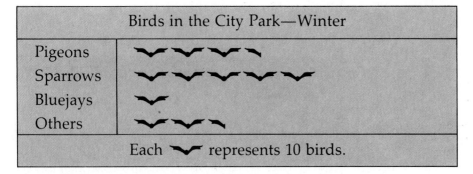

Birds in the City Park—Winter

Pigeons	
Sparrows	
Bluejays	
Others	

Each ⌣ represents 10 birds.

1. How many birds does ⌐ represent?

2. Give the number of each kind of bird the club members saw.

In May, the club members made another trip to the park.
Their findings on this trip are shown in the graph below.

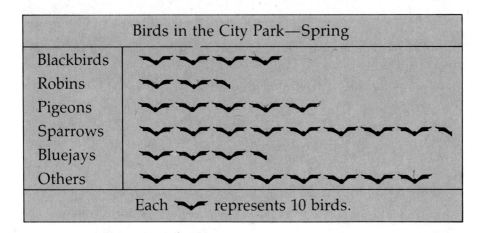

Birds in the City Park—Spring

Blackbirds	
Robins	
Pigeons	
Sparrows	
Bluejays	
Others	

Each ⌣ represents 10 birds.

3. How many more sparrows did they see in the spring than in the winter?

4. How many more pigeons did they see in the spring than in the winter?

☆ 5. How many more birds in all did they see in the spring than in the winter?

The science club decided to make a study of the trees in the state park. They chose one part of the park and collected data on the trees in it. The picture graph shows the kinds and numbers of the trees they found.

Trees in the State Park	
Oak	🌳🌳🌳🌳🌳🌳
Maple	🌳🌳🌱
Hickory	🌳🌳🌳🌳
Pine	🌳🌳🌳🌳🌳🌳🌳🌳
Sycamore	🌳🌱
Others	🌳🌳🌳🌳🌳🌳🌳🌳🌳🌳

Each 🌳 represents 20 trees.

1. How many trees does 🌱 represent?

2. How many more oak trees than maple trees were there?

3. Give the number of each kind of tree.

Can you find the mass of each block in these problems?

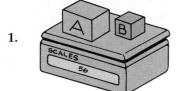
1.

Block A has a mass 6 times as great as block B. Blocks A and B together have a mass of 56 grams.

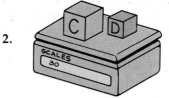
2.

Block C has a mass 3 grams more than twice block D. Blocks C and D together have a mass of 30 grams.

Presenting data—circle graphs

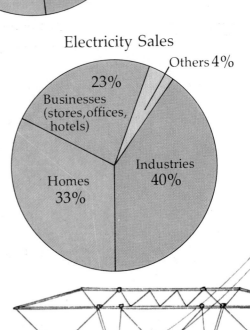

This circle graph shows the ways energy was used in the United States in a recent year.

Energy Use in the United States

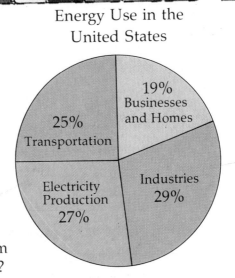

25% Transportation

19% Businesses and Homes

Industries 29%

Electricity Production 27%

1. What was the greatest amount of energy used for?

2. What was $\frac{1}{4}$ of the energy used for?

3. What do you think is the sum of the percents on the graph? Add to see if you are correct.

This circle graph shows the percent of a utility company's electricity that is bought by different kinds of customers.

Electricity Sales

Others 4%

23% Businesses (stores, offices, hotels)

Industries 40%

Homes 33%

4. Which group buys the most electricity?

5. Which group buys almost $\frac{1}{3}$ of the electricity?

6. Suppose the graph represents $50 000 in total sales. What is the cost of the electricity bought by businesses? By industries?

Cut out a circle that has a radius of 6 cm.

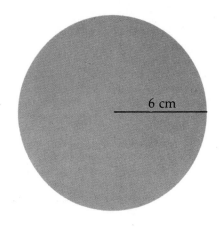

6 cm

Fold it four times.

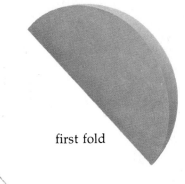

first fold   second fold   third fold   fourth fold

Unfold the circle. Think of the whole circle as representing 24 hours. Each part represents $1\frac{1}{2}$ hours. Color your circle to show how long you spend in each of these activities.

1. sleeping

2. attending school

3. playing

4. eating

5. other

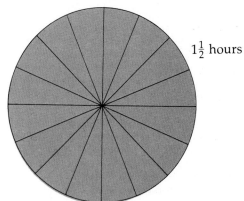

$1\frac{1}{2}$ hours

24 Hours Total

Self-check

1. Which color received the most votes?

2. Which color received 10 votes?

3. How many votes did orange receive?

4. How many students wear sizes over 8?

5. How many wear sizes under 5?

6. How many wear sizes in the 5 or 6 group?

Students' Favorite Colors

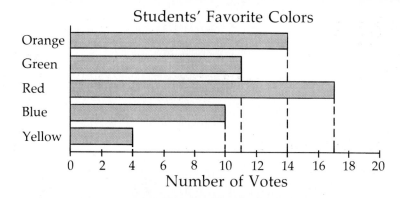

Number of Votes

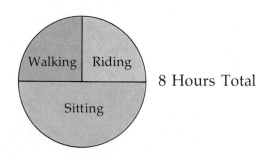

Answers for Self-check—page 337

Test

1. What was the number of breaths after 20 seconds?

2. What was the number of breaths after 60 seconds?

3. How long did it take to reach 25 breaths per minute?

How many hours were spent in each activity?

4. riding

5. walking

6. sitting

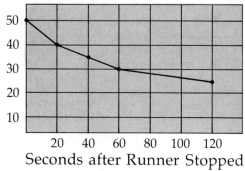

Seconds after Runner Stopped

8 Hours Total

Which estimate is better, **A** or **B**?

One thousand

1. 1000 days
   A almost 3 years
   B almost 30 years

2. 1000 page book
   A about 2 cm thick
   B about 5 cm thick

One million

3. 1 000 000 cm
   A 1 kilometer
   B 10 kilometers

4. 1 000 000 hours
   A about 10 years
   B about 110 years

One billion

5. 1 000 000 000 m
   A 2.5 times around the earth
   B 25 times around the earth

6. 1 000 000 000 seconds
   A over 30 years
   B over 300 years

Check your pulse rate (heartbeats per minute).
On your next birthday, about how many times will your heart have beat since you were born?

Exponents

$$10^2 \quad 10 \times 10 = 100$$
$$10^3 \quad 10 \times 10 \times 10 = 1000$$
$$10^4 \quad 10 \times 10 \times 10 \times 10 = 10000$$
$$10^5 \quad 10 \times 10 \times 10 \times 10 \times 10 = 100$$
$$10^6 \quad 10 \times 10 \times 10 \times 10 \times 10$$

Part of the writing on the chalkboard was erased. The teacher asked a student to replace the part that was erased.

The small raised numerals (2, 3, 4 in 10^2, 10^3, 10^4) are called **exponents**. They tell how many tens have been multiplied.

1. Copy the last two equations from the chalkboard and see if you can give the missing parts.

2. Give the missing words.

    For 10^2, we read ten to the second power, or ten squared.
    For 10^3, we read ten to the third power, or ten cubed.
    For 10^4, we read ten to the fourth power.
    For 10^5, we read ten to the ?   ? .
    For 10^6, we read ten to the ?   ? .

The numbers 10^2, 10^3, 10^4, . . . are called **powers of ten**.

Give the missing numbers.

Example: $10^2 = 100$

1. $10^3 = $ ▓▓▓
2. $10^4 = $ ▓▓▓
3. $10^5 = $ ▓▓▓
4. $10^6 = $ ▓▓▓
5. $10^7 = $ ▓▓▓
6. $10^8 = $ ▓▓▓
7. $10^9 = $ ▓▓▓
8. $10^{10} = $ ▓▓▓
9. $10^{11} = $ ▓▓▓

Solve the equations.

Examples: $5 \times 10^2 = 500$ $5 \times 10^3 = 5000$

10. $8 \times 10^2 = n$
11. $8 \times 10^3 = n$
12. $8 \times 10^4 = n$
13. $2 \times 10^2 = n$
14. $2 \times 10^3 = n$
15. $2 \times 10^4 = n$
16. $7 \times 10^5 = n$
17. $4 \times 10^6 = n$
18. $8 \times 10^7 = n$

Write each number as a power of ten.

Examples: $100 = 10^2$ $1000 = 10^3$

19. 10 000
20. 10 000 000
21. 100 000
22. 100 000 000
23. 1 000 000
24. 1 000 000 000

Write each number as in the examples.

Examples: $600 = 6 \times 10^2$ $6000 = 6 \times 10^3$

25. 300
26. 3000
27. 30 000
28. 900
29. 9000
30. 90 000
31. 800 000
32. 8 000 000
33. 80 000 000

Suppose a book has an average of 108 names listed in each column, with 4 columns per page. The book has 340 pages. How many books are needed to list all the people in a state or nation that has a population of 22 million?

More practice, page 394, Set C

When a power is expressed as a product of a number between 1 and 10 and a power of 10, the number is expressed in **scientific notation**.

Give the missing numbers.

Facts about the earth

		Standard numeral	Scientific notation
	Estimated population for a recent year	4 000 000 000	4×10^9
	Circumference	about 40 000 000 m	4×10^7 m
1.	Surface area	almost 500 000 000 km²	$5 \times$ ▥ km²
2.	Mass	over 5 000 ... 000 metric tons (21 zeros)	$5 \times$ ▥ metric tons
3.	Maximum distance to the sun and back	over 300 000 000 km	$3 \times$ ▥ km

Give the missing numbers.

Facts about the universe

		Standard numeral	Scientific notation
1.	Distance around our sun	over 4 000 000 000 km	4 × ▦ km
2.	Distance to one of the nearest stars (Alpha Centauri)	nearly 40 000 000 000 000 km	4 × ▦ km
3.	Other groups of stars (galaxies) detected	at least 500 000 000 000	▦ × ▦
4.	Distance across the Milky Way galaxy	18 zeros over 9 000 ... 000 km	▦ × ▦ km

Answers for Self-check   1. millions   2. trillions   3. 1000   4. 100 000   5. 10 000   6. 7000
7. 9 000 000   8. 10^6 9. 10^5 10. 10^{10} 11. 8 × 10^5 12. 5 × 10^8

Self-check

Give the name of the largest period of each number.

1. 37 000 000   2. 127 000 000 000 000   3. One billion is how many millions, 10, 100, or 1000?

Give the missing numbers.

Example: $10^3 = 1000$ Example: $6 \times 10^2 = 600$

4. $10^5 = $ ▓▓▓   5. $10^4 = $ ▓▓▓   6. $7 \times 10^3 = n$ 7. $9 \times 10^6 = n$

Write each number as a power of ten.

8. 1 000 000   9. 100 000   10. 10 000 000 000

Write each number in scientific notation.

11. 800 000   12. 500 000 000

Answers for Self-check—page 347

Test

Give the name of the largest period of each number.

1. 73 000 000 000   2. 184 000 000   3. One million is how many thousands, 10, 100, or 1000?

Give the missing numbers.

Example: $10^7 = 10\ 000\ 000$ Example: $5 \times 10^3 = 5000$

4. $10^3 = $ ▓▓▓   5. $10^6 = $ ▓▓▓   6. $3 \times 10^4 = n$ 7. $7 \times 10^5 = n$

Write each number as a power of ten.

8. 100 000 000   9. 10 000   10. 1 000 000

Write each number in scientific notation.

11. 4 000 000   12. 7 000 000 000

Grouping by Fives

Grouping rules:

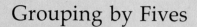

1. Put 5 beans on a stick.
2. Put 5 sticks in a box.

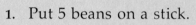

Follow the grouping rules and give the missing numbers.

	Beans	Boxes	Sticks	Single beans
	7 beans		1	2
	14 beans		2	4
	38 beans	1	2	3
1.	17 beans		▓	▓
2.	48 beans	▓	▓	▓
3.	69 beans	▓	▓	▓

You can count beans using this "code."   3 2 4

boxes sticks single beans

Continue the counting to 444.

1	2	3	4	10	11	12	13	14	20	21	22	23	24
30	31	32	33	34	40	41	42	43	44	100	101	102	103
104	110	111	112	113	114	...							

Volume

Getting started

The **volume** of a space figure
is the number of cubic units
in the figure.

Volume = 12 cubic units

A cube that is one centimeter on each edge is a **cubic centimeter**.

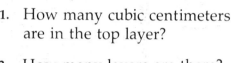

1 cubic centimeter (cm³)

How many cubic centimeters are there in the box? How many more will it hold?

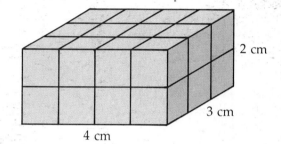

How many cubic centimeters in all can be placed in the box?

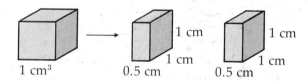

1. How many cubic centimeters are in the top layer?

2. How many layers are there?

3. What is the volume of the box?

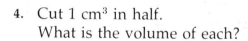

4. Cut 1 cm³ in half. What is the volume of each?

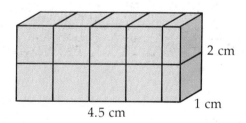

5. What is the volume of this figure?

6. What is the volume of this figure?

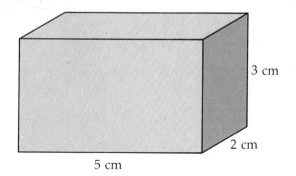

Finding the volume of boxes

What is the volume of the shoe box?

Finding the answer

The volume *(V)* of a box
is the product of the length *(l)*,
the width *(w)*, and the height *(h)*.

Length: 30 cm
Width: 14 cm
Height: 9 cm

$$V = l \times w \times h \qquad V = 30 \times 14 \times 9 \qquad V = 3780$$

The volume of the box is 3780 cm³.

Other examples

l = 7 cm
w = 1.5 cm
h = 3 cm
$V = 7 \times 1.5 \times 3$
   = 31.5 cm³

l = 3.4 cm
w = 2 cm
h = 0.9 cm
$V = 3.4 \times 2 \times 0.9$
   = 6.12 cm³

Find the volume of each box in cubic centimeters.

1.

4 cm
4 cm
4 cm

2.
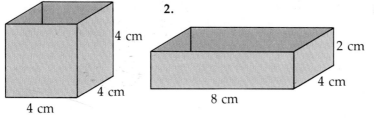
2 cm
4 cm
8 cm

3.
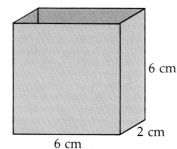
6 cm
6 cm
2 cm

4.
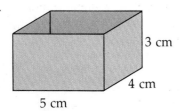
3 cm
4 cm
5 cm

5.
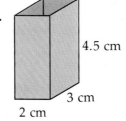
4.5 cm
3 cm
2 cm

6.
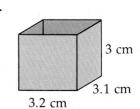
3 cm
3.1 cm
3.2 cm

Find the volume of each container.

1.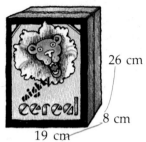
26 cm
8 cm
19 cm

2.
25 cm
20 cm
7.5 cm

3.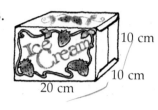
10 cm
20 cm
10 cm

4.
6 cm
15 cm
16.5 cm

5.
7 cm
2 cm
5.5 cm

6.
40 cm
38 cm
38 cm

7. l = 15 cm
w = 8 cm
h = 8 cm

8. l = 10.8 cm
w = 7.0 cm
h = 5.5 cm

9. l = 4 m
w = 1.5 m
h = 2 m

10. l = 8 m
w = 2 m
h = 0.1 m

11. l = 20 cm
w = 20 cm
h = 2.5 cm

12. l = 50 cm
w = 22 cm
h = 18 cm

13. A room is 4 m long, 3 m wide, and 2.5 m high. What is the volume in cubic meters (m^3)?

☆ 14. Choose a box. Measure its length, width, and height to the nearest centimeter. Find the volume of the box.

Measure the length, width, and height of your classroom to the nearest tenth of a meter. Find the volume of the room. Divide by the number of persons in the room. How many cubic meters of air, to the nearest cubic meter, are there for each person?

More practice, page 395, Set B

Volume and capacity

The volume of liquids is often expressed in units of **capacity**.
Common units of capacity are **liters** (ℓ), **kiloliters** (kl),
and **milliliters** (ml).

Volume	Capacity
1 cm³	1 ml
1000 cm³	1 ℓ = 1000 ml
1 m³	1 kl = 1000 ℓ

Cubic decimeter (dm³)

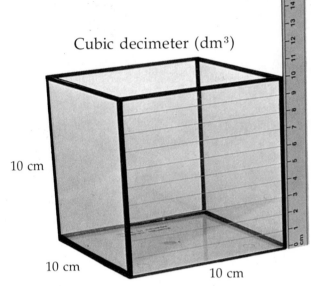

10 cm

10 cm   10 cm

Cubic centimeter (cm³)

1 cm

1 cm

1 cm

Volume: 1 cm³ Capacity: 1 ml

Volume: 1000 cm³ Capacity: 1 ℓ

Find or describe some
containers that will hold
almost these amounts.

1. 1 ml

2. 1 ℓ

3. 1 kl

4. 250 ml

5. 10 ℓ

6. 5 ml

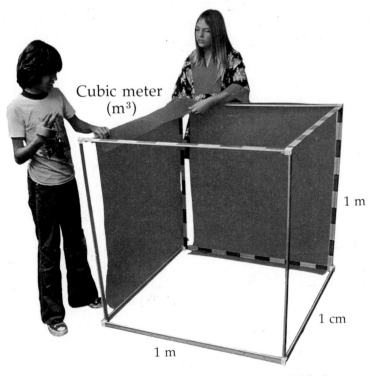

Cubic meter
(m³)

1 m

1 m

1 cm

1 m

1 cm

Volume: 1 m³ Capacity: 1 kl or 1000 ℓ

Give the number of units of capacity for each object.

1. 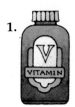 small bottle: 50 cm³ ▓ ml

2. 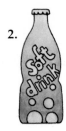 soft drink bottle: 355 cm³ ▓ ml

3. juice glass: 150 cm³ ▓ ml

4. bleach bottle: 4000 cm³ ▓ ℓ

5. water jug: 20 000 cm³ ▓ ℓ

6. 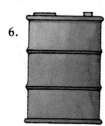 oil drum: 160 000 cm³ ▓ ℓ

7.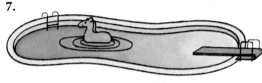

swimming pool:
1742 m³
▓ kl

8.

Boeing 747 fuel tanks:
178 m³
▓ kl

Find the capacity of each container in liters.

9.
20 cm
20 cm
50 cm

Volume = 50 × 20 × 20
       = 20 000 cm³
Capacity = ▓ ℓ

10.
20 cm
25 cm
25 cm
▓ ℓ

11.
10 cm
50 cm
80 cm
▓ ℓ

Volume and mass

One cubic centimeter of water
has a mass of one gram.

One milliliter of water
has a mass of one gram.

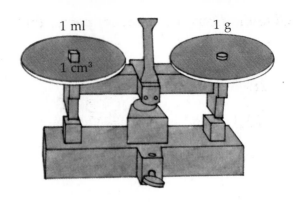

1 ml   1 g
1 cm³

One cubic decimeter of water
has a mass of one kilogram.

One liter of water has
a mass of one kilogram.

1000 g = 1 kg

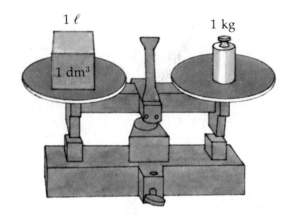

1 ℓ   1 kg
1 dm³

Copy and complete the table below.

	Amount of water	Mass
	1 ℓ	1000 g
1.	270 ml	▧
2.	▧	3 kg
3.	▧	1 g
4.	500 ml	▧
5.	▧	10 g
6.	2.7 ℓ	▧
7.	1 kl	▧

8. 100 ml of water has a mass of 100 g.
The mass of mercury is 13.6 times as
great as the mass of water. What is
the mass of 100 ml of mercury?

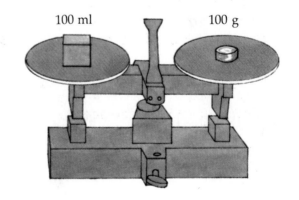

100 ml   100 g

Give the mass of water, in grams, that each container would hold.

1.

20 ml

2.

250 ml

3.

325 ml

4.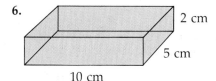

1000 ml

5.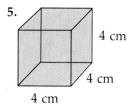

4 cm
4 cm
4 cm

6.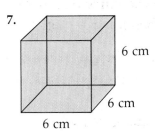

2 cm
5 cm
10 cm

7.

6 cm
6 cm
6 cm

Solve the problems.

8. Gasoline has a mass of about 0.7 times the mass of water. What is the mass in grams of 50 ℓ of gasoline?

9. Milk has a mass of about 1.03 times the mass of water. What is the mass of 500 ml of milk?

☆ 10. Fill a small container with water. Find the mass of the container and water. Empty the water and refill the container with another liquid such as oil, honey, or liquid soap. Find the mass of the filled container. Is the second liquid lighter or heavier than the water?

1 m³ of air has a mass of about 1.29 kg. What is the approximate mass of the air in your classroom?

Self-check

Find the volume of each box.

1. 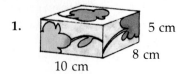 5 cm

8 cm

10 cm

2. $l = 5$ cm
$w = 5$ cm
$h = 5$ cm

3. $l = 8$ cm
$w = 4$ cm
$h = 2.5$ cm

Give the capacity of each object.

4. Volume:
15 cm³

▓▓ ml
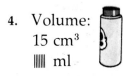

5. Volume:
38 000 cm³

▓▓ ℓ
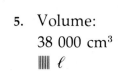

6.

Volume: 12 m³
▓▓ kl

Give the mass of water each container will hold.

7. 50 ml
▓▓ g
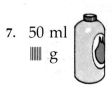

8. 310 ml
▓▓ g
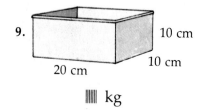

9.

10 cm

10 cm

20 cm

▓▓ kg

Answers for Self-check—page 357

Test

Find the volume of each box.

1. 10 cm

5 cm

5 cm

2. $l = 18$ cm
$w = 8$ cm
$h = 2$ cm

3. $l = 10$ cm
$w = 10$ cm
$h = 3.5$ cm

Give the capacity of each object.

4. 250 cm³
▓▓ ml

5. 12 000 cm³
▓▓ ℓ

6. 200 m³
▓▓ kl

Give the mass of water each container will hold.

7. 475 ml
▓▓ g

8. 3800 ml
▓▓ kg

9.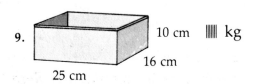

10 cm ▓▓ kg

16 cm

25 cm

Finding the Volume of a Rock

A Put an empty juice can in a waterproof container. Fill the juice can level to the brim with water.

rock

B Carefully put a rock in the can of water.

C Find the number of milliliters of water that overflowed.

D The volume of the overflow water is the same as the volume of the rock.

450 ml

1 liter

450 cm³

Find the volume of some rocks or other heavy objects using this method.

Level 34 review

Find the sums.

Find the differences.

1.

| 4 | | 6 |

Receive Pay out
$4 + {}^-6 = n$

2.
| 3 | 5 |

$^-3 + 5 = n$

3. $5 + {}^-2 = 3$
$^-2 + 5 = 3$
$3 - {}^-2 = n$

4. S   A   A
$^-4 - 2 = n$

5. Pick a card without looking. What are the possible outcomes?

6. Are the outcomes in exercise 5 equally likely?

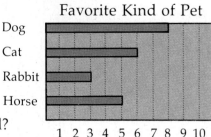
| 1 | 2 |
| 3 | 4 |

7. What is the probability of tossing heads?

8. Which kind of pet received the most votes?

9. How many votes did the horse receive?

10. How many people voted in all?

Favorite Kind of Pet

Dog
Cat
Rabbit
Horse

1 2 3 4 5 6 7 8 9 10
Number of Votes

Write the standard numeral.

11. Two million, four hundred twenty thousand

12. five billion

Give the missing numbers. Examples: $10^4 = 10\ 000$; $4 \times 10^3 = 4000$

13. $10^6 = $ ▓

14. $10^5 = $ ▓

15. $5 \times 10^6 = $ ▓

16. $8 \times 10^2 = $ ▓

Write each number as a power of ten. Example: $100\ 000 = 10^5$

17. 1 000 000

18. 1000

19. 100 000 000

Write each number in scientific notation. Example: $30\ 000 = 3 \times 10^4$

20. 700 000

21. 30 000 000

22. 9 000 000

Give the volume of each box.

23. $l = 4$ cm
$w = 2$ cm
$h = 3$ cm

24. $l = 6$ m
$w = 5$ m
$h = 8$ m

25. $l = 10$ cm
$w = 4$ cm
$h = 2.5$ cm

Give the mass of these amounts of water.

26. 500 ml

27. $1\ \ell$

Appendix

Inches, feet, yards, miles

Here are some nonmetric units
of length:

Units of Length		
Unit	Symbol	Relation
inch	in.	12 in. = 1 ft
foot	ft	1 ft = 12 in.
yard	yd	1 yd = 3 ft
mile	mi	1 mi = 5280 ft
		1760 yd

Estimate each of these lengths.
Then measure to check your estimates.

1. your height in inches
2. your armspan in inches
3. the height of the classroom door in feet
4. the length and width of your classroom in feet
5. the length of a hallway of your school in yards
6. the distance to a nearby city in miles (Ask your teacher
   for the information to check your guess.)

Give the unit you would use to measure each of these lengths.

7. length of your book
8. length of a car
9. distance from New York to San Francisco
10. length of a nail
11. length of a football field
12. height of a mountain

Use the table on page 362 to answer the questions.

1. How many inches are in a yard?

2. How many feet are in a mile?

3. A football field is 100 yd long.
   How many feet is this?

4. A basketball player is 6 ft 10 in. tall.
   How many inches is this?

5. One track event is the 880 yd race.
   How many feet is this?

6. A track star runs two 880 yd races.
   How many miles is this?

7. One track event is a $\frac{1}{4}$ mile race.
   How many yards is this?

8. A person is 72 in. tall.
   How many feet is this?
   How many yards?

Find the length of each segment in inches.
Give each answer to the nearest inch, the nearest
half inch, and the nearest quarter inch.

9. ├─────────────────────┤   10. ├───────────┤

11. ├──────────────────────────┤   12. ├──────────┤

13. ├───────────────────┤   14. ├───────────────┤

15. Draw a segment $4\frac{5}{8}$ in. long.

Finding area

Unit of area   **Problem**

Actual size

1 square inch
1 in.²

1. A picture is 24 in. long and 16 in. wide.

   What is its area in square inches?

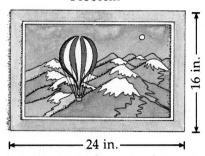

Reduced from actual size

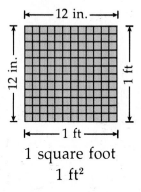

1 square foot
1 ft²

2. A garden is 15 ft long and 12 ft wide. What is its area in square feet?

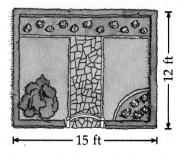

Reduced from actual size

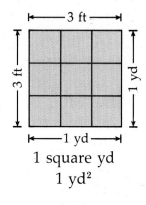

1 square yd
1 yd²

3. A room is 9 yd wide and 12 yd long.

   What is its area in square yards?

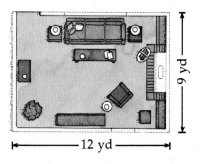

Reduced from actual size

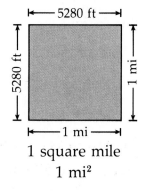

1 square mile
1 mi²

4. A state park is 14 mi long and 9 mi wide.

   What is its area in square miles?

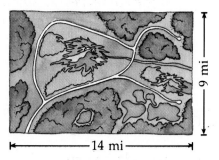

Use the pictures of the units on page 364 to answer the questions.

1. How many square inches are in a square foot?
2. How many square feet are in a square yard?
3. How many square yards are in a square mile?

Which unit would you use to measure these areas?

4. the front of your math book
5. your state
6. the floor of your classroom
7. a city park
8. a sheet of notebook paper
9. a football field

10. The area of a piece of land 88 yd long and 55 yd wide is 1 **acre**. What is the area of an acre in square yards?

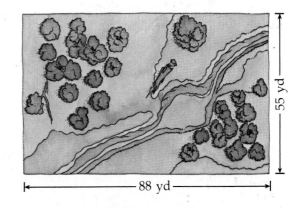

11. A house is to be built on a square lot that is 40 yd on each side. What is the area of the lot in square yards? Is the lot larger or smaller than $\frac{1}{3}$ acre?

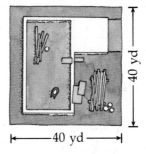

☆ Find each of these areas.

12. your classroom
13. the chalkboard in your classroom
14. your desk top
15. some other surface of your choice

Temperature–degrees Fahrenheit

Temperature is sometimes measured in degrees Fahrenheit (° F).

This Fahrenheit thermometer shows some useful temperature measurements.

70° Comfortable room — temperature

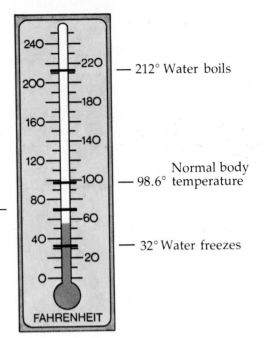

— 212° Water boils

Normal body
— 98.6° temperature

— 32° Water freezes

FAHRENHEIT

Choose the best temperature estimate for each item. Use the information shown on the thermometer to help you.

1. hot chocolate

    A 50° F

    B 100° F

    C 180° F

2. ice cream

    A 10° F

    B 40° F

    C 60° F

3. cool fall day

    A 10° F

    B 50° F

    C 90° F

4. warm bath water

    A 75° F

    B 125° F

    C 200° F

5. hot summer day

    A 55° F

    B 75° F

    C 95° F

6. a day when the snow is just beginning to melt

    A 0° F

    B 35° F

    C 65° F

7. inside an oven with a cake baking

    A 99° F

    B 125° F

    C 350° F

8. inside a freezer where ice cubes are made

    A 25° F

    B 35° F

    C 50° F

Give the number for each ▥ .

1. Normal body temperature is ▥ °F.

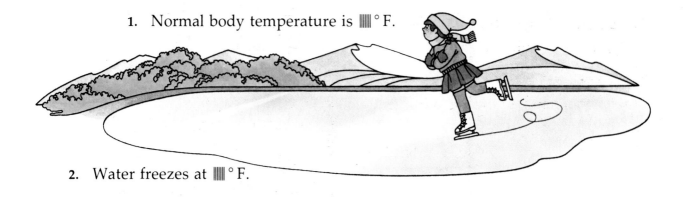

2. Water freezes at ▥ °F.

3. Water boils at ▥ °F.

4. Comfortable room temperature is about ▥ °F.

Use a Fahrenheit thermometer to find these temperatures.

5. cold water from a faucet

6. hot water from a faucet

7. "palm temperature" (Hold the thermometer inside your fist for 2 minutes.)

8. "light bulb temperature" (Hold the thermometer 2 in. from a light bulb for 2 minutes.)

9. today's indoor temperature

10. today's outdoor temperature

☆ 11. Record the temperature in °F at noon each day for 5 days. Make a graph to show your findings.

☆ 12. Consult a world almanac and find the normal monthly high temperatures for your locality for each month of the year. Make a graph to show your findings.

Volume

Cubic inches (in.³), cubic feet (ft³), and cubic yards (yd³) are units of volume. A cubic inch is a cube whose edges are 1 inch long.

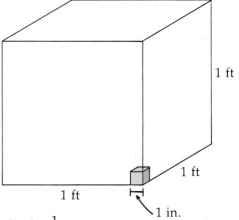

Cubic inch

1 in.
1 in.
1 in.

The scale drawing shows a comparison of the sizes of a cubic inch and a cubic foot.

$1 \text{ ft}^3 = 1728 \text{ in.}^3$ $1 \text{ yd}^3 = 27 \text{ ft}^3$

Use the volume formula, $V = l \times w \times h$, for exercises 1–5.
Find the volume.

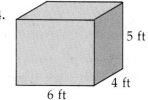

1 ft
1 ft
1 ft
1 in.

Scale: $\frac{1}{8}$ in. = 1 in.

Example:

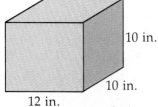

10 in.
10 in.
12 in.

$V = 12 \times 10 \times 10 = 1200 \text{ in.}^3$

1.
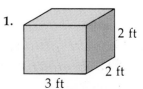
2 ft
2 ft
3 ft

2.
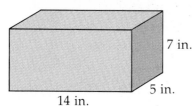
7 in.
5 in.
14 in.

3.
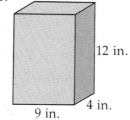
12 in.
9 in.
4 in.

4.

5 ft
6 ft
4 ft

5.

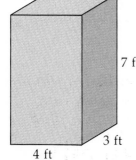
7 ft
3 ft
4 ft

Solve the problems.

1. What is the volume of a room that is 18 ft long, 12 ft wide, and 18 ft high?

2. A suitcase is 24 in. long, 20 in. wide, and 5 in. deep. How many cubic inches does it hold?

3. How much more than a cubic foot does the suitcase in exercise 2 hold?

4. A classroom is 30 ft long, 24 ft wide, and 12 ft high. What is the volume of the room in cubic feet?

5. Give the volume of the classroom in exercise 4 in cubic yards.

6. A standard brick is 8 in. long, $2\frac{1}{4}$ in. thick, and $3\frac{3}{4}$ in. wide. What is the volume of the brick?

8. How many cubic inches are in a cubic yard?

☆ 9. A box is 6 in. wide and 6 in. high. How long is the box if its volume is 1 cubic foot?

7. What is the volume of a shipping box that has a length of 17 in., a width of 11 in., and a height of 11 in.?

☆ 10. Concrete is often sold by the cubic yard. How many cubic yards of concrete are needed for a sidewalk 60 ft long, 3 ft wide, and 4 in. thick?

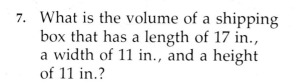

Capacity

Some common units of capacity
are shown below.

1 cup
(8 ounces)

1 tablespoon

1 pint

1 quart   1 gallon

---

1 fluid ounce (oz) = 2 tablespoons (T)
1 cup = 8 fluid ounces
1 pint (pt) = 2 cups
1 quart (qt) = 2 pints
1 gallon (gal) = 4 quarts

Give the missing numbers.

1. 2 cups = ▥ oz
2. 5 gal = ▥ qt
3. 1 gal = ▥ pt
4. 16 T = ▥ cup
5. 1 cup = ▥ T
6. 1 gal = ▥ cups
7. $\frac{1}{2}$ gal = ▥ qt
8. 4 cups = ▥ oz
9. 1 T = ▥ oz
10. 16 pt = ▥ gal
11. 32 oz = ▥ qt
12. $2\frac{1}{2}$ gal = ▥ qt

Give the missing numbers.

13. It takes ▥ quarts to fill 2 gallons.
14. 1 quart of juice fills ▥ cups.
15. 1 pint of cough syrup fills ▥ tablespoons.
16. 1 gallon and 2 pints fill ▥ quarts.
17. 1 quart and 2 cups fill ▥ pints.
18. 2 pints and 4 cups fill ▥ quarts.

Solve the problems.

1. Linda bought 6 pint
   bottles of orange soda. How many
   quarts was this?

2. How many cups of root beer
   are in six 12-ounce
   cans of root beer?

3. A punch bowl holds $1\frac{1}{2}$ gallons.
   How many quarts does it hold?

4. One can holds 28 ounces of tomato
   juice. Another can holds 1 quart of
   tomato juice. Which can holds more
   juice? How many ounces more?

5. A recipe calls for 1 cup plus 2 tablespoons
   of water. How many tablespoons of water
   is this in all?

6. The volume of a gallon container is
   231 cubic inches. What is the volume
   in cubic inches of a 1-quart milk carton?

☆ 7. A container has a volume of 1 ft³
   (1728 in.³). How many gallons will
   the container hold? (Use 1 gal = 231 in.³)
   Round the answer to the nearest tenth.

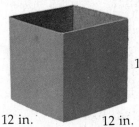

12 in.

12 in.   12 in.

Ounces, pounds, and tons

A tennis ball weighs about 2 ounces.

A quart of milk weighs about 2 pounds.

A small truck weighs about 2 tons.

> 1 pound (lb) = 16 ounces (oz)
> 1 ton = 2000 pounds

Give the number of ounces for each weight.

1. 1 lb
2. $\frac{1}{4}$ lb
3. $\frac{3}{4}$ lb
4. 10 lb
5. 5 lb
6. $\frac{1}{2}$ lb
7. 2 lb
8. 1 ton

Give the number of pounds for each weight.

9. 32 oz
10. 8 oz
11. 10 tons
12. 18 oz
13. 48 oz
14. 2 tons
15. 2 oz
16. 30 tons

Complete each sentence with the correct word, **ounce, pound,** or **ton**.

17. It takes about 7 nickels to weigh 1 __?__ .
18. A large blue whale may weigh about 160 __?__ .
19. A small car weighs about 2400 __?__ .
20. A hamburger may weigh about $\frac{1}{4}$ __?__ .
21. A small can of orange juice weighs about 6 __?__ .
22. A large elephant may weigh about 10 000 __?__ .
23. It takes about 14 table-tennis balls to weigh 1 __?__ .
24. A large turkey may weigh about 20 __?__ .

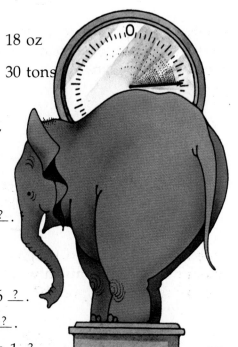

Solve the problems.

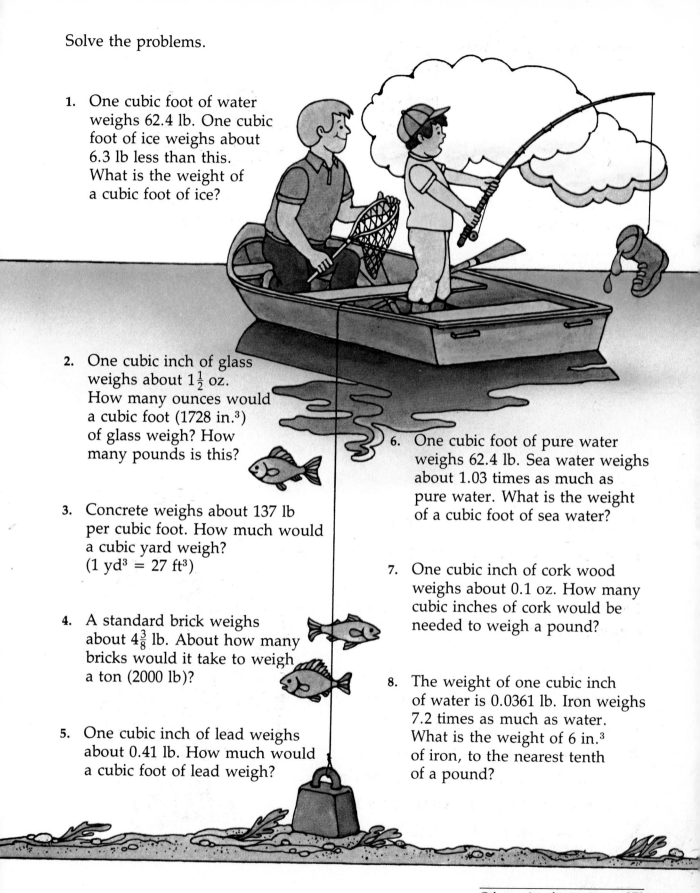

1. One cubic foot of water weighs 62.4 lb. One cubic foot of ice weighs about 6.3 lb less than this. What is the weight of a cubic foot of ice?

2. One cubic inch of glass weighs about $1\frac{1}{2}$ oz. How many ounces would a cubic foot (1728 in.^{3}) of glass weigh? How many pounds is this?

3. Concrete weighs about 137 lb per cubic foot. How much would a cubic yard weigh? (1 yd^3 = 27 ft^3)

4. A standard brick weighs about $4\frac{3}{8}$ lb. About how many bricks would it take to weigh a ton (2000 lb)?

5. One cubic inch of lead weighs about 0.41 lb. How much would a cubic foot of lead weigh?

6. One cubic foot of pure water weighs 62.4 lb. Sea water weighs about 1.03 times as much as pure water. What is the weight of a cubic foot of sea water?

7. One cubic inch of cork wood weighs about 0.1 oz. How many cubic inches of cork would be needed to weigh a pound?

8. The weight of one cubic inch of water is 0.0361 lb. Iron weighs 7.2 times as much as water. What is the weight of 6 in.^{3} of iron, to the nearest tenth of a pound?

More Practice

Add.

	A	B	C	D	E	F	G	H	I	J
1.	2 + 3	1 + 5	5 + 2	3 + 2	0 + 4	1 + 2	3 + 4	6 + 3	1 + 1	2 + 5
2.	5 + 4	2 + 2	4 + 2	6 + 9	5 + 3	8 + 2	3 + 1	0 + 2	7 + 4	3 + 3
3.	8 + 3	2 + 9	0 + 7	4 + 5	1 + 4	9 + 5	4 + 6	7 + 2	8 + 8	9 + 3
4.	4 + 3	5 + 7	2 + 0	5 + 1	3 + 7	8 + 1	2 + 8	6 + 1	0 + 9	2 + 4
5.	9 + 6	2 + 6	4 + 4	8 + 5	0 + 5	9 + 2	7 + 0	1 + 3	3 + 5	1 + 9
6.	3 + 0	7 + 3	0 + 0	0 + 6	4 + 9	7 + 6	6 + 4	0 + 3	4 + 1	5 + 5
7.	7 + 9	0 + 8	1 + 6	8 + 4	2 + 7	9 + 1	4 + 0	5 + 6	4 + 7	6 + 2
8.	0 + 1	9 + 4	7 + 1	5 + 0	6 + 6	1 + 7	7 + 5	6 + 8	8 + 0	5 + 8
9.	9 + 7	2 + 1	1 + 0	3 + 6	8 + 9	1 + 8	6 + 7	9 + 0	9 + 9	6 + 0
10.	9 + 8	4 + 8	8 + 6	6 + 0	3 + 9	8 + 7	7 + 7	5 + 9	6 + 5	7 + 8

Set A   For use after page 21

Add.

1. 57 + 38	2. 65 + 48	3. 574 + 77	4. 344 + 98	5. 264 + 339	6. 485 + 854
7. 345 + 675	8. 564 + 573	9. 767 + 359	10. 842 + 479	11. 1287 + 736	12. 5413 + 397
13. 3409 + 6687	14. 2643 + 9972	15. 4531 + 7298	16. 18 644 + 23 976	17. 52 131 + 17 986	18. 64 328 + 27 683
19. 34 75 + 26	20. 324 471 + 589	21. 641 309 + 766	22. 1432 76 + 228	23. 3761 8412 + 3798	24. 7641 2837 + 4278
25. 143 72 642 + 271	26. 386 743 292 + 64	27. 1852 2322 476 + 28	28. 7421 364 8211 + 34	29. 4456 3124 6718 + 2421	30. 7049 2733 1841 + 3976

Set B   For use after page 23

Add.

1. 14.7 + 26.7	2. 5.7 + 3.9	3. 2.64 + 8.05	4. 7.37 + 5.89	5. 22.6 + 18.5	6. 12.15 + 39.78
7. 32.6 + 49.7	8. 0.83 + 0.79	9. 9.64 + 7.48	10. 3.126 + 4.793	11. 2.465 + 7.375	12. 19.214 + 15.689
13. 0.538 + 0.769	14. 0.824 + 19.278	15. 5.761 + 24.978	16. 34.682 + 45.939	17. 0.549 + 7.899	18. 56.308 + 72.854
19. 5.6 13.2 + 4.2	20. 12.7 10.5 + 7.8	21. 4.532 2.648 + 7.305	22. 0.76 0.82 + 0.34	23. 24.48 39.72 + 18.46	24. 47.34 9.76 + 22.33
25. 3.571 4.768 + 2.488	26. 28.760 5.489 + 48.731	27. 76.43 8.38 + 29.92	28. 9.324 15.463 + 78.283	29. 83.261 7.988 + 3.421	30. 0.764 0.983 + 0.768

Subtract.

	A	B	C	D	E	F	G	H	I	J
1.	8 −3	5 −1	12 −7	10 −3	7 −5	8 −7	9 −1	4 −0	6 −3	11 −3
2.	3 −1	1 −0	14 −8	7 −2	12 −4	16 −7	6 −0	9 −5	4 −2	10 −6
3.	11 −8	8 −2	6 −1	3 −2	8 −4	15 −8	7 −6	8 −0	10 −4	11 −2
4.	6 −4	1 −1	11 −5	12 −9	7 −0	5 −2	13 −6	10 −2	9 −6	3 −3
5.	10 −7	6 −2	2 −0	5 −4	8 −1	15 −9	17 −8	7 −7	9 −3	10 −1
6.	2 −2	12 −5	14 −6	7 −1	9 −0	16 −9	11 −7	9 −4	4 −1	13 −7
7.	12 −3	2 −1	13 −5	12 −8	3 −0	8 −5	17 −9	5 −5	9 −2	10 −5
8.	10 −9	5 −0	7 −3	4 −4	15 −6	10 −8	0 −0	6 −5	18 −9	9 −7
9.	13 −9	7 −4	11 −9	6 −6	4 −3	9 −8	15 −7	14 −5	8 −8	13 −8
10.	11 −4	9 −9	13 −4	14 −9	8 −6	14 −7	11 −6	16 −8	5 −3	12 −6

Set A   For use after page 25

Subtract.

1.	2.	3.	4.	5.	6.
438 − 172	873 − 346	727 − 243	649 − 483	327 − 195	561 − 173

7.	8.	9.	10.	11.	12.
905 − 463	630 − 214	422 − 138	784 − 535	806 − 379	925 − 638

13.	14.	15.	16.	17.	18.
3721 − 1360	7059 − 2263	8133 − 4097	4629 − 1137	6423 − 3715	3401 − 1623

19.	20.	21.	22.	23.	24.
9843 − 6371	8540 − 5827	6127 − 2632	7283 − 4926	4395 − 3637	5182 − 1739

25.	26.	27.	28.	29.
32 706 − 21 273	84 311 − 37 158	125 503 − 76 426	748 392 − 374 637	604 320 − 416 463

Set B   For use after page 27

Subtract.

1.	2.	3.	4.	5.	6.
7.5 − 3.6	61.4 − 32.8	0.76 − 0.49	38.1 − 26.4	9.32 − 4.27	18.05 − 8.63

7.	8.	9.	10.	11.	12.
0.53 − 0.26	9.38 − 2.92	15.6 − 4.8	72.5 − 28.3	64.1 − 36.3	0.364 − 0.228

13.	14.	15.	16.	17.	18.
5.137 − 1.453	0.73 − 0.45	5.06 − 1.93	0.742 − 0.568	9.33 − 2.97	30.00 − 15.75

19.	20.	21.	22.	23.	24.
71.38 − 52.85	50.41 − 32.37	8.384 − 5.926	43.5 − 16.7	30.02 − 11.69	0.051 − 0.032

25.	26.	27.	28.	29.	30.
7.137 − 2.562	81.5 − 73.6	0.604 − 0.238	65.83 − 28.67	9.417 − 5.346	8.209 − 3.794

31. 6.042 − 3.766   32. 52.31 − 28.14   33. 0.608 − 0.482   34. 91.05 − 36.11

Multiply.

	A	B	C	D	E	F	G	H	I	J
1.	4 ×3	2 ×2	1 ×5	7 ×4	0 ×5	6 ×8	3 ×9	5 ×5	6 ×3	2 ×5
2.	7 ×8	6 ×0	5 ×4	3 ×3	1 ×4	7 ×5	0 ×3	4 ×9	5 ×3	6 ×4
3.	9 ×8	1 ×7	0 ×0	8 ×5	2 ×3	5 ×6	7 ×2	8 ×8	2 ×9	6 ×7

4. 4×4 5. 9×6 6. 8×3 7. 7×9 8. 2×6 9. 4×8

10. 2×8 11. 2×4 12. 1×9 13. 6×6 14. 9×5 15. 8×6

16. 9×9 17. 7×3 18. 2×0 19. 4×5 20. 6×5 21. 3×4

22. 7×6 23. 9×4 24. 3×6 25. 5×2 26. 5×7 27. 4×0

Multiply.

1. 7×100 2. 3×10 3. 38×10 4. 45×100 5. 6×300

6. 32×100 7. 48×10 8. 7×1000 9. 14×1000 10. 9×20

11. 15×10 12. 26×100 13. 80×10 14. 73×100 15. 92×100

16. 30×20 17. 6×500 18. 7×600 19. 3×800 20. 8×200

21. 50×60 22. 40×80 23. 80×90 24. 2000×5 25. 6000×4

26. 70×600 27. 4000×4 28. 50×40 29. 56×100 30. 400×8

31. 20×50 32. 70×20 33. 80×400 34. 40×30 35. 3000×9

36. 900×3 37. 200×40 38. 5×700 39. 80×50 40. 70×30

41. 60×80 42. 90×30 43. 80×200 44. 700×60 45. 3000×4

46. 30×60 47. 8000×4 48. 90×70 49. 40×900 50. 80×80

Multiply.

1.	45 × 2	**2.**	125 × 6	**3.**	86 × 3	**4.**	38 × 4	**5.**	76 × 5	**6.**	236 × 7
7.	376 × 5	**8.**	831 × 7	**9.**	293 × 5	**10.**	792 × 6	**11.**	648 × 4	**12.**	507 × 9
13.	3125 × 3	**14.**	6204 × 5	**15.**	5346 × 8	**16.**	8138 × 6	**17.**	4595 × 3	**18.**	7118 × 4

Multiply.

1.	34 × 28	**2.**	76 × 42	**3.**	26 × 95	**4.**	51 × 39	**5.**	64 × 75	**6.**	23 × 89
7.	236 × 45	**8.**	615 × 22	**9.**	586 × 32	**10.**	453 × 57	**11.**	814 × 36	**12.**	734 × 53
13.	921 × 48	**14.**	842 × 26	**15.**	768 × 43	**16.**	345 × 71	**17.**	624 × 33	**18.**	547 × 26
19.	1367 × 48	**20.**	7053 × 32	**21.**	2651 × 58	**22.**	8116 × 29	**23.**	3264 × 93	**24.**	4467 × 37
25.	6243 × 46	**26.**	5317 × 39	**27.**	9613 × 45	**28.**	7538 × 61	**29.**	2769 × 72	**30.**	6832 × 54

Multiply.

1.	734 × 210	**2.**	256 × 419	**3.**	309 × 561	**4.**	483 × 320	**5.**	538 × 265	**6.**	819 × 347
7.	348 × 362	**8.**	452 × 565	**9.**	681 × 405	**10.**	273 × 960	**11.**	740 × 320	**12.**	568 × 853
13.	825 × 468	**14.**	939 × 348	**15.**	266 × 854	**16.**	398 × 292	**17.**	671 × 735	**18.**	817 × 636

Multiply.

1. 6.9
    × 0.7

2. 32.6
    × 0.4

3. 56.72
    ×   8

4. 4.36
    × 0.2

5. 82.7
    ×   3

6. 7.11
    × 0.5

7. 28.2
    ×   9

8. 34.51
    × 0.6

9. 8.19
    ×   7

10. 24.17
    × 0.3

11. 48.6
    × 0.3

12. 62.3
    ×   5

13. 82.5
    × 0.2

14. 9.36
    ×   4

15. 5.84
    × 0.5

16. 142.6
    × 0.7

17. 3684
    × 0.8

18. 5.013
    × 0.6

19. 25.66
    ×   9

20. 472.3
    ×   5

21. 3.19
    × 0.2

22. 9.8
    × 0.7

23. 6.108
    ×   4

24. 82.71
    × 0.5

25. 701.4
    × 0.3

26. 5.03
    × 0.01

27. 1.36
    × 0.22

28. 93.4
    × 0.31

29. 7.41
    × 3.6

30. 289
    × 0.44

31. 4.16
    ×   38

32. 62.5
    × 4.2

33. 9.62
    ×   29

34. 79.1
    × 0.52

35. 8.06
    × 0.36

36. 7.3
    × 6.4

37. 21.5
    × 9.2

38. 3.81
    ×   56

39. 84.3
    × 0.46

40. 639
    × 0.28

41. 5.07
    × 2.6

42. 48.6
    ×   74

43. 8.51
    × 5.7

44. 37.9
    × 2.6

45. 7.08
    × 0.25

46. 2.98
    × 4.3

47. 6.04
    × 0.38

48. 59.5
    × 6.4

49. 9.48
    × 2.7

50. 3.06
    × 0.89

Set A   For use after page 79

Multiply.

1. 0.072   2. 0.341   3. 8.5   4. 0.08   5. 0.291
    × 0.6   × 0.02   × 0.06   × 0.04   × 0.7

6. 0.462   7. 0.092   8. 6.43   9. 0.0003   10. 0.084
    × 0.002   × 0.46   × 0.003   ×   28   × 0.92

11. 9.92   12. 0.0037   13. 0.002   14. 0.038   15. 0.0083
    × 0.02   × 0.08   × 0.029   × 0.064   × 0.14

16. 0.061   17. 2.82   18. 0.048   19. 0.582   20. 0.0009
    × 2.5   × 0.0006   × 0.087   × 0.07   ×   37

21. 0.073   22. 5.68   23. 0.039   24. 4.01   25. 0.059
    × 6.4   × 0.09   × 0.047   × 0.007   × 0.72

Set B   For use after page 83

Multiply.

1. 76.5   2. 32.7   3. 8.34   4. 18.4   5. 47.63
    ×   4   × 0.6   × 0.7   ×   9   × 0.2

6. 15.6   7. 9.14   8. 71.3   9. 5.92   10. 4.05
    × 0.32   × 4.5   × 2.6   × 0.64   × 38

11. 87.23   12. 3.87   13. 28.9   14. 7.195   15. 56.31
    × 2.7   × 0.53   × 6.2   × 0.4   × 0.45

16. 3.02   17. 62.7   18. 0.83   19. 0.27   20. 8.32
    × 1.35   × 3.01   × 0.05   × 0.006   × 2.89

21. 0.0043   22. 0.0038   23. 0.0094   24. 7.16   25. 48.7
    × 0.006   ×   1.5   × 0.007   × 0.52   × 3.11

Find the area of each rectangle.

1.
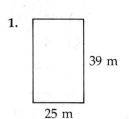
39 m
25 m

2.
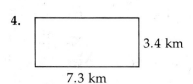
22 cm
74 cm

3.
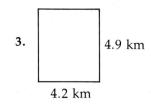
4.9 km
4.2 km

4.
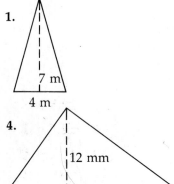
3.4 km
7.3 km

5.
43 m
56 m

6.
25 cm
11 cm

Find the area of each triangle.

1.
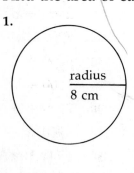
7 m
4 m

2.
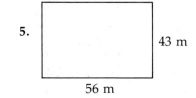
22 cm
36 cm

3.
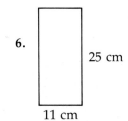
16 cm
9 cm

4.
12 mm
26 mm

5.
58 cm
36 cm

6.
48 cm
52 cm

Find the area of each circle.

1.
radius
8 cm

2.
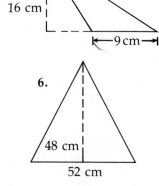
radius
25 mm

3.
radius
3.8 m

4.
diameter
6 cm

5.
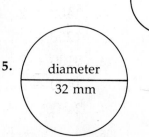
diameter
32 mm

6.
diameter
18 m

Set A   For use after page 119

Divide.

1. $18 \div 3$	2. $5 \div 5$	3. $10 \div 2$	4. $6 \div 3$	5. $7 \div 1$
6. $35 \div 5$	7. $9 \div 3$	8. $4 \div 1$	9. $18 \div 2$	10. $8 \div 2$
11. $0 \div 4$	12. $4 \div 4$	13. $25 \div 5$	14. $3 \div 3$	15. $15 \div 3$
16. $36 \div 4$	17. $8 \div 1$	18. $6 \div 1$	19. $8 \div 4$	20. $0 \div 3$
21. $1 \div 1$	22. $24 \div 3$	23. $20 \div 5$	24. $5 \div 1$	25. $6 \div 2$
26. $16 \div 2$	27. $12 \div 2$	28. $28 \div 4$	29. $14 \div 2$	30. $30 \div 5$
31. $20 \div 4$	32. $45 \div 5$	33. $12 \div 4$	34. $0 \div 5$	35. $32 \div 4$
36. $27 \div 3$	37. $10 \div 5$	38. $24 \div 4$	39. $40 \div 5$	40. $12 \div 3$
41. $0 \div 1$	42. $2 \div 2$	43. $21 \div 3$	44. $15 \div 5$	45. $0 \div 2$
46. $4 \div 2$	47. $3 \div 1$	48. $16 \div 4$	49. $2 \div 2$	50. $9 \div 1$
51. $9 \div 9$	52. $24 \div 8$	53. $30 \div 6$	54. $14 \div 7$	55. $0 \div 8$
56. $24 \div 6$	57. $7 \div 7$	58. $45 \div 9$	59. $8 \div 8$	60. $35 \div 7$
61. $16 \div 8$	62. $0 \div 6$	63. $56 \div 7$	64. $48 \div 6$	65. $27 \div 9$

Set B   For use after page 121

Divide.

1. $120 \div 4$	2. $360 \div 6$	3. $350 \div 5$	4. $280 \div 7$
5. $400 \div 5$	6. $320 \div 8$	7. $180 \div 9$	8. $210 \div 3$
9. $420 \div 7$	10. $540 \div 6$	11. $240 \div 4$	12. $150 \div 5$
13. $360 \div 9$	14. $150 \div 3$	15. $480 \div 6$	16. $200 \div 4$
17. $180 \div 6$	18. $450 \div 9$	19. $240 \div 8$	20. $350 \div 7$
21. $160 \div 2$	22. $240 \div 3$	23. $120 \div 6$	24. $270 \div 9$
25. $300 \div 5$	26. $280 \div 4$	27. $490 \div 7$	28. $560 \div 8$
29. $2700 \div 3$	30. $2500 \div 5$	31. $1600 \div 4$	32. $2400 \div 6$
33. $1600 \div 8$	34. $2100 \div 7$	35. $4500 \div 5$	36. $7200 \div 9$
37. $3200 \div 4$	38. $1400 \div 2$	39. $5400 \div 9$	40. $5600 \div 7$
41. $2000 \div 5$	42. $1200 \div 3$	43. $4000 \div 8$	44. $1800 \div 2$
45. $6300 \div 7$	46. $8100 \div 9$	47. $4200 \div 6$	48. $2500 \div 5$
49. $4500 \div 9$	50. $1400 \div 7$	51. $1800 \div 3$	52. $3600 \div 4$
53. $56\,000 \div 8$	54. $24\,000 \div 6$	55. $28\,000 \div 4$	56. $15\,000 \div 3$
57. $21\,000 \div 3$	58. $40\,000 \div 5$	59. $35\,000 \div 7$	60. $18\,000 \div 6$

Divide.

1. 5)316   2. 4)330   3. 2)113   4. 3)146   5. 6)237

6. 3)1534   7. 8)2595   8. 4)2853   9. 7)4390   10. 9)4071

11. 4)3385   12. 6)2517   13. 8)2283   14. 5)3783   15. 3)1177

16. 5)2417   17. 7)3628   18. 9)3389   19. 6)4369   20. 2)1979

21. 7)18 995   22. 5)41 621   23. 6)35 227   24. 8)29 458   25. 4)25 934

26. 4)20 505   27. 3)22 235   28. 8)36 737   29. 7)45 047   30. 6)23 258

Divide.

1. 24)1812   2. 93)4475   3. 56)2093   4. 42)2360   5. 38)2447

6. 71)2516   7. 63)1522   8. 29)1695   9. 58)3617   10. 81)3812

11. 64)2761   12. 36)3144   13. 75)4755   14. 82)4272   15. 47)3594

16. 43)2087   17. 57)4306   18. 94)3486   19. 65)2881   20. 28)1945

21. 37)2900   22. 62)3481   23. 83)5066   24. 76)3270   25. 95)2570

26. 54)3531   27. 73)3807   28. 68)2479   29. 94)4325   30. 85)6125

Divide.

1. 46)10 637   2. 72)32 481   3. 33)26 915   4. 86)29 357   5. 52)32 457

6. 68)25 438   7. 38)19 919   8. 91)39 317   9. 43)26 448   10. 74)54 762

11. 84)43 351   12. 51)16 378   13. 76)42 869   14. 29)22 715   15. 37)23 798

16. 56)27 395   17. 45)17 512   18. 82)51 012   19. 31)22 414   20. 66)34 147

21. 73)66 503   22. 67)43 428   23. 41)21 701   24. 54)15 853   25. 85)63 928

26. 92)48 414   27. 83)21 769   28. 55)42 469   29. 63)30 354   30. 42)31 773

Divide. Check your answers.

1. 3)0.966   2. 7)36.4   3. 5)235.5   4. 2)1.506   5. 6)50.04

6. 8)29.52   7. 9)4.212   8. 3)7.95   9. 4)0.344   10. 7)4.277

11. 4)29.48   12. 3)27.3   13. 6)163.2   14. 7)239.4   15. 8)373.6

16. 5)31.5   17. 2)166.6   18. 4)369.6   19. 6)2.64   20. 3)217.2

21. 57)142.5   22. 38)26.6   23. 92)38.64   24. 26)15.6   25. 45)40.5

26. 63)81.9   27. 71)39.76   28. 84)67.2   29. 32)14.72   30. 56)207.2

31. 37)103.6   32. 91)6.37   33. 65)5.85   34. 86)455.8   35. 73)671.6

36. 46)243.8   37. 62)223.2   38. 74)19.24   39. 53)25.44   40. 85)60.35

Annex zeros as needed and divide until the remainder is zero.

1. 5)8   2. 6)3.3   3. 4)3.8   4. 2)1.3   5. 5)37

6. 4)18   7. 8)3.4   8. 6)5.1   9. 2)0.17   10. 4)71

11. 6)7.5   12. 4)8.5   13. 5)73   14. 20)3.64   15. 60)93

16. 15)1.98   17. 26)5.33   18. 34)69.7   19. 72)38.7   20. 85)27.37

21. 54)8.37   22. 38)47.5   23. 16)5.2   24. 14)86.1   25. 25)3.62

26. 42)157.5   27. 64)246.4   28. 55)15.18   29. 36)84.6   30. 24)9

31. 75)193.5   32. 82)142.27   33. 95)45.22   34. 46)333.5   35. 35)167.3

Divide.

1. $0.5\overline{)3.25}$ 2. $6.2\overline{)3.658}$ 3. $0.34\overline{)0.7854}$ 4. $7.6\overline{)33.136}$

5. $8.3\overline{)2.1082}$ 6. $0.92\overline{)0.3358}$ 7. $0.26\overline{)0.494}$ 8. $5.4\overline{)19.98}$

9. $0.04\overline{)0.2248}$ 10. $0.7\overline{)44.94}$ 11. $0.63\overline{)1.575}$ 12. $3.7\overline{)2.812}$

13. $5.8\overline{)21.46}$ 14. $9.3\overline{)5.673}$ 15. $0.85\overline{)0.3655}$ 16. $41.\overline{)35.67}$

17. $6.4\overline{)3.072}$ 18. $0.39\overline{)2.1879}$ 19. $0.47\overline{)3.384}$ 20. $8.2\overline{)296.84}$

Divide.

1. $1.8\overline{)10.8}$ 2. $0.34\overline{)8.5}$ 3. $0.07\overline{)3.64}$ 4. $0.004\overline{)0.8}$

5. $0.57\overline{)1.653}$ 6. $0.009\overline{)0.36}$ 7. $0.16\overline{)8.8}$ 8. $0.48\overline{)36}$

9. $8.2\overline{)492}$ 10. $7.5\overline{)270}$ 11. $0.005\overline{)1.5}$ 12. $0.64\overline{)32}$

13. $0.003\overline{)2.1}$ 14. $5.9\overline{)206.5}$ 15. $0.43\overline{)30.1}$ 16. $0.17\overline{)13.6}$

17. $4.6\overline{)207}$ 18. $0.006\overline{)4.2}$ 19. $0.35\overline{)9.8}$ 20. $9.4\overline{)611}$

Use the cross-products method and tell whether
each pair of fractions is equivalent.

1. $\frac{2}{3}, \frac{9}{15}$ 2. $\frac{1}{5}, \frac{4}{20}$ 3. $\frac{3}{4}, \frac{1}{2}$ 4. $\frac{7}{8}, \frac{2}{16}$ 5. $\frac{3}{7}, \frac{9}{21}$

6. $\frac{2}{11}, \frac{6}{22}$ 7. $\frac{3}{6}, \frac{3}{4}$ 8. $\frac{1}{4}, \frac{40}{100}$ 9. $\frac{3}{23}, \frac{6}{46}$ 10. $\frac{2}{5}, \frac{4}{35}$

11. $\frac{7}{10}, \frac{70}{100}$ 12. $\frac{7}{15}, \frac{14}{30}$ 13. $\frac{9}{16}, \frac{18}{30}$ 14. $\frac{12}{14}, \frac{6}{7}$ 15. $\frac{8}{32}, \frac{1}{4}$

Solve these equations.

16. $\frac{3}{8} = \frac{n}{24}$ 17. $\frac{1}{3} = \frac{n}{30}$ 18. $\frac{4}{5} = \frac{16}{n}$ 19. $\frac{1}{10} = \frac{7}{n}$

20. $\frac{0}{4} = \frac{n}{16}$ 21. $\frac{7}{13} = \frac{14}{n}$ 22. $\frac{1}{8} = \frac{n}{32}$ 23. $\frac{7}{9} = \frac{56}{n}$

24. $\frac{5}{12} = \frac{10}{n}$ 25. $\frac{2}{11} = \frac{8}{n}$ 26. $\frac{5}{6} = \frac{n}{30}$ 27. $\frac{8}{8} = \frac{n}{9}$

Set A   For use after page 193

Give the lowest-terms fraction for each.

1. $\frac{7}{21}$ 2. $\frac{14}{35}$ 3. $\frac{4}{8}$ 4. $\frac{2}{16}$ 5. $\frac{8}{36}$ 6. $\frac{10}{14}$

7. $\frac{10}{15}$ 8. $\frac{6}{8}$ 9. $\frac{10}{12}$ 10. $\frac{15}{24}$ 11. $\frac{12}{27}$ 12. $\frac{8}{20}$

13. $\frac{5}{30}$ 14. $\frac{6}{24}$ 15. $\frac{10}{18}$ 16. $\frac{12}{42}$ 17. $\frac{4}{20}$ 18. $\frac{5}{45}$

19. $\frac{21}{27}$ 20. $\frac{12}{20}$ 21. $\frac{7}{49}$ 22. $\frac{24}{28}$ 23. $\frac{14}{16}$ 24. $\frac{24}{56}$

25. $\frac{16}{18}$ 26. $\frac{15}{21}$ 27. $\frac{12}{36}$ 28. $\frac{20}{25}$ 29. $\frac{13}{39}$ 30. $\frac{11}{22}$

Set B   For use after page 195

Write as improper fractions.

1. $3\frac{1}{5}$ 2. $5\frac{1}{2}$ 3. $6\frac{1}{3}$ 4. $2\frac{7}{8}$ 5. $4\frac{3}{7}$ 6. $2\frac{7}{10}$

7. $8\frac{2}{3}$ 8. $9\frac{1}{5}$ 9. $4\frac{3}{10}$ 10. $12\frac{1}{2}$ 11. $7\frac{3}{5}$ 12. $3\frac{9}{10}$

13. $6\frac{2}{7}$ 14. $5\frac{3}{8}$ 15. $7\frac{3}{4}$ 16. $9\frac{1}{7}$ 17. $4\frac{5}{8}$ 18. $8\frac{3}{4}$

19. $2\frac{31}{100}$ 20. $8\frac{17}{100}$ 21. $3\frac{2}{9}$ 22. $6\frac{3}{7}$ 23. $7\frac{4}{9}$ 24. $14\frac{1}{2}$

25. $5\frac{1}{7}$ 26. $6\frac{5}{8}$ 27. $4\frac{2}{7}$ 28. $10\frac{3}{5}$ 29. $9\frac{1}{6}$ 30. $30\frac{2}{3}$

Set C   For use after page 197

Give a mixed numeral for each improper fraction.

1. $\frac{11}{2}$ 2. $\frac{29}{3}$ 3. $\frac{47}{8}$ 4. $\frac{27}{5}$ 5. $\frac{38}{7}$ 6. $\frac{50}{6}$

7. $\frac{25}{4}$ 8. $\frac{39}{8}$ 9. $\frac{56}{9}$ 10. $\frac{71}{6}$ 11. $\frac{17}{3}$ 12. $\frac{232}{7}$

13. $\frac{45}{10}$ 14. $\frac{19}{6}$ 15. $\frac{123}{5}$ 16. $\frac{322}{4}$ 17. $\frac{19}{8}$ 18. $\frac{55}{3}$

19. $\frac{53}{2}$ 20. $\frac{176}{7}$ 21. $\frac{257}{6}$ 22. $\frac{191}{9}$ 23. $\frac{39}{10}$ 24. $\frac{620}{100}$

25. $\frac{93}{6}$ 26. $\frac{151}{4}$ 27. $\frac{122}{10}$ 28. $\frac{930}{100}$ 29. $\frac{304}{9}$ 30. $\frac{234}{5}$

Find the sums and differences.

1. $\frac{1}{3}$ $+\frac{1}{2}$
2. $\frac{1}{2}$ $+\frac{3}{4}$
3. $\frac{1}{4}$ $+\frac{2}{5}$
4. $\frac{3}{8}$ $+\frac{1}{4}$
5. $\frac{4}{6}$ $+\frac{1}{2}$
6. $\frac{3}{7}$ $+\frac{4}{7}$
7. $\frac{3}{4}$ $+\frac{5}{8}$

8. $\frac{3}{5}$ $-\frac{1}{2}$
9. $\frac{2}{3}$ $-\frac{1}{4}$
10. $\frac{1}{2}$ $-\frac{1}{4}$
11. $\frac{2}{3}$ $-\frac{1}{2}$
12. $\frac{13}{16}$ $-\frac{3}{4}$
13. $\frac{3}{4}$ $-\frac{1}{6}$
14. $\frac{7}{10}$ $-\frac{3}{5}$

15. $\frac{3}{4}$ $-\frac{1}{5}$
16. $\frac{3}{12}$ $-\frac{1}{4}$
17. $\frac{5}{16}$ $+\frac{1}{8}$
18. $\frac{7}{10}$ $-\frac{3}{100}$
19. $\frac{3}{8}$ $-\frac{1}{4}$
20. $\frac{5}{6}$ $-\frac{5}{12}$
21. $\frac{7}{9}$ $-\frac{2}{3}$

22. $\frac{1}{2}$ $\frac{2}{3}$ $+\frac{5}{6}$
23. $\frac{3}{4}$ $\frac{1}{6}$ $+\frac{1}{2}$
24. $\frac{2}{3}$ $\frac{3}{4}$ $+\frac{1}{2}$
25. $\frac{5}{16}$ $\frac{1}{2}$ $+\frac{5}{8}$
26. $\frac{1}{3}$ $\frac{7}{12}$ $+\frac{3}{4}$
27. $\frac{1}{2}$ $\frac{3}{10}$ $+\frac{2}{5}$
28. $\frac{3}{5}$ $\frac{1}{4}$ $+\frac{1}{2}$

Find the sums.

1. $15\frac{2}{3}$ $+7\frac{3}{4}$
2. $8\frac{1}{2}$ $+9\frac{1}{4}$
3. $21\frac{2}{5}$ $+32\frac{1}{10}$
4. $43\frac{3}{7}$ $+72\frac{3}{14}$
5. $64\frac{3}{8}$ $+38\frac{1}{4}$
6. $9\frac{2}{5}$ $+3\frac{1}{4}$

7. $11\frac{7}{10}$ $+39\frac{1}{2}$
8. $63\frac{1}{2}$ $+28$
9. $47\frac{2}{3}$ $+38\frac{5}{6}$
10. $84\frac{1}{12}$ $+57\frac{2}{3}$
11. $76\frac{3}{5}$ $+97\frac{1}{10}$
12. $56\frac{2}{5}$ $+99\frac{3}{4}$

13. $64\frac{5}{9}$ $+58\frac{2}{3}$
14. $28\frac{1}{2}$ $+75\frac{2}{9}$
15. $19\frac{1}{7}$ $+36\frac{3}{14}$
16. $234\frac{5}{12}$ $+186\frac{1}{3}$
17. $348\frac{1}{6}$ $+279\frac{1}{8}$
18. $687\frac{6}{10}$ $+328\frac{4}{10}$

19. $1\frac{2}{3}$ $9\frac{5}{6}$ $+7\frac{1}{2}$
20. $24\frac{1}{5}$ $37\frac{3}{4}$ $+19\frac{1}{2}$
21. $47\frac{1}{10}$ $36\frac{2}{5}$ $+84\frac{3}{4}$
22. $148\frac{1}{2}$ $685\frac{5}{8}$ $+345\frac{3}{4}$
23. $721\frac{1}{3}$ $349\frac{5}{6}$ $+572\frac{1}{2}$
24. $814\frac{1}{6}$ $289\frac{2}{3}$ $+376\frac{3}{4}$

Set A   For use after page 209

Subtract.

1. 13
   $- 9\frac{2}{3}$

2. $21\frac{1}{4}$
   $- 14\frac{3}{8}$

3. $7\frac{2}{9}$
   $- 3\frac{1}{3}$

4. $32\frac{1}{3}$
   $- 15\frac{1}{8}$

5. $47\frac{3}{14}$
   $- 29\frac{1}{7}$

6. $51\frac{7}{8}$
   $- 38\frac{1}{4}$

7. $70\frac{1}{2}$
   $- 36\frac{3}{4}$

8. $45\frac{5}{6}$
   $- 28\frac{2}{3}$

9. $81\frac{3}{5}$
   $- 43\frac{1}{2}$

10. $22\frac{3}{4}$
    $- 16\frac{3}{8}$

11. 93
    $- 56\frac{5}{8}$

12. $64\frac{2}{3}$
    $- 49\frac{5}{12}$

13. $26\frac{3}{4}$
    $- 17\frac{7}{8}$

14. $82\frac{1}{10}$
    $- 54\frac{3}{5}$

15. $43\frac{1}{4}$
    $- 27\frac{2}{3}$

16. $54\frac{3}{4}$
    $- 16\frac{7}{10}$

17. $65\frac{1}{6}$
    $- 37\frac{2}{9}$

18. $76\frac{1}{4}$
    $- 29\frac{7}{6}$

19. $34\frac{2}{3}$
    $- 27\frac{1}{6}$

20. 21
    $- 7\frac{1}{2}$

21. $50\frac{1}{16}$
    $- 22\frac{1}{4}$

22. $75\frac{1}{3}$
    $- 46\frac{2}{15}$

23. $83\frac{2}{5}$
    $- 54\frac{3}{4}$

24. $47\frac{1}{6}$
    $- 19\frac{3}{8}$

Set B   for use after page 215

Multiply.

1. $\frac{1}{3} \times \frac{3}{4}$
2. $\frac{1}{6} \times \frac{1}{7}$
3. $\frac{3}{5} \times \frac{1}{3}$
4. $\frac{2}{9} \times \frac{3}{7}$
5. $\frac{3}{2} \times \frac{1}{4}$

6. $\frac{1}{10} \times \frac{7}{10}$
7. $\frac{3}{9} \times \frac{9}{3}$
8. $\frac{7}{8} \times \frac{0}{2}$
9. $\frac{5}{6} \times \frac{3}{5}$
10. $\frac{2}{7} \times \frac{1}{2}$

11. $\frac{5}{3} \times \frac{4}{7}$
12. $\frac{7}{12} \times \frac{3}{8}$
13. $\frac{7}{8} \times \frac{1}{3}$
14. $\frac{3}{10} \times \frac{1}{10}$
15. $\frac{6}{7} \times \frac{4}{3}$

16. $\frac{3}{5} \times \frac{2}{5}$
17. $\frac{5}{8} \times \frac{3}{4}$
18. $\frac{5}{9} \times \frac{1}{1}$
19. $\frac{4}{7} \times \frac{7}{12}$
20. $\frac{7}{15} \times \frac{3}{5}$

Set C   For use after page 217

Multiply.

1. $1\frac{1}{2} \times 3\frac{2}{3}$
2. $4\frac{1}{5} \times 7\frac{1}{2}$
3. $1\frac{1}{4} \times 1\frac{1}{4}$
4. $\frac{7}{8} \times 1\frac{3}{4}$
5. $6\frac{1}{9} \times \frac{3}{5}$

6. $15 \times 3\frac{1}{5}$
7. $3\frac{7}{8} \times 1\frac{5}{9}$
8. $5\frac{1}{6} \times 30$
9. $8 \times \frac{1}{4}$
10. $24 \times \frac{1}{12}$

11. $32 \times 3\frac{1}{8}$
12. $3\frac{1}{10} \times 4\frac{7}{10}$
13. $7\frac{3}{8} \times \frac{2}{7}$
14. $6\frac{2}{5} \times 7\frac{1}{2}$
15. $4\frac{4}{9} \times 45$

16. $6\frac{2}{3} \times \frac{9}{14}$
17. $2\frac{2}{15} \times 6\frac{1}{2}$
18. $4\frac{1}{5} \times 6\frac{2}{3}$
19. $16 \times 3\frac{1}{4}$
20. $8\frac{3}{4} \times 6\frac{2}{7}$

Give the reciprocal of each number.

1. $\frac{1}{3}$ 2. $\frac{3}{5}$ 3. $\frac{1}{8}$ 4. $\frac{7}{9}$ 5. $\frac{3}{4}$ 6. $\frac{1}{5}$ 7. 4 8. $3\frac{1}{2}$

9. $5\frac{1}{4}$ 10. $\frac{5}{6}$ 11. $\frac{4}{9}$ 12. $\frac{3}{100}$ 13. $2\frac{3}{4}$ 14. $6\frac{4}{5}$ 15. 3 16. $9\frac{1}{2}$

17. $\frac{7}{3}$ 18. $4\frac{2}{5}$ 19. 7 20. $\frac{3}{8}$ 21. $\frac{2}{9}$ 22. $\frac{9}{5}$ 23. $\frac{15}{28}$ 24. $5\frac{1}{3}$

25. $\frac{17}{43}$ 26. $2\frac{7}{8}$ 27. $\frac{5}{3}$ 28. $\frac{11}{4}$ 29. $12\frac{1}{3}$ 30. $\frac{5}{8}$ 31. $\frac{32}{29}$ 32. $10\frac{1}{2}$

33. $\frac{9}{11}$ 34. 2 35. $\frac{52}{35}$ 36. $\frac{5}{9}$ 37. $\frac{21}{100}$ 38. $\frac{10}{7}$ 39. $3\frac{1}{4}$ 40. $9\frac{2}{3}$

Divide.

1. $\frac{3}{4} \div \frac{1}{3}$ 2. $\frac{7}{10} \div \frac{1}{4}$ 3. $\frac{3}{8} \div \frac{3}{7}$ 4. $\frac{7}{6} \div \frac{2}{3}$ 5. $1 \div \frac{4}{5}$ 6. $8 \div \frac{1}{4}$

7. $\frac{5}{6} \div \frac{1}{3}$ 8. $\frac{5}{12} \div \frac{2}{3}$ 9. $\frac{3}{16} \div \frac{1}{8}$ 10. $\frac{4}{15} \div \frac{3}{5}$ 11. $\frac{3}{10} \div \frac{7}{10}$ 12. $\frac{9}{8} \div \frac{3}{4}$

13. $\frac{7}{20} \div \frac{1}{10}$ 14. $\frac{2}{9} \div \frac{1}{18}$ 15. $\frac{4}{9} \div \frac{7}{9}$ 16. $21 \div \frac{7}{8}$ 17. $\frac{3}{4} \div 9$ 18. $\frac{1}{2} \div 5$

19. $\frac{2}{3} \div \frac{4}{9}$ 20. $\frac{7}{10} \div \frac{1}{10}$ 21. $\frac{1}{3} \div \frac{1}{15}$ 22. $\frac{3}{7} \div \frac{4}{21}$ 23. $\frac{7}{8} \div \frac{3}{7}$ 24. $\frac{5}{12} \div \frac{3}{4}$

25. $\frac{5}{8} \div 10$ 26. $\frac{1}{6} \div \frac{2}{3}$ 27. $\frac{3}{5} \div \frac{3}{10}$ 28. $24 \div \frac{8}{9}$ 29. $\frac{9}{10} \div \frac{3}{8}$ 30. $\frac{7}{20} \div 5$

Divide.

1. $3\frac{1}{3} \div \frac{1}{2}$ 2. $10 \div 1\frac{3}{5}$ 3. $1 \div 3\frac{1}{2}$ 4. $1\frac{2}{5} \div 1\frac{2}{3}$ 5. $3\frac{1}{8} \div 5$

6. $\frac{1}{5} \div 4\frac{1}{2}$ 7. $3\frac{1}{6} \div \frac{2}{3}$ 8. $1\frac{1}{12} \div \frac{3}{4}$ 9. $6\frac{1}{2} \div \frac{5}{12}$ 10. $4\frac{1}{5} \div \frac{7}{10}$

11. $6 \div 9$ 12. $4\frac{2}{3} \div \frac{7}{9}$ 13. $1\frac{1}{8} \div 1\frac{1}{2}$ 14. $\frac{1}{6} \div 1\frac{1}{18}$ 15. $2\frac{3}{4} \div \frac{5}{12}$

16. $2\frac{1}{10} \div 3\frac{2}{5}$ 17. $6\frac{1}{5} \div \frac{8}{5}$ 18. $7\frac{1}{2} \div \frac{1}{3}$ 19. $3 \div 5$ 20. $7 \div 1\frac{1}{8}$

21. $5 \div 2\frac{1}{7}$ 22. $4 \div 8$ 23. $3\frac{2}{3} \div \frac{11}{3}$ 24. $5\frac{1}{3} \div \frac{8}{9}$ 25. $4\frac{2}{5} \div 1\frac{1}{10}$

Jeremy Roeder

Write a decimal for each fraction.

1. $\frac{1}{8}$ 2. $\frac{19}{25}$ 3. $\frac{3}{16}$ 4. $\frac{7}{8}$ 5. $\frac{43}{50}$ 6. $\frac{15}{32}$

7. $\frac{7}{20}$ 8. $\frac{11}{16}$ 9. $\frac{3}{5}$ 10. $\frac{3}{2}$ 11. $\frac{1}{4}$ 12. $\frac{27}{50}$

13. $\frac{4}{25}$ 14. $\frac{9}{25}$ 15. $\frac{3}{4}$ 16. $\frac{4}{5}$ 17. $\frac{3}{8}$ 18. $\frac{9}{16}$

19. $\frac{27}{2}$ 20. $\frac{7}{5}$ 21. $\frac{5}{16}$ 22. $\frac{17}{8}$ 23. $\frac{13}{10}$ 24. $\frac{7}{50}$

25. $\frac{11}{5}$ 26. $\frac{1}{16}$ 27. $\frac{11}{10}$ 28. $\frac{9}{20}$ 29. $\frac{37}{25}$ 30. $\frac{21}{8}$

Set B   For use after page 249

Write a mixed decimal for each fraction.

1. $\frac{4}{7}$ 2. $\frac{5}{8}$ 3. $\frac{3}{10}$ 4. $\frac{3}{7}$ 5. $\frac{2}{9}$ 6. $\frac{5}{3}$

7. $\frac{4}{11}$ 8. $\frac{3}{14}$ 9. $\frac{5}{7}$ 10. $\frac{5}{16}$ 11. $\frac{6}{7}$ 12. $\frac{4}{9}$

13. $\frac{7}{3}$ 14. $\frac{7}{15}$ 15. $\frac{3}{11}$ 16. $\frac{4}{7}$ 17. $\frac{10}{3}$ 18. $\frac{13}{12}$

19. $\frac{9}{4}$ 20. $\frac{3}{16}$ 21. $\frac{7}{9}$ 22. $\frac{5}{14}$ 23. $\frac{13}{6}$ 24. $\frac{5}{16}$

25. $\frac{1}{16}$ 26. $\frac{2}{11}$ 27. $\frac{8}{7}$ 28. $\frac{8}{3}$ 29. $\frac{3}{11}$ 30. $\frac{11}{16}$

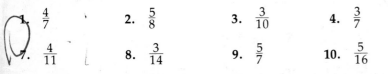

optional

Set C   For use after page 251

Write a lowest-terms fraction or mixed numeral for each decimal.

1. 0.8   2. 3.25   3. 5.5   4. 0.03   5. 2.75   6. 0.06

7. 4.125   8. 0.44   9. 0.7   10. 0.004   11. 0.65   12. 0.400

13. 0.075   14. 6.375   15. 3.45   16. 9.31   17. 8.002   18. 0.35

19. 0.425   20. 7.016   21. 8.66   22. 0.82   23. 0.008   24. 6.95

Find the number for n.

1. $\frac{3}{8} = \frac{n}{40}$ 2. $\frac{2}{9} = \frac{22}{n}$ 3. $\frac{n}{20} = \frac{12}{60}$ 4. $\frac{5}{7} = \frac{45}{n}$ 5. $\frac{5}{n} = \frac{30}{90}$

6. $\frac{n}{28} = \frac{3}{4}$ 7. $\frac{15}{39} = \frac{5}{n}$ 8. $\frac{5}{n} = \frac{35}{42}$ 9. $\frac{16}{n} = \frac{2}{3}$ 10. $\frac{3}{n} = \frac{18}{72}$

11. $\frac{n}{14} = \frac{28}{56}$ 12. $\frac{15}{n} = \frac{60}{64}$ 13. $\frac{63}{72} = \frac{7}{n}$ 14. $\frac{3}{6} = \frac{39}{n}$ 15. $\frac{10}{16} = \frac{5}{n}$

16. $\frac{2}{4} = \frac{n}{28}$ 17. $\frac{3}{n} = \frac{18}{60}$ 18. $\frac{12}{90} = \frac{2}{n}$ 19. $\frac{n}{64} = \frac{4}{8}$ 20. $\frac{n}{32} = \frac{3}{96}$

21. $\frac{7}{13} = \frac{42}{n}$ 22. $\frac{16}{40} = \frac{2}{n}$ 23. $\frac{4}{n} = \frac{12}{48}$ 24. $\frac{63}{n} = \frac{7}{9}$ 25. $\frac{2}{n} = \frac{10}{70}$

Write a percent for each decimal or fraction.

1. $\frac{1}{25}$ 2. $\frac{3}{10}$ 3. $\frac{7}{20}$ 4. $\frac{9}{10}$ 5. $\frac{2}{5}$ 6. $\frac{4}{25}$

7. 0.09 8. 0.70 9. 0.38 10. 0.06 11. 0.99 12. 0.4

13. $\frac{11}{50}$ 14. $\frac{5}{12}$ 15. $\frac{1}{20}$ 16. $\frac{3}{2}$ 17. $\frac{4}{5}$ 18. $\frac{17}{24}$

19. 3.15 20. 0.05 21. 0.77 22. 2.25 23. 9.32 24. 0.86

25. $\frac{6}{25}$ 26. $\frac{9}{7}$ 27. $\frac{12}{16}$ 28. $\frac{8}{5}$ 29. $\frac{7}{50}$ 30. $\frac{2}{3}$

Write a decimal and lowest-terms fraction for each percent.

1. 1% 2. 9% 3. 12% 4. 15% 5. 20% 6. 25%

7. $45\frac{1}{2}\%$ 8. $36\frac{1}{2}\%$ 9. $54\frac{1}{2}\%$ 10. $92\frac{1}{2}\%$ 11. $83\frac{1}{2}\%$ 12. $14\frac{1}{2}\%$

13. 70% 14. 35% 15. 65% 16. 142% 17. 138% 18. 102%

19. 115% 20. 160% 21. 11% 22. 75% 23. $68\frac{1}{2}\%$ 24. 18%

25. $72\frac{1}{2}\%$ 26. $40\frac{1}{2}\%$ 27. 154% 28. 175% 29. 125% 30. $50\frac{1}{2}\%$

Set A   For use after page 273

Solve.

1. 30% of 50
2. 40% of 15
3. 50% of 36
4. 20% of 75

5. 3% of 100
6. 13% of 80
7. 62% of 39
8. $32\frac{1}{2}$% of 54

9. 75% of 44
10. 12% of 150
11. 48% of 82
12. 9% of 1500

13. $10\frac{1}{2}$% of 50
14. 2% of 1200
15. 71% of 58
16. $22\frac{1}{2}$% of 93

17. 130% of 200
18. 110% of 811
19. $86\frac{1}{2}$% of 300
20. 14% of 450

21. 25% of 500
22. 6% of 2500
23. $15\frac{1}{2}$% of 60
24. 49% of 100

25. 50% of 3500
26. $45\frac{1}{2}$% of 100
27. 120% of 500
28. 180% of 70

29. $63\frac{1}{2}$% of 40
30. 200% of 300
31. 7% of 8000
32. $57\frac{1}{2}$% of 200

33. 15% of 2000
34. 26% of 400
35. 11% of 3500
36. 175% of 600

Set B   For use after page 275

Solve.

1. 10% of 80
2. 25% of 24
3. 50% of 30
4. $33\frac{1}{3}$% of 90

5. 20% of 75
6. 10% of 50
7. 25% of 40
8. 40% of 10

9. 25% of 32
10. 50% of 70
11. $33\frac{1}{3}$% of 120
12. 20% of 80

13. 30% of 20
14. 40% of 50
15. 10% of 70
16. 5% of 40

17. 20% of 35
18. $33\frac{1}{3}$% of 18
19. 50% of 320
20. 25% of 60

21. 40% of 45
22. 5% of 60
23. 30% of 90
24. 20% of 90

25. 50% of 240
26. 30% of 200
27. 40% of 15
28. 10% of 650

29. 25% of 360
30. 20% of 300
31. 50% of 450
32. $33\frac{1}{3}$% of 270

Find the sums.

1. $5 + {}^-3 = n$
2. ${}^-7 + 2 = n$
3. ${}^-8 + {}^-1 = n$
4. $4 + {}^-2 = n$

5. ${}^-5 + 7 = n$
6. $11 + {}^-3 = n$
7. $2 + {}^-9 = n$
8. ${}^-4 + 13 = n$

9. $6 + {}^-3 = n$
10. $9 + {}^-5 = n$
11. ${}^-7 + {}^-8 = n$
12. ${}^-3 + 15 = n$

13. ${}^-12 + 7 = n$
14. $3 + {}^-7 = n$
15. $10 + {}^-2 = n$
16. ${}^-4 + {}^-9 = n$

17. ${}^-5 + 8 = n$
18. ${}^-2 + {}^-3 = n$
19. ${}^-5 + 11 = n$
20. $9 + {}^-3 = n$

Find the differences.

	S	A	A
1. $3 - {}^-2 = n$
2. ${}^-4 - 3 = n$
3. $6 - {}^-1 = n$
4. ${}^-3 - {}^-2 = n$

	S	A	A
5. $2 - {}^-5 = n$
6. ${}^-7 - 3 = n$
7. $3 - 8 = n$
8. $1 - {}^-4 = n$

	S	A	A
9. ${}^-6 - {}^-2 = n$
10. $1 - {}^-9 = n$
11. ${}^-5 - 6 = n$
12. ${}^-2 - 7 = n$

	S	A	A
13. $8 - {}^-4 = n$
14. ${}^-6 - {}^-8 = n$
15. ${}^-3 - 7 = n$
16. $5 - 8 = n$

Solve the equations.

1. $3 \times 10^3 = n$
2. $5 \times 10^2 = n$
3. $7 \times 10^5 = n$
4. $6 \times 10^4 = n$

5. $9 \times 10^2 = n$
6. $8 \times 10^6 = n$
7. $2 \times 10^3 = n$
8. $3 \times 10^4 = n$

9. $7 \times 10^3 = n$
10. $6 \times 10^5 = n$
11. $3 \times 10^2 = n$
12. $8 \times 10^5 = n$

Write each number as in the example.

Example: $700 = 7 \times 10^2$

13. 400
14. 5000
15. 800
16. 30 000

17. 500 000
18. 70 000
19. 9000
20. 200 000 000

21. 60 000
22. 2000
23. 300 000
24. 8 000 000

Set A   For use after page 347

Write each number in scientific notation.

1. 30 000
2. 5000
3. 600 000
4. 900

5. 9 000 000
6. 70 000
7. $\overset{\text{23 zeros}}{400 \ldots 000}$
8. 50 000 000

9. $\overset{\text{34 zeros}}{200 \ldots 000}$
10. 3 000 000
11. 500 000 000
12. 8 000 000 000

13. 400
14. 60 000 000
15. 900 000 000
16. 3 000 000 000

Set B   For use after page 353

Find the volume of each box.

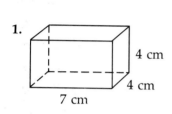

1. 4 cm, 4 cm, 7 cm

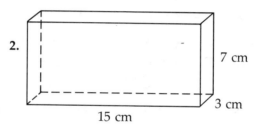

2. 3 cm, 7 cm, 15 cm

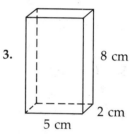

3. 8 cm, 2 cm, 5 cm

4. $l = 5.6$ m
   $w = 3.8$ m
   $h = 2.1$ m

5. $l = 9$ cm
   $w = 4$ cm
   $h = 6$ cm

6. $l = 11.3$ cm
   $w = 5.6$ cm
   $h = 3.5$ cm

7. $l = 7.3$ cm
   $w = 5.2$ cm
   $h = 3.9$ cm

8. $l = 6.5$ cm
   $w = 2.3$ cm
   $h = 8.5$ cm

9. $l = 30$ cm
   $w = 20$ cm
   $h = 10$ cm

10. $l = 3$ cm
    $w = 7$ cm
    $h = 0.2$ cm

11. $l = 8$ cm
    $w = 3.6$ cm
    $h = 2$ cm

12. $l = 5$ cm
    $w = 4.2$ cm
    $h = 0.5$ cm

13. $l = 20$ m
    $w = 3$ m
    $h = 0.1$ m

14. $l = 15$ cm
    $w = 2$ cm
    $h = 3$ cm

15. $l = 9$ cm
    $w = 2.5$ cm
    $h = 2$ cm

Table of Measures

Metric System | English System

──────────────── Length ────────────────

Metric System		English System	
1 millimeter (mm)	$\frac{1}{10}$ centimeter (cm) $\frac{1}{1000}$ meter (m)	1 foot (ft)	12 inches (in.)
1 centimeter (cm)	10 millimeters (mm)	1 yard (yd)	36 inches (in.) 3 feet (ft)
1 decimeter (dm)	100 millimeters (mm) 10 centimeters (cm)	1 mile (mi)	5280 feet (ft) 1760 yards (yd)
1 meter (m)	1000 millimeters (mm) 100 centimeters (cm) 10 decimeters (dm)	1 nautical mile	6076 feet (ft) 1852 meters (m)
1 kilometer (km)	1000 meters (m)		

──────────────── Area ────────────────

Metric System		English System	
1 square meter (m²)	100 square decimeters (dm²) 10 000 square centimeters cm²)	1 square foot	144 square inches (in.²)
1 hectare (ha)	$\frac{1}{100}$ square kilometer (km²) 10 000 square meters (m²)	1 square yard (yd²)	9 square feet (ft²) 1296 square inches (in.²)
1 square kilometer (km²)	1 000 000 square meters (m²) 100 hectares (ha)	1 acre (A)	43 560 square feet (ft²) 4 840 square yards (yd²)
		1 square mile (mi²)	640 acres (A)

──────────────── Volume ────────────────

Metric System		English System	
1 cubic decimeter (dm³)	$\frac{1}{1000}$ cubic meter (m³) 1000 cubic centimeters (cm³) 1 liter (ℓ)	1 cubic foot (ft³)	1728 cubic inches (in.³)
1 cubic meter (m³)	1 000 000 cubic centimeters (cm³) 1 000 cubic decimeters (dm³)	1 cubic yard (yd³)	27 cubic feet (ft³) 46 656 cubic inches (in.³)

──────────────── Capacity ────────────────

Metric System		English System	
1 teaspoon	5 milliliters (ml)	1 cup (c)	8 fluid ounces (fl oz)
1 tablespoon	12.5 milliliters (ml)	1 pint (pt)	16 fluid ounces (fl oz) 2 cups (c)
1 liter (ℓ)	1000 milliliters (ml) 1000 cubic centimeters (cm³) 1 cubic decimeter (dm³) 4 metric cups	1 quart (qt)	32 fluid ounces (fl oz) 4 cups (c) 2 pints (pt)
1 kiloliter (kl)	1000 liters (ℓ)	1 gallon (gal)	128 fluid ounces (fl oz) 16 cups (c) 8 pints (pt) 4 quarts (qt)

──────────────── Mass ────────────────

Metric System		English System	
1 gram (g)	1000 milligrams (mg)	1 pound (lb)	16 ounces (oz)
1 kilogram (kg)	1000 grams (g)	1 ton (T)	2000 pounds (lbs)
1 metric ton (t)	1000 kilograms (kg)		

Glossary

addend   Any one of a set of numbers to be added. In the equation 4 + 5 = 9, the numbers 4 and 5 are addends.

addition   An operation that combines a first number and a second number to give exactly one number. The two numbers are called addends, and the result is called the sum of the addends.

angle   Two rays from a single point.

$$A$$

approximation   One number is an approximation of another number if the first number is suitably "close" (according to context) to the other number.

area   The area of a closed figure or region is the measure of that region as compared to a given selected region called the unit, usually a square region in the case of area.

associative (grouping) principle   When adding (or multiplying) three numbers, you can change the grouping and the sum (or product) is the same.

Examples: 2 + (8 + 6) = (2 + 8) + 6
3 × (4 × 2) = (3 × 4) × 2

average   The average of a set of numbers is the quotient resulting when the sum of the numbers in the set is divided by the number of addends.

bisect   To divide in half or find the midpoint.

centimeter   A unit of length. One centimeter is 0.01 meter.

circle   The set of all points in a plane which are a specified distance from a given point called the center or center point.

center point   circle

circumference   The distance around a circle.

common factor   When a number is a factor of two different numbers, it is said to be a common factor of the two numbers.

common multiple   A number is a common multiple of two numbers if it is a multiple of each of the numbers.

commutative (order) principle   When adding (or multiplying) two numbers, the order of the addends (or factors) does not affect the sum (or product).

Examples: 4 + 5 = 5 + 4
3 × 6 = 6 × 3

composite number   Any whole number greater than 1 that is not prime.

congruent figures   Geometric figures that have the same size and shape.

congruent triangles

coordinates   Number pair used in graphing.

coordinate axes   Two number lines intersecting at right angles at 0.

cube   A rectangular prism (box) such that all faces are squares.

decimal   Any base-ten numeral that uses place value to represent a number.

degree   A unit of angle measure.

denominator   The number indicated by the numeral below the line in a fraction symbol.

diagonal   A segment joining two nonadjacent vertices of a polygon. In the figure, the diagonal is segment AB.

$$A \qquad B$$

diameter   A chord that passes through the center point of the circle. The diameter is segment AB.

distributive (multiplication-addition) principle   This principle is sometimes described in terms of "breaking apart" a number before multiplying.

Example: 6 × (20 + 4) = (6 × 20) + (6 × 4)

dividend   In the problem 33 ÷ 7, 33 is called the dividend.

Example:
```
      4  ← quotient
   7)33  ← dividend
     28
      5  ← remainder
```
divisor

division   An operation related to multiplication as illustrated:

3 × 4 = 12
12 ÷ 4 = 3
12 ÷ 3 = 4

divisor   In the problem 33 ÷ 7, 7 is called the divisor.

edge   An edge of a space figure is one of the segments making up any one of the faces of a space figure.

face → ← edge

equality (equals; or =)   A mathematical relation of being exactly the same.

equally likely outcomes   Outcomes that have the same chance of occurring.

equation   A mathematical sentence involving the use of the equality symbol.

Examples: 5 + 4 = 9; 7 + □ = 8; n + 3 = 7.

equivalent fractions   Two fractions are equivalent when it can be shown that they each can be used to represent the same amount of a given object. Also, two fractions are equivalent if these two products are the same:

$$3 \times 8 \longrightarrow 24$$
$$4 \times 6 \longrightarrow 24$$

equivalent sets   Two sets that may be placed in a one-to-one correspondence.

estimate   To find an approximation for a given number. (Sometimes a sum, a product, etc.)

even numbers   The whole-number multiples of 2 (0, 2, 4, 6, 8, 10, 12, . . .).

exponent   In the symbol 10^3, the "3" is the exponent. It indicates that 10 is used as a factor three times. Thus: $10^3 = 10 \times 10 \times 10 = 1000$
$$5^4 = 5 \times 5 \times 5 \times 5 = 625$$

face   The face of a given space figure is any one of the plane geometric figures (regions) making up the space figure. *See* edge.

factor   In the equation $6 \times 7 = 42$, 6 and 7 are factors of 42. *See* multiplication.

fraction   A symbol for a fractional number, such as $\frac{2}{3}, \frac{3}{4}, \frac{1}{2}$, and so on.

fractional number   The one number we think about for each set of equivalent fractions.

graph   (1) A set of points associated with a given set of numbers or set of number pairs. (2) A picture used to illustrate a given collection of data. The data might be pictured in the form of a bar graph, a circle graph, a line graph, or a pictograph. (3) To draw the graph of.

greater than (>)   One of the two basic inequality relations.

  Example: $8 > 5$, read 8 is greater than 5.

greatest common factor   The largest, or greatest, number that is a factor of each of two numbers.

height of a triangle   The height of a triangle from any vertex is the perpendicular distance from that vertex to the opposite side (usually called the base). In the figure, the length of $\overline{CD}$ is the height of the triangle from vertex C to base $\overline{AB}$.

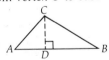

hexagon   A six-sided polygon.

hypotenuse   The side opposite the right angle in a right triangle.

improper fraction   A fraction in which the numerator is greater than or equal to the denominator.

  Examples: $\frac{8}{5}, \frac{6}{6}, \frac{12}{3}, \frac{7}{7}$

inequality (<, ≠, >)   In arithmetic, a relation indicating that the two numbers are not the same.

integers   The whole numbers together with their negatives: $\{. . . , ^-3, ^-2, ^-1, 0, 1, 2, 3, . . .\}$

least common denominator   The least common multiple of two denominators. The least common denominator for $\frac{3}{4}$ and $\frac{5}{6}$ is 12.

least common multiple   The smallest non-zero number that is a multiple of each of two given numbers. The least common multiple of 4 and 6 is 12.

legs of a right triangle   The two sides of a right triangle other than the hypotenuse.

length   (1) A number indicating the measure of one line segment with respect to another line segment, called the unit. (2) Sometimes used to denote one dimension (usually the greater) of a rectangle.

less than (<)   One of the two basic inequality relations. Example: $5 < 8$, read 5 is less than 8.

lowest terms   A fraction is in lowest terms if the numerator and denominator of the fraction have no common factor greater than 1.

meter   The basic unit of length in the Metric System.

midpoint   A point that divides a line segment into two parts of the same size.

mixed-decimal numeral   Numerals such as $0.7\frac{1}{2}$ and $0.33\frac{1}{3}$.

mixed numeral   Symbols such as $2\frac{1}{2}$ and $5\frac{1}{4}$.

multiple   A first number is a multiple of a second number if there is a whole number that multiplies by the second number to give the first number.

  Example: 24 is a multiple of 6 since $4 \times 6 = 24$.

multiplication   An operation that combines two numbers, called factors, to give one number called the product.

negative number   A number which will add to a positive number to give a sum of zero.

  For example: $5 + ^-5 = 0$, $19 + ^-19 = 0$

number pair   Any pair of numbers. Each pair of numbers can be matched with a unique point in the coordinate plane.

numeral   A symbol for a number.

numerator   The number indicated by the numeral above the line in a fraction symbol.

odd number   Any whole number that is not even.

  Examples: 1, 3, 5, 7, . . .

one principle   Any number multiplied by 1 is that same number. Sometimes called the identity principle for multiplication.

parallel lines   Two lines which lie in the same plane and do not intersect.

parallelogram   A quadrilateral with its opposite sides parallel.

pentagon   A five-sided polygon.

percent (%)   Per 100; for each; $\frac{1}{100}$.

perimeter   The sum of the lengths of the sides of a given polygon.

period   In arithmetic, each set of three digits indicated by spaces when writing a numeral is called a period.

Example:

$$\overline{3\ 4\ 2} \quad \overline{6\ 7\ 4} \quad \overline{2\ 0\ 8}$$

millions'   thousands'   units'
period   period   period

perpendicular lines   Two lines that intersect in right angles are perpendicular to each other.

pi (π)   The ratio of the circumference to the diameter of a circle; approximately 3.14.

place value   A system used for writing numerals for numbers, using only a definite number of symbols or digits. In the numeral 3257 the 5 stands for 50; in the numeral 36 289 the 6 stands for 6000.

polygon   A closed geometric figure made up of line segments. A regular polygon has congruent sides and congruent angles.

prime number   A number greater than 1 whose only factors are itself and 1. Examples: 2, 3, 5, 7

probability   The probability that an event will occur in a set of equally likely outcomes is the number of ways the event can occur divided by the total number of possible outcomes. For example, the probability that a 3 or a 4 will turn up in a single toss of a die is $\frac{2}{6}$ since there are 2 ways the event can occur and there are 6 possible equally likely outcomes.

product   The result of the multiplication operation. In $6 \times 7 = 42$, 42 is the product of 6 and 7.

protractor   An instrument used for measuring angles.

quadrilateral   A four-sided polygon.

quotient   The number (other than the remainder) that is the result of the division operation. It may be thought of as a factor in a multiplication equation.

radius   (1) Any segment from the center point to a point on the circle. (2) The distance from the center point to any point on the circle.

radius

A B

ratio   A pair of numbers used in making certain comparisons. The ratio of 3 to 4 is written $3:4$ or $\frac{3}{4}$.

ray   A ray is a certain part of a line.

ray

reciprocal   Two numbers are reciprocals of one another if their product is 1. Example: $\frac{4}{7}$ and $\frac{7}{4}$ are reciprocals of each other.

rectangle   A quadrilateral that has four right angles.

rhombus   A parallelogram with 4 congruent sides.

right angle   An angle that has the measure of 90 degrees.

right triangle   A triangle that has one right angle.

Roman numerals   Numerals used by the Romans. Used primarily to record numbers rather than for computing. Examples: IV, IX, XIV, L, C, M.

rotation   A motion in which a given figure is turned about a fixed point.

scale drawing   A drawing constructed so the ratio of all the dimensions in the drawing to those of the actual object is the same.

segment   Two points on a line and all the points on that line that are between the two points.

sequence   A collection or set of numbers given in a specific order. Such numbers are commonly given according to some rule or pattern.

set   undefined; usually thought of as a group or collection.

similar figures   Two figures that have the same shape.   △   △ similar figures

skew lines   Two lines that are not in the same plane.

solution   The number or numbers which result from solving an equation or a given problem.

square   A quadrilateral that has four right angles and four sides that are the same length.

subtraction   An operation related to addition as illustrated:

$$7 + 8 = 15 \begin{cases} 15 - 8 = 7 \\ 15 - 7 = 8 \end{cases}$$

sum   The result obtained by adding any set of numbers.

symmetric figure   A plane figure which can be folded in half so that the two halves match.

tangent   A line is tangent to a circle if the two figures are in one plane and have exactly one point in common.

tessellation   A repeated pattern of regions that can cover a plane.

translation   A motion in which each point of a figure is moved the same distance and in the same direction.

trapezoid   A quadrilateral with at least one pair of parallel sides.

triangle   A three-sided polygon.

unit   An amount or quantity adopted as a standard of measurement.

vertex   The point that the two rays of an angle have in common.

vertex →

volume   The measure, obtained using an appropriate unit (usually a cube), of the interior region of a space figure.

whole number   Any number in the set {0, 1, 2, 3, 4, 5, 6, 7, 8, 9, 10, 11, 12, 13, 14, . . .}

zero principle   Any number added to zero is that same number. (Also called the identity principle for addition.)

Index